Titanic
The Long Night

DIANE HOH

SCHOLASTIC INC.
New York Toronto London Auckland Sydney

No part of this publication may be reproduced in whole or in part, or stored in a retrieval system, or transmitted in any form or by any means, electronic, mechanical, photocopying, recording, or otherwise, without written permission of the publisher. For information regarding permission, write to Scholastic Inc., Attention: Permissions Department, 555 Broadway, New York, NY 10012.

ISBN 0-590-33123-X

12 11 10 9 8 7 6 5 4 3 2 1   8 9/9 0 1 2 3/0

Printed in the U.S.A.
First Scholastic printing, March 1998

This book is dedicated to my mother
Regis Niver Eggleston,
a truly unsinkable woman.

Prologue

There were two things Elizabeth remembered most about that long, fateful night. The first was the sound of terrified cries for help. Those cries echoed in her nightmares, no matter how soundly she slept. The second was the fierce, penetrating cold. For the rest of her life, a sharp, icy wind or a sudden dive in temperature would transport her back to lifeboat number six.

It rested on the flat, black sea while its passengers, shivering and huddled together for comfort, watched the great ship *Titanic*'s lights blink and then, finally, with the bow completely submerged, go out. Even with the bright, golden lights gone, the ship, hanging nearly perpendicular in the water, its stern aloft as if pointing to the black, star-studded sky above, was still clearly visible to the survivors drifting in the open sea. They continued to watch with wide, disbelieving eyes as the liner, touted as "unsinkable," sank, taking with it more than one thousand passengers.

It sank quietly, as if unwilling to create any more of a stir than it already had. Or, a dazed Elizabeth had thought, as if it were ashamed to be such a bitter disappointment.

And then it was gone, that most magnificent of all oceangoing vessels, gone forever.

There were so many painful memories of that night, memories that brought her sharply awake in the middle of the night, sweating and terrified. A light being turned on in a dark room reminded her of the way the ship's lights had stayed on for so long. Hearing certain ragtime melodies brought back an image of the *Titanic*'s band, gathered at the entrance to the Grand Staircase while the lifeboats were being loaded. A late-night black sky studded with brilliant stars sent her back to the sea again.

But always, throughout her life, it was the icy, penetrating cold Elizabeth remembered most clearly about that long, terrible night.

Chapter 1

During one last argument, Elizabeth Farr tried desperately to convince her parents to allow her to stay on in London with her cousins, instead of returning to New York. It was an argument she lost as always, and the Farr family left Waterloo Station at nine forty-five A.M. on the White Star Line boat train for Southampton. During the seventy-nine-mile journey through English villages with names like Surbiton, Woking, and Basingstoke, Elizabeth remained sullenly silent. She was still silent when they arrived at dockside shortly before eleven-thirty in the morning.

But the sullen pout left her face when she saw the great ship *Titanic* anchored in the harbor. There were other, smaller ships there, too. But the one whose maiden voyage would carry

1

her and her parents back to New York towered over all of them. The word that sprang first into Elizabeth's mind was "majestic." It was enormous, its four huge funnels marching along the boat deck like giant soldiers on guard. It was the most beautiful ship she had ever seen, and she had seen several. This had not been her first trip abroad.

"Eleven stories high," her father commented, seeing the look on Elizabeth's face. "If you stood it on end, it would rival the tallest buildings in the world. It's something, isn't it?"

It was indeed something. But Elizabeth was still stinging from the morning's argument. "If you stood it on end," she countered crisply, "it would sink."

For the rest of her life, whenever she remembered that remark, she would flush with anguish.

Glancing around, Elizabeth saw with satisfaction that she was not the only first-class passenger who looked excited. Others, as unaccustomed to being impressed as she was, were nevertheless staring and exclaiming, some over the sheer size of the oceangoing vessel, others over its shining beauty.

The first-class passengers walked along the gently sloping gangway to the main entrance on B deck, amidships. A man Elizabeth's father addressed as "Chief Steward Latimer" and a purser's clerk were there to greet them and direct or escort them to their cabins on C deck.

They passed through the entrance and walked quickly down the blue-carpeted corridors.

Elizabeth Langston Farr was used to luxury. The only child of a wealthy New York banker and his equally wealthy wife, she had never known anything else. But even she was not prepared for the impressive, lavish accommodations on board the new ship *Titanic*.

Only her residual anger kept her from exclaiming with delight when confronted by the elegant foyer at the foot of the wide, curved staircase on B deck. It kept her from making any comment when she saw the large, four-poster bed in her cabin, the patterned wall-covering on the upper walls, and the rich, dark paneling on the lower walls. She pretended not to be impressed by the dainty, antique desk well supplied with fine linen stationery bearing the ship's letterhead, or the heavy, ornate, raised molding around the doors. Angry at being treated like a child, she had made up her mind not to let one pleasant comment about this trip escape her lips. But that was more difficult than she had expected, given the beauty and luxury of the ship.

She had her own bathroom, fully equipped with thick, white towels, tiny bars of wrapped soap, and beautiful antique light fixtures. She could easily be in one of the finest hotels in Paris or London.

But she was determined not to let her pleasure show. "It's just a ship," she said when she moved through the doorway into her parents' room. There was disdain in her voice. "Not a hotel. Why waste all of this on people who are probably going to be seasick, anyway?" She was referring to her mother who, although the ship was still firmly moored, was already paler than usual. "I think it's ostentatious."

"No one's going to be seasick," her father said, removing his hat. His wife was sitting on a maroon velvet chaise lounge situated at the foot of the canopied bed. "And," he added drily, "considering what I paid for these accommodations, I would hardly expect less than 'all of this.'"

"It's such bad form to discuss money, Martin," his wife protested, lying back against the chaise. But then she lifted her head to glance around. Their cabin was larger than Elizabeth's. The canopied bed was further sheltered by velvet draperies hanging at all four corners, the smooth, thick bedspread a rich, embossed fabric. A finely cut crystal chandelier hung from the ceiling, the carved walnut paneling shone against the light, a brass firebox against one wall was polished to a brilliant golden shine. A delicate glass vase filled with pastel-colored fresh flowers sat on a table in the center of the room. "I must say, you can't fault the taste. These are exquisite furnishings. As impressive as any I've seen in the better hotels."

Elizabeth pulled free a pin securing the camel-hair wool hat that matched her traveling suit. She tossed the hated hat on a chair and removed the pins that held her long, pale hair in place, letting it tumble across her shoulders. "You mean the *best* hotels, Mother. When were you ever in anything less?"

"Elizabeth," her father warned, "your mother isn't feeling well. I'm sure she would appreciate a change in your tone of voice."

"Well, she can't be seasick yet," Elizabeth replied childishly, turning to go back into her own cabin. "We're still anchored." And without waiting for a reprimand, she left them, closing the door after her. She didn't slam it, though she wanted to, but the resounding click as the door shut was almost as satisfying.

Still in her suit, she flopped down on the bed on her stomach, resting her head on a soft, fat bed pillow. How could they expect her to be in good spirits during this trip, when they knew as well as she did what was awaiting her in New York? That stupid debut! An endless round of parties and dinners, in the company of shallow girls and arrogant, impeccably dressed young men who would scrutinize each of the debutantes as if they were examining a new gold wristwatch. Some of the young women would be promptly dismissed as being too plain, others because their parents weren't important enough. Her mother would see to it that Elizabeth wore a different dress and hairdo every night. She would have to endure banal conversation, bland food, and boring company. She had no interest in any of it. But her mother was adamant, and her father, usually so supportive, had so far refused to take a stand on Elizabeth's behalf.

The debut was bad enough. What was worse was, sometime shortly after the "season" ended, she was expected to marry Alan Reed, a wealthy banker ten years her senior. Alan was a decent sort, even if his hairline was receding and his waistcoats getting a bit tight around the middle. Though he was just twenty-seven years old, he seemed much older. He didn't like to dance, he thought traveling was a waste of money, and in spite of having gone to the best private schools, his conversation was limited to two topics: dogs and banking. During the long hours she had spent with Alan, he had mentioned an endless amount of times that the bank his father owned was growing by leaps and bounds. He had also said, without much conviction, that he was glad he had studied banking as his father wanted him to rather than pursuing a career in veterinary medicine as he'd once thought he wanted.

Elizabeth was sure that was a lie. There was no enthusiasm in his voice when he discussed banking, none at all.

Alan was not a horrid person, but he was missing a spine.

"If you make me marry him," she had told her parents, "I'll kill myself!" Then, "On second thought, I won't have to. I'll die of boredom within six months."

"Alan will take good care of you," her mother had argued.

"I can take care of myself."

"Nonsense! You've never taken care of yourself."

Which, Elizabeth had to admit reluctantly, if only to herself, was true enough. But she could learn, couldn't she? She wanted to stand on her own two feet. Not that she knew any other girls her age who did. Most of her friends would be engaged halfway through the social season, and would marry in June. "Suitable" matches, of course. Their parents always had a heavy hand in making sure all the money they spent on gowns and dinners and parties bore fruit. Pity the poor girl who came to the end of the season without a beau in tow. The only avenue left at that point was a prompt dispatch to Europe, where she might get lucky and capture a member of royalty, no matter how undistinguished the title.

The only independent woman Elizabeth knew was her great-aunt Bess, for whom she had been named. Bess had never married, and was in her early fifties now. She lived alone in an enormous house in Westchester that smelled of cats and lily of the valley, a sickening combination. She treated all six of her huge, hostile cats as if they were her children, but had no patience at all with real children. Elizabeth had been frightened of her for years. Bess Langston was not a very good example of the "independent woman" Elizabeth envisioned herself becoming someday. There had to be a more pleasant way of living on one's own. All Elizabeth wanted was the chance to find it.

How was she ever going to do that, with her parents orchestrating her life?

She was planning on using this time on board the *Titanic* to change their minds, to beg them to let her attend Vassar College in September to study journalism, instead of marrying Alan. It wasn't as if she were asking to go back to Europe. Poughkeepsie, New York, wasn't that far from home. Monica Beaumont, a girl one year ahead of Elizabeth at Miss Chatsworth's School in Manhattan, was a student at Vassar, and she often came home by herself on the train on weekends. Monica was studying biology, and said that she loved college.

I would, too, Elizabeth thought now, hearing her mother calling her from the next room. I know I would love it. They *have* to let me go. They just have to.

But they had refused to let her stay in London, and she'd had no choice in that matter. She had no money of her own. Not until she was twenty-one. If she made them too angry, they would disown her. It wasn't the money itself she cared about, but the freedom it would provide. So she had to be careful. If she were penniless, she could never go to college.

They had to change their minds about the debut and the marriage, and let her go to school. She would spend every waking moment on this floating hotel working toward that end. No making friends, no playing shuffleboard, no swimming, even though she loved swimming and had been amazed to discover that the *Titanic* actually had a swimming pool. She would have positively no fun at all until she persuaded them to let her make her own choices.

She left the bed then, went to the dressing table, sat on the plush, green velvet bench and peered into the mirror. She knew without being told that she would be one of the prettier debutantes. This was not conceit, it was simple fact. It had nothing to do with her, since she'd inherited her fair skin, deep blue eyes, and pale hair from her mother, who was still pretty and would have been a great beauty had she had more of what Elizabeth thought of as "sparkle." Her mother did not sparkle. It was Elizabeth's firm opinion that her mother's apparent lack of personality was the direct result of her husband's strong, almost overwhelming presence. He was the competent one, the popular one, the accomplished one of the pair. If there had ever been a shining light in Nola Langston's eyes, it had been overshadowed long ago by the brilliance of Martin Farr's light.

Elizabeth was determined not to make the same mistake. If she ever married at all (and she wasn't sure that she would), she hoped to find a mate who would see her as a partner, rather than as someone subservient to his needs and wishes.

She had expressed that idea aloud to her mother, only once.

"Don't be ridiculous," her mother had responded. "If women were meant to express their opinions, we'd be allowed to vote."

"As we should be!" Elizabeth had replied hotly.

Now, she took a deep breath and let it out slowly. Then she carefully, studiously, rearranged her hair in a proper upsweep, pinning it carefully in place, got up from the dressing table, and taking one last, satisfied look around at the roomy, tastefully decorated cabin, left to explore the ship. Without a hat.

At the same time that Elizabeth and her family were leaving London's Waterloo Station for Southampton that morning, a tall, very thin young man in a worn tweed jacket and cap, his arms loaded down with a large, leather portfolio and a trio of large boxes tied with string, left Paris on the *Train Transatlantique* for Cherbourg, France, a six-hour trip. But when the train arrived at Gare Maritime in Cherbourg, there was no sign of the great ship *Titanic* that Max Whittaker had read so much about. Impatient under the very best of circumstances, he glowered from beneath thick, dark eyebrows as the announcement came that embarkation on the tenders, originally scheduled to leave at four-thirty, would be delayed at least an hour. Something about the new ship having some trouble in Southampton.

"Perfect!" Max muttered under his breath. How good could this highly touted ship be if it couldn't even make it out of Southampton without problems? It hadn't been his idea to procure passage on a maiden voyage. The problem with maiden voyages was, if there were any manufacturing mistakes to be worked out, they hadn't been discovered yet. He would have preferred passage on a more sea-tested ship. But he was totally, completely broke after his year of studying art in Paris. He had had to swallow his pride and contact his grandmother for passage home. That seemed preferable to contacting his parents, who were still angry with him. The *Titanic* was his grandmother's choice. Also the first-class accommodations, which Max wouldn't have selected for himself. Too many snobs, most of whom knew very little about art. All a painting had to be was expensive, and they'd gladly hang it on their walls. His parents included.

He wasn't the only one upset about the delay. Others complained aloud. Some people got up and, paying someone to watch their baggage, strolled off to explore. Others shrugged and headed for the nearby casino. A young couple set off along the Grand Jetée, keeping their eyes on the ocean for some sign of the great liner.

Sighing with irritation, Max dropped one of the larger boxes onto the ground and sat down on top of it, stretching his long legs out in front of him. "I should have stayed in Paris," he told a small boy playing with a few shiny marbles. The boy frowned up at him, clearly not understanding English. Max repeated his statement, this time in French, and the boy smiled and nodded. "*Oui, oui, Paris,*" he cried. Then he went back to his marbles.

Max sat, staring glumly out at the sea, willing the ship to appear. His legs were already beginning to cramp.

At about that time, in County Cork, Ireland, a young girl and two male companions were cheerfully making their way south by a variety of means. Katie Hanrahan had never been so excited. She was not only going to America to seek her fortune, an adventure in itself, but she was making the trip on a great new ship, the *Titanic*. Everyone in Ballyford had talked about the wondrous new vessel. And all seemed to want to take a trip on it, though few could afford even a third-class passage. Fortunately for Katie, her da had done well this year, thanks be to the dairy cows and the milk and cheese they provided. And although her ma and da said they hated to see her go, they agreed that America was the place for Katie. So, on her sixteenth birthday on the first day of March, her da had surprised her with a steerage ticket on the maiden voyage of the majestic new ship, the *Titanic*.

Katie had never been on a ship in her life. "But Da," she had cried to her father when she opened the ticket envelope, "what if the ship should sink? I cannot swim a stroke!"

Her father had laughed and answered jovially, "Ah, Katie-girl, have you not heard? The miracle ship *Titanic* cannot sink!"

She had found that reassuring. Her da was always right.

But it was truly Brian Kelleher she must thank for this journey. She wouldn't have been allowed to go if Brian, nearly a grown man at twenty, hadn't agreed to go along and seek his fortune as well. According to Katie's da, who had worked alongside Brian on the farm for two years now, Brian was "a strong, steady bloke, and that's the truth of it."

Of course, she hadn't known that Brian would be bringing along his younger brother, Paddy. Patrick Kelleher was as different from his older brother as a sheep from a cow. Katie had never taken to Paddy. A true rascal, especially with girls. Everyone knew it. Brian was quiet, like her, but Paddy wasn't.

And then she found, to her surprise, that she was grateful for Paddy's lighthearted company during the trip. He was a master at keeping their spirits up during the long, taxing trip, and that was the truth of it. He sang while they traveled first by wooden cart, told jokes while they rode next in the back of a lorry, played pranks on Brian while they traveled on foot. During that tiring trek, their luggage became so burdensome, Katie thought her back was going to break. Paddy took the luggage from her, carrying it along with his own, until they were lucky enough to hitch a ride on another lorry. Paddy *was* a rascal, but he was good company.

They were almost to Queenstown, where they would stay with a friend of Brian's da until it was time to board the ship. "Better to get there early," her ma had said as she hugged Katie good-bye, "than to miss this chance."

It had been hard leaving her ma and da, always so good to her, and going off into the unknown. And she would miss Moira and Sean and Mary and the newest Hanrahan, Siobhan, not yet two.

But it was time. Her ma was right. This *was* her chance, and she'd have been a fool not to take it. Her uncle Malachy and his wife, Lottie, had agreed that she could stay with them in Brooklyn while she made her place in America. That was good fortune. Without relatives in the new country, her da would never have let her go.

The chill rain had stopped at last, and as the skies cleared, Katie could see in the distance the unfinished spire of St. Coleman's Cathedral, Queenstown.

Her heart swelled with excitement . . . and fear. Her adventure was about to begin.

Chapter 2

On the boat deck astern, facing the docks, Elizabeth watched in fascination as six tugboats began to maneuver the massive *Titanic* from its moorings. From where she stood, leaning over the railing, she had a bird's-eye view. The tugs seemed dwarfed, no larger than a child's bathtub toys. The ship moved slowly . . . slowly. Then, still with the help of the tugboats, it made a ninety-degree turn, which felt to Elizabeth like the final, easy turn of a carousel ride. Now the ship was ready to go forward. The tugs slacked off, and the ship began to head out, away from the docks.

Elizabeth moved to the port side for a better look. There were two much smaller ships anchored on the port side. The rush of water as the *Titanic* pulled away was too much for one of the ships, the *New York*, and it began bobbing up and down in agitation. Its ropes snapped with a loud cracking sound. As the larger ship increased its speed, the *New York*, now free to follow if it chose, was pulled broadside. It looked from above as if the two ships would collide momentarily.

Elizabeth, watching from the railing, gasped and took a step backward, anticipating the collision. Others standing near her did the same.

The *Titanic* slowed, then halted in the water, then moved almost imperceptibly astern, back toward the dock, away from the smaller ship.

Elizabeth's reaction was, Why isn't my father up here, watching this? After all his talk about this ship being the greatest in the world, we have barely left the dock and already it's in trouble! A faint hope arose within her that the trip would be canceled and they would all be forced to return to London.

The runaway *New York* drifted down river slightly, but one of the tugs had somehow managed to toss a wire or a rope on board. That was followed by other lines, until the tugs had regained control. Elizabeth continued to watch as the *New York* was allowed to drift further. It ended up with its bow pointing toward a floating bridge and was safely moored there until the powerful *Titanic* had left the area.

Though all of this seemed to Elizabeth to

have happened in minutes, it had actually taken much longer. As the ship once again got underway, she heard the bugle announcing luncheon. Glancing down in surprise at the tiny, round gold watch worn on a delicate chain around her neck, she realized departure had been delayed by more than an hour by the near-collision between the two ships. She couldn't wait to see her father. He hated delays.

When she arrived at the stateroom, she had to endure a brief lecture from her mother, who seemed aghast that Elizabeth had gone exploring on her own. "What will people think, seeing someone your age wandering about as if you had no chaperone?"

"That I'm a wild, irresponsible person who should be made to walk the plank," Elizabeth retorted. Then, more calmly, "They won't think anything, Mother. They have more important things on their minds." And she told them how the captains of both the *Titanic* and the tugs had narrowly averted disaster.

Her mother frowned. She asked her husband nervously, "You don't think that means this ship is too large to be handled efficiently, do you, Martin? You know, that's why the Logans didn't book passage. Amanda felt she would be safer on a smaller ship."

"Amanda Logan is a neurotic bag of nerves," her husband answered shortly. "She'd worry throughout the entire trip no matter what kind of ship she was on." Facing the dresser mirror as he gave his black bow tie one final adjustment, he added, "And didn't you hear what Elizabeth said? She said Captain Smith did a fine job of negotiating his way around the smaller ship. That should reassure you, my dear."

Elizabeth's mother didn't look reassured. But she did look beautiful, as always, in a silk dress of periwinkle blue, its high collar edged with Irish lace, the same lace edging the cuffs of the long, full sleeves. "Come along, then," she said to her husband and daughter. "The bugle blew a good fifteen minutes ago. We'll be hard-pressed to find decent seats in the dining salon."

Although there were elevators between decks, her father insisted on taking the Grand Staircase to D deck as they had not yet had a chance to study it in the rush of embarking. He had heard, he told them, that it rivaled anything seen in the best hotels.

He was right, Elizabeth conceded. She particularly liked the natural light streaming in through the wrought iron and glass dome overhead, which prevented that dark, closed-in feeling she'd experienced on other ships. The staircase curved similarly to one she had seen in an enormous mansion in Atlanta, Georgia, during a visit to friends, and the railings were intricately carved with wrought iron insets. At the midway point, where the lower railings began to swirl gently outward on either side, there was a large, stately carved panel on the landing containing a clock, surrounded by two embossed figures her father explained were meant to symbolize Honor and Glory crowning Time. Elizabeth had no idea what that meant, but she decided she liked the carving. On each landing as they descended, there were paintings on the walls, gold-plated light fixtures, and comfortable chairs and tables should one need to rest.

There were people seated in the white-paneled reception room, relaxing before going on through the double doors into the dining room and luncheon. Voices and laughter provided a pleasant sound.

Her mother's concern about the difficulty of finding seating in the dining room, Elizabeth realized as they stood in the entrance, had been just plain silly. The room, which her father stated was the largest room afloat, was enormous, over one hundred feet in length, with small, cozy alcoves and leaded floor-to-ceiling windows. While she had expected long, narrow tables and perhaps wooden, straight-backed chairs, what she saw instead were groups of smaller, white-clothed tables and elegant chairs upholstered in a luxurious green fabric. Thick beige carpet lay underfoot. Lush green plants provided a tropical look, and crystal and china adorned the tables. The vast room, which could easily seat five hundred, was bright and welcoming, although Elizabeth would have been happier had she seen more people her own age sitting at the tables.

The ship was so steady that her water glass never bobbled once on the white tablecloth, nor did her salmon mousse slide about on her fork as she lifted it to her mouth. The food was delicious, and the sea air had made her ravenously hungry. If it hadn't been for what was facing her at the end of this trip, and for the strained relationship between herself and her parents, she would have been quite content.

"There, now!" her father said heartily, lifting his wine glass. "Isn't this everything I said it would be?" He beamed a broad smile first at his wife, then his daughter.

Elizabeth quickly erased the smile by complaining, "I don't see very many people my age."

"Perhaps someone nice will board in Cherbourg," her mother said hastily, clearly not wanting an argument to begin in public. "A lovely young French girl. That would give you an excellent opportunity to practice your language skills."

Elizabeth set her glass down on the table. "I speak French like a native, Mother. And what does it really matter, since I will never have occasion to use it? Alan Reed has no interest in travel. It's all he can do just to make the trip from his house in Manhattan to his estate in Tarrytown."

"Please, Elizabeth," her mother pleaded in a low voice, "not here. Would you be kind enough to let us enjoy our meal?" Turning from her daughter to her husband, she added in a more cheerful tone, "Isn't this lamb magnificent? So tender. I wonder if it would be possible to get the recipe from the cook?"

I've been dismissed, Elizabeth told herself. Roast lamb is more important to them than I am. Though she was still hungry, she refused to eat another bite. Her parents pretended not to notice.

After lunch, they went up to the first-class lounge on B deck for coffee. On their way to the elevator, they found the corridors crowded with passengers exploring the ship, intent on learning their way around. Most were too accustomed to luxury to exclaim openly. Still, the expressions on all of the faces were admiring, and some were full of wonder as they peered into this room or that.

There were people playing cards in the lounge, a large, carpeted room with wall sconces, arched doorways, patterned upholstered chairs, and elaborately carved wooden paneling on the walls and ceiling. Others engaged in conversation, striking up acquaintanceships that would last throughout the trip.

Unwilling to sit with only adults, Elizabeth invented a headache. She excused herself and walked the length of the room to the aft first-class staircase, where she left the lounge. A cool breeze caressed her face as she went to the rail and stood there, looking out over the water. The sea was still smooth, a silken sheet of dark blue. She could taste salt on her lips. Around her, couples strolled, hand in hand, talking and laughing. A pang of envy shot through Elizabeth. She knew there were honeymooning couples aboard, and she tried to envision herself and Alan Reed strolling among them. Impossible. Alan hated traveling, that was the first thing. The second thing was she couldn't picture Alan laughing and talking as freely and easily as these couples seemed to be doing.

Elizabeth sighed. Better to jump over the railing right now and disappear forever beneath the surface than spend her entire life in the dull, dreary company of Alan Reed.

Then she straightened up, took a deep breath of salty air, and shook her head vehemently. Nonsense! Alan wasn't important enough to make her do something so stupid.

She had her whole life ahead of her, and she was going to see to it herself that she spent it the way *she* wanted. Whatever that took.

Her father came up, accompanied her to the enclosed promenade on A deck, and rented a chair and a lap robe for her. "A nice relaxing rest," he said gently. "Just what the doctor ordered." He gave her an awkward pat on the head as he turned to leave. Then he spoiled it by adding, "Your head is uncovered, Elizabeth. Would you like me to run down to your cabin and bring you a hat?"

Every other woman on deck was wearing a hat.

"No, Father," Elizabeth said, sliding down beneath the lap robe. "The hat is what gave me the headache in the first place." Not true. But if she could invent a headache, she could certainly invent the reason for it. "Don't worry, no one's going to throw me overboard because my head is bare."

She heard the sigh that followed him off deck. She couldn't help feeling sorry for him. Bad enough he hadn't had the son he wanted, who would follow him into the banking business. Now his daughter was being difficult.

She stayed in the deck chair all afternoon, drinking endless cups of hot tea and brooding about her future. It wasn't until the ship slowed as they approached Cherbourg that she tossed the lap robe aside, climbed to her feet, and left the promenade to walk along the starboard rail where she could watch the embarkation. She could see the long seawall straight ahead, and peered more closely to look for the tenders that would bring passengers aboard. There they were, sitting low in the shallow waters along the shore. The small boats were already loaded. She wondered how long the passengers had been waiting. Probably an hour or more.

The sun hadn't set yet. It turned the water along the low shore into liquid gold for a brief period. Then dusk quickly descended as the tenders made for the ship. Elizabeth imagined how the *Titanic* must look from where they were. The ship's lights had all come on, hundreds, perhaps thousands of them, and were turning the ship into a fairyland castle sitting high in the water.

She was still standing at the rail, watching with interest at seven-thirty, when the bugle sounded for dinner. Her stomach was growling with hunger, and she was curious about why her parents hadn't come looking for her. Her mother, who spent hours getting herself ready for any occasion, knew Elizabeth would have to bathe and change before the evening meal. Odd that her father hadn't come to peel her away from the railing.

Elizabeth turned and went inside, to stand at

a distance opposite the entrance to watch as the first-class passengers from Cherbourg came on board. She was hoping there would be another girl her age, of almost any nationality. If the girl didn't speak English or French, they'd find some other way to communicate. But at least she'd have someone besides her parents for company on board.

There *was* someone her age, or near her age. Unfortunately, not a female. A young man, very tall, almost too thin, in a worn tweed jacket and matching cap pulled low over his light brown hair, which needed cutting. The minute he came through the doorway, Elizabeth knew he was in the wrong place. Not only were his clothes far too worn for first class, but he was carrying his own baggage: what looked to be a portfolio of some kind, and several boxes tied with string. First-class passengers did *not* tote their own luggage. She wondered how he had gotten past the staff greeting arriving passengers. Didn't they check to see what class ticket the new arrivals carried?

She wondered if he even spoke English or French. There were many nationalities traveling on this ship. Some were emigrating to America; others were on their way to visit relatives. If the young man was Norwegian or Swedish or German, Elizabeth would be at a loss. She spoke only English and French.

She glanced around as the tall young man struggled to balance his boxes. No one seemed to be paying any attention to him. Perhaps in all the confusion of this new group of passengers boarding, he had slipped by the crew. He must not have understood the class designation on his ticket.

As he neared, she took a step forward and, intending to be helpful, asked, "Excuse me. Do you speak English?"

He lifted his head to look at her over the tower of black boxes, but didn't answer. His eyes were a deep, dark blue, thickly lashed. But they seemed to Elizabeth uncomprehending.

"Well," she said gently, "I think you might be in the wrong area of the ship. Does your ticket read first class?"

Still no answer. His face was so lean, his cheekbones sculpted so acutely, Elizabeth wondered if he might be starving. How had he afforded this trip at all? Even a third-class passage on the *Titanic* would require funds he could have used for food.

The dark blue eyes regarded her carefully. She saw no comprehension in them.

Elizabeth took pity on him. Calling a steward to assist him might be a humiliation. Deciding that even a second-class passenger probably wouldn't be carrying his own luggage, she tried to think where the third-class entrance might be. She had no idea. She hesitated, wondering if she should interfere at all. Then she thought how mortified she herself would feel if she were mistakenly at the wrong entrance, and made up her mind. In that same, gentle tone of voice, she said, "Would you excuse me for a minute? Don't go anywhere. I'll be right back."

She hurried over to a nearby, uniformed steward directing a group of passengers to their cabins. "Could you please tell me where the third-class entrance might be?" she asked, keeping her voice low so the young man wouldn't hear.

Barely restraining surprise at such a question coming from someone so well-dressed, the steward answered politely, "There's two I know of, miss. Aft on C deck, D deck on the bow."

Nodding and thanking him, Elizabeth returned to the passenger. "Come with me," she said briskly. "I'll direct you to a third-class entrance. We'll take the elevator to C deck." She added, almost as an afterthought, "Then I've got to rush back up and get ready for dinner or my parents will have everyone on the ship looking for me."

He still had not spoken a word when the lift stopped at C deck, and the door opened. But as she pointed aft and told him good-bye, he managed somehow to free a hand long enough to tip his tweed cap to her and nod a thank-you before striding off along the corridor.

Feeling satisfied, even a little smug at proving she *could* be useful on her own, Elizabeth returned to her stateroom to change for dinner.

Chapter 3

Wednesday, April 10, 1912

Knowing her father had little patience on an empty stomach, Elizabeth resisted the urge to discuss her impending debut and marriage to Alan Reed while they were all changing for dinner. She regarded this strategy as prudent rather than cowardly. The best military generals plotted their moves carefully. She would do no less. She was determined to win this war.

She wore her apricot silk, its collar high around her throat, its sleeves full and to the elbow. It was the most feminine dress she owned, and she knew how becoming it was. She hadn't seen anyone who looked especially interesting board at Cherbourg, but she had been distracted by that confused young man from third class. It was possible that while she was helping him, someone fascinating had boarded. If so, that person would most likely be in the dining room. She should look her best, just in case. The apricot silk brought out the peach tones in her skin and the reddish highlights in her hair.

"Tomorrow night," her mother said as she fastened a mother-of-pearl comb in her own blond upsweep, "I should like to dine in the à la carte restaurant. Mrs. Widener tells me the cuisine is extraordinary. But tonight I prefer the dining room. Someone we know may have boarded in Cherbourg. The Jarvises were touring the Continent this spring, and Lily Bascomb rented a house in the south of France for the entire month of March. Wouldn't it be lovely if they were all on board?"

Since Elizabeth couldn't tolerate her mother's friend Miss Bascomb, a silly, vain woman who talked of nothing but herself, she made no comment. She thought it interesting, even surprising, that she and her mother were thinking alike. They so seldom did. But now they were both hoping someone interesting had boarded at Cherbourg.

Elizabeth's apricot-dyed shoes pinched her toes, forcing her to take tiny, mincing steps.

"Good heavens, Elizabeth!" her mother said. "Must you walk like that?"

"You ordered the shoes a half size too small. They hurt."

"Then change them," her father interjected.

"Heaven knows you've got plenty of others in your wardrobe room. If I were as astute a businessman as everyone thinks I am, I'd invest in an Italian shoe company."

Nola Farr looked shocked. "Martin! Those shoes were custom-dyed specifically for that dress. And they are *not* the wrong size. Elizabeth is just being melodramatic."

"Tell my *toes* that," Elizabeth said. But she repositioned her feet in the shoes enough to allow her a normal gait. She didn't want to waste any time arguing on something as insignificant as shoes. There were far more important issues to discuss with her parents.

The dining room was more crowded than it had been earlier in the day. Mr. Farr shared information garnered from one of the stewards that one hundred and forty-two first-class passengers had boarded in Cherbourg. But the enormous room was also more festive. Now that darkness had fallen, the lights were on, sending a soft glow across the tables. Elizabeth found herself wishing she were making this trip with someone other than her parents.

The thought took her by surprise. Romance hadn't been on her mind lately. She'd been concentrating too hard on removing Alan Reed from her life to even think about putting someone else *in*.

But there was something about this magical

ship gliding across the Atlantic Ocean that made her think about strolling on the promenade hand in hand with someone wonderful. Someone who understood her. (And *liked* her.) Maybe it was the soft, golden glow cast by the lights, or the love songs being played by the orchestra now and again, or the sight of honeymooning couples seated in the cozy alcoves, holding hands across the table and gazing into each other's eyes.

Whatever it was, Elizabeth felt a sudden wash of loneliness sweep over her, and she shivered.

Her father noticed and said, "You should have worn a shawl."

"I shouldn't have worn these *shoes*." Elizabeth shifted position again to ease the cramping in her toes, and as she did so, she saw, across the room, the third-class passenger she had helped. He was seated at a table with Mr. Benjamin Guggenheim, a friend of Elizabeth's father's.

At first, she thought she was mistaken. How could that passenger be sitting in the first-class dining salon? But as she continued to look, she knew there was no mistaking those finely chiseled cheekbones. He was still in need of a haircut, and although he had changed into a dinner jacket, he was wearing it over a white turtleneck sweater, the only man in the entire room dressed so informally. He probably didn't know any better.

What was he doing *here*? According to the pamphlet they'd been given with their tickets, there was supposed to be a very clear separation of classes on board. Second-class passengers had their own dining room, also on D deck, but near the bow, and third-class passengers, like this fellow, were supposed to eat in their own dining room on E deck. Not that she cared where anyone ate. But if someone ... a waiter, perhaps ... checked and discovered a third-class passenger dining in the first-class salon, it could be positively mortifying for the young man.

It seemed obvious that he must not understand a word of English.

"Well," her father, standing at Elizabeth's elbow, said then, "I do see someone we know. Two people, actually. And their table isn't yet full. Shall we join them?"

It made sense to Elizabeth that he led the way then to Mr. Benjamin Guggenheim's table. After all, the man was an acquaintance of her father's. She had met him herself twice, and wouldn't need to be introduced.

What did not make sense, however, was the way her father turned to the young man in the turtleneck, who had politely risen to acknowledge the presence of ladies, and said with a smile, "And this, if I'm not mistaken, is Jules Whittaker's slightly wayward son, Maxwell. Max, isn't it?" Mr. Farr extended his hand. As the two shook hands, Elizabeth's father added, "Studying art in Paris, weren't you? Always the rebel, eh, Max?"

Elizabeth stared, unaware that her jaw had dropped. He was an *American*? The son of someone her father knew? He spoke English, and he wasn't poor? But then, what —?

She knew who Jules Whittaker was. He owned one of the largest fur salons in New York and another in Los Angeles. Her mother adored him . . . or maybe it was his furs she adored. Jules Whittaker was a very wealthy man. His son, rebel or not, wouldn't be traveling third class . . . unless Daddy had disowned him. But if that were true, her own father would know it, and wouldn't be speaking to the son in such a civil, even friendly, voice.

Elizabeth knew the Whittakers slightly. She also knew they had a son. She even knew the son's name was Max, and that he had a talent for art. But she had never met him.

So. The tall, thin, confused, third-class passenger she'd "helped" earlier that evening wasn't third class at all, and hadn't been the tiniest bit confused. He was as wealthy and privileged as *she* was. How mortifying. For *her*, not for him. How could she have made such a mistake?

"Enid Whittaker is near collapse," Elizabeth remembered her mother reporting at breakfast one morning late in August last year. "That younger son of theirs, the one who's always been so difficult, is giving her palpitations." This was the young man she'd been talking about? This Max standing in front of her, smiling?

"That boy has spirit," her father had answered in August. "He's just sowing his wild oats. They'd be well-advised to leave him alone, let him stand on his own two feet for a change."

Elizabeth had been angry about that. Why was it he didn't feel the same way about his daughter standing on *her* own two feet? Now, she struggled with her chagrin over mistaking Jules Whittaker's son for a third-class passenger. Remembering how he had remained so completely silent while she directed him to third class, Elizabeth flushed with anger. He could have *said* something — before she made a complete fool of herself.

Of course, she *had* made the mistake of judging him by his appearance. Bad, bad mistake. But he could have set her straight. Why hadn't he? He must have been laughing at her the whole time.

She remained miserably mute when they were introduced, barely nodding her head. She looked away, fixing an aloof stare on the ornate ceiling above his head. But she knew he was still smiling.

She hated him.

"I'm sure your parents will be relieved," Elizabeth's mother said. "I know your mother's been beside herself, with you off in France alone." Her voice lacked its usual warmth. Elizabeth knew why. The shagginess of his haircut, the turtleneck sweater . . . one of those things all by itself would have set her mother's teeth on edge. The two combined were simply too much. She was, of course, completely civil. Nola's Rules of Etiquette were on display. But she was not as friendly as she would normally be to the son of an acquaintance.

Elizabeth wondered if Max Whittaker noticed. Probably not. Probably wouldn't care, anyway, about a woman who had a fool for a daughter.

The fool daughter had no choice but to be equally civil to the Whittaker's errant son. Her mother would expect nothing less of her. And Elizabeth didn't want to waste time back in the stateroom listening to a lecture on manners. If she didn't face her parents tonight regarding their plans for her, the entire first day at sea would be a waste. She couldn't afford that.

The only thing she learned about Max Whittaker during that endless dinner was that he was intelligent and could carry on a spirited conversation. He entertained them all with witty tales of his adventures living among the poor artists in Paris. Even as he lifted a forkful of filet mignon to his lips, he said, "You can make a surprisingly palatable tomato soup with nothing more than catsup and water. Very cheap, and very filling."

What Elizabeth couldn't figure out and was unwilling to ask was how Max Whittaker, who had apparently defied his parents, could afford first-class passage on the *Titanic*. Had his parents forgiven him for rejecting Harvard and choosing instead to live among the bohemians in Paris? She could imagine the message inserted in the fine linen envelope containing his first-class ticket: "All is forgiven. Come home."

She tried her best to ignore him, but his stories *were* interesting. Then, too, she told herself she might be forced to follow his example and cut all ties with her own parents if they refused to listen to her wishes. Perhaps she could learn something about living on one's own if she listened carefully to Max Whittaker. Although she couldn't imagine eating tomato soup made from catsup and water.

They all left the dining room together. They were passing through the lounge when Max

Whittaker suddenly appeared at her side and asked quietly, "Helped any more third-class passengers since I saw you last?"

Elizabeth felt her cheeks flush scarlet. Fortunately, her parents had paused to talk for a moment with Second Officer Lightoller, and were unaware of their daughter's discomfort.

"No," she snapped in response. Not content to leave it at that, she added under her breath, "And if you're really Jules Whittaker's son, I would think you could afford a decent haircut!" With that, she picked up the hem of her apricot dress and swept out of the lounge with her head held high.

She heard laughter behind her. She didn't turn around. But she knew it was coming from him.

Chapter 4

Wednesday, April 10, 1912

Katie couldn't sleep. Her body ached from the rigors of the long trip and she was physically exhausted, but her mind was racing. She lay in the narrow bed under the eaves in Tommy Bascomb's attic in Queenstown and willed morning to come quickly. Then, at last she would be on her way to America!

It would be hard, leaving her beautiful country. She had lived here sixteen years and one month, surrounded by family and friends. And she had been happy. But Ireland had little to offer a young girl except marriage and children, and she wasn't ready for that yet. She wanted to see some of the world first. She wanted to see America, where the streets were paved with gold.

At first, her ma thought she was addlepated.

"Sure, and why would you be wantin' to traipse off to a big, rough place like America where there's nothin' but strangers?"

Katie couldn't explain, though she'd tried. Her da understood. "Make your fortune while you're young, Katie-girl." Hadn't there been a note of wistfulness in his voice? "You wait too long, it'll pass you by."

And then he had given her the ticket for her birthday, while her mother got teary-eyed at the kitchen table, having long since accepted the fact of Katie's leaving.

Tommy Bascomb, Brian's da's friend with whom they were staying overnight, said, "There's money to be made in America. I'd go meself if I thought they could use another butcher. But I hear they've got plenty, and here I own me own shop. But three fine young people like yourselves can make your mark, and that's the truth of it. Even you," he had added, addressing Katie directly. "A comely young lass like yourself should have no trouble finding a rich husband."

Katie had bristled. "'Tis not a husband I'm seekin'," she had said hotly. "I'm goin' to make me *own* fortune!"

Brian had laughed uproariously, as had Tommy. Only Paddy had defended her, saying firmly, "She's quick-minded, and she's healthy and strong. She'll do fine in America."

"Aye, but she's a *girl*," Tommy had protested.

Katie turned restlessly in bed. What if he was right? What if Brian and Tommy knew something about the way of the world that she didn't? Doom and disaster could be awaiting her in the new country. And then there was the great ship itself. If the *Titanic* was as big as everyone said it was, how could it be expected to stay afloat all the way to America?

She didn't know how to swim.

Katie laughed softly to herself. Even if she could swim, the waters of the Atlantic at this time of year were so icy, the strongest swimmer would flounder, arms and legs frozen after only seconds in the frigid sea. Knowing how to swim would be useless.

"It's unsinkable," she reminded herself in a whisper meant to reassure. "The *Titanic* is unsinkable. Da said so."

Remembering her father's wholehearted support of her adventure comforted Katie, and she finally fell asleep.

Elizabeth became increasingly tense as she waited alone in the stateroom for her parents to return. What was taking them so long? She could almost hear the giant clock on the Grand Staircase ticking away her life. *Tick . . . tick . . .*

tick ... Elizabeth Farr has ... *tick, tick* ... no say in ... *tick, tick* ... her own future.

"Oh, yes I *do!*" she muttered under her breath. She began pacing back and forth. The apricot silk swirled around her ankles, making a soft, whispering sound that seemed to Elizabeth yet another "*tick, tick* ..."

She was still pacing when her parents arrived, laughing over some remembered witticism of Max Whittaker's as they entered their cabin. Elizabeth knew it had come from Max because her mother was saying, "I know he's given poor Enid a difficult time, but he really is quite charming."

Elizabeth stiffened. Charming? Max Whittaker?

"Where have you been?" she asked as she stepped from her cabin into theirs. "I've been back for *hours!*"

Unperturbed, her father pulled his gold pocket watch free and glanced at it. "You left us exactly twenty minutes ago. Twenty minutes does not constitute an hour, Elizabeth, let alone several."

"Well, it seemed like it," she replied, flopping into a wine velvet upholstered chair. "You *knew* I wanted to talk to you."

"I knew no such thing," her mother said, slipping out of her gold slippers and collapsing wearily onto the chaise lounge. "Martin, did you know Elizabeth wished to speak to us?"

"Elizabeth always wishes to speak to us. Unfortunately, it's always on the same subject." Elizabeth's father, still standing in the middle of the cabin, smiled warily at her. "I dare say I'm right? Or are we about to get lucky and simply talk about this great ship and what a pleasant day at sea it's been?" He took a seat on the green velvet banquette against the wall opposite Elizabeth's chair. "That would be so refreshing."

"I'm not going to marry Alan Reed," Elizabeth said quickly. "And I'm not making my debut, either. I want to go to college. To Vassar. You *have* to let me."

Her father's eyebrows arched. "*Have* to?"

Her mother, one hand to her forehead, said, "Oh, Elizabeth, how many times have we had this pointless discussion? We've had such a lovely day. Must you ruin it?"

Elizabeth kept talking. "I don't want to get married, not now. And if I did, it wouldn't be to anyone as boring as Alan."

"Alan is a sweet man. Your father and I have met few gentlemen we've liked as well."

"Then perhaps you could adopt him." Elizabeth's voice was cold. "And let *me* go to Vassar."

"Mind your tongue," her father warned, his

smile completely gone now. "We're only trying to see that you're well taken care of, Elizabeth. However . . ."

Elizabeth's heart leaped with hope.

"Perhaps, since you're already spoken for," her father continued, "we could cancel your formal debut. If you really hate the idea so intensely."

Nola Farr shot upright on the chaise lounge. "Martin, you can't be serious! Plans have been made, gowns and shoes ordered. I've already accepted invitations in Elizabeth's name! What would people think?"

Elizabeth stood up. "They would think, Mother, that you were letting *me* decide which parties I wanted to attend."

"You would have declined every invitation."

"Yes, I would have. Because I don't want to be put on display like an exhibit at a World's Fair. And Father is right. The whole point of debuting into society, whether anyone admits it or not, is to find a husband. Since you've already picked one out for me and made all the arrangements, why do I have to go through a debut?"

Her mother looked confused for a moment. Then her brow cleared, and she answered almost triumphantly, "Because this is how we *do* things."

Elizabeth knew what "we" meant. The privileged of society. Wasn't that why they were on this most impressive of all ocean liners in the first place, traveling in such luxury? And they weren't the only ones. They were in the company of John Jacob Astor, one of the richest men in the United States, and his young wife, along with Mr. Isadore Strauss, owner of Macy's department store, and his wife, and Benjamin Guggenheim. There was at least one countess on board. And they all did things a certain way. Her mother's way.

Elizabeth thought, But I want to make my own way. Within reason, of course. She would admit she needed their support. Luxurious living was something she had learned to take for granted. She knew, just as her parents seemed to, that she would not be good at being poor. But right at the moment, the price she had to pay for privilege seemed much too high. Marriage to a man she didn't love? Didn't even especially like?

"I won't marry him," she repeated. "I'd rather jump overboard."

"I hear," her father said easily, lighting his pipe, "that the waters of the Atlantic are especially cold this time of year."

"And you'd ruin your dress, dear," Elizabeth's mother said, sending a conspiratorial smile her husband's way.

"Don't *do* that!" Elizabeth said. "Don't treat me like a two-year-old!"

"If you dislike it so much," her father said, "you'd be well-advised to hold onto your temper, unlike most two-year-olds."

"Oh!" Elizabeth cried in frustration. Fighting angry tears, she ran back to her own cabin.

She didn't stay there long. In the adjoining cabin, she could hear her father chuckling and knew her parents were not taking her announcement seriously. It was her own fault. Her father was right. She had acted like a two-year-old. But it was so frustrating, not being taken seriously. Even if she hadn't raised her voice, they still wouldn't have changed their minds about Alan.

And she knew why. Because neither of her parents trusted her to take care of herself and to choose her own husband. They were afraid she'd pick some handsome but grasping fortune hunter instead of someone who already had his own fortune and had no need of hers.

I wouldn't *do* that, Elizabeth told the dresser mirror as she passed it. I have more common sense than that.

She knew why her mother worried. There had been that one boy last summer . . . Joshua Lawrence . . . but her mother had overreacted to that. It had been perfectly innocent. Elizabeth hardly knew him. Joshua worked on the ice truck that served their neighborhood. He was terribly good-looking — all the girls said so — and he was very friendly. After only two days on the job, he knew the names of everyone in the neighborhood. Elizabeth's mother had been shocked when, as the Farrs were leaving their brownstone one day last June, Joshua had called from the back of the truck as it passed, "Mornin', Elizabeth."

Perhaps that was when her mother had approached Alan Reed for the first time.

Joshua wasn't a fortune hunter. He was just a friendly person. It would have been rude not to return his greeting.

But it had been impossible to convince her mother that he and Elizabeth had exchanged only the barest civilities, and nothing more. The solution, from Nola Farr's point of view, was to marry her daughter off, as quickly as possible, to someone who didn't need her money. Enter Alan Reed.

Pulling a pale yellow mohair shawl from one of the dresser drawers and tossing it around her shoulders, Elizabeth left the cabin and took the stairs up to A deck. If she was going to look at the sea, she wanted to feel the cool air and taste the salt on her lips.

It was after ten o'clock, but the open promenade was busy with strollers, many of them holding hands or linked arm in arm. The pang of wistfulness overtook Elizabeth again. How lucky they were to have each other.

"Looking for wayward travelers in need of assistance?" a deep voice at her shoulder asked.

She knew who it was immediately, and deliberately refused to turn her head. Her mother wasn't around, so there was no reason to be polite. "This is a sea voyage," she said, her voice as chilly as the air sweeping in from the vast, black ocean. The shawl was proving woefully inadequate. "So I am looking at the sea."

"Mind if I join you?"

"Yes. I do mind. Very much. Go away." The words were barely out of her mouth when she sensed his presence at her left elbow, as if she hadn't even spoken.

"Tsk, tsk, Elizabeth," Max Whittaker scolded. "Deplorable manners! What would your mother say?"

"Do you see my mother anywhere around here? I believe I'm alone. And I would prefer to stay that way." Elizabeth remained staring steadfastly out over the glistening, flat sea. It looked smooth enough to skate on, and indeed the immense ship moved across the water with none of the rocking motion Elizabeth had experienced on other crossings.

"Nice night. Aren't you cold in that flimsy thing?"

He was referring to her shawl. His comment seemed much too personal. As if her comfort were any of his concern. Perhaps if she ignored him, he would go away.

He didn't go away. Instead, he astonished her by saying suddenly, "So, getting married, are you?"

Taken by surprise, Elizabeth whirled around. "No, I am *not* getting married! And if I were, what concern would that be of yours? Have you been asking questions about me?"

"Your mother told me you were betrothed," he said casually, as if he hadn't noticed her anger. "I think she was warning me away." He laughed lightly. "Must be the turtleneck. She disapproved. Looked at me pretty much the same way you did when you saw me come aboard."

Annoyed by the presumption that she and her mother thought alike, Elizabeth snapped, "Well, it wasn't the turtleneck then. You weren't wearing it when you came on board."

He laughed again, louder this time. "Quite right, I wasn't." He hesitated, then added seriously, "If I apologize for misleading you and taking advantage of your good will, will you apologize for judging me by my appearance?"

Although his accusation rankled, Elizabeth couldn't help noticing that his eyes laughed when his mouth did, something she had always found attractive.

Still, she didn't really feel like forgiving him. Unless ... "I suppose I *could* forgive you," she answered slowly, turning her gaze back to the sea. "But you'll have to earn my forgiveness."

"And how, exactly, do I do that?"

Elizabeth smiled. "You can start by telling me all about your life in Paris. You can tell me what it's like for someone raised with money to strike out on his own and live on very little. That is, unless your parents were supporting you financially. Then I wouldn't be interested."

"They were not supporting me. I worked as a waiter in Paris to support myself."

Elizabeth propped an elbow on the railing and rested her chin against it, and only then did she turn her face to meet his gaze. "Then tell me," she insisted. "Tell me what it's like to be on one's own. And if you do a good job, perhaps I'll forgive you."

Max began talking.

Chapter 5

Thursday, April 11, 1912

When Elizabeth awoke on her second day at sea, it took her several moments to realize where she was. There was no noticeable bobbing to tell her she was on the ocean, and the warm wood paneling was much like that of any hotel room. She could have been safely on land in London, Paris, Zurich, or New York.

But she wasn't. That realization dawned on her as she recalled the last thing Max Whittaker had said to her last night. After listening intently for over an hour to his tales of Paris, Elizabeth had been summoned by her father. "It's after eleven," he had called from the first-class entrance. "Come along, Elizabeth." She had politely, if reluctantly, thanked Max for the stimulating conversation, and as she walked away, hugging her arms around her to keep warm, he had called, "Smooth sailing, Elizabeth!"

Remembering now where she was, Elizabeth yawned and stretched slowly. As entertaining as Max's stories had been, she knew herself well enough to realize that living in a garret somewhere, without heat or hot water, as Max had done this past year, was not for her. Max might not care a great deal about ready access to a long, soothing hot bath, but Elizabeth was painfully aware that she would be miserable without it. If her parents refused to pay her tuition at Vassar, she wouldn't be able to go. Even if she were willing to live in a hovel and work to pay her own way, what sort of work could she find? She had no experience, no training, no qualifications.

It's not my fault, she thought as she dressed in a long, white knife-pleated skirt and a white long-sleeved middy top.

But Max had been raised the same way she had. And yet he had spoken of eating week-old vegetables discarded by restaurants, and lighting his room by candlelight, and painting with fingers so cold, his knuckles ached. He had spoken of these hardships as if he had dealt with them all of his life.

But I'm *not* Max, Elizabeth told herself. I don't want to freeze in a garret. All I'm asking for is an education! My parents shouldn't have told me "yes" throughout my life to everything any girl could want, if they were going to turn around and tell me "no" to the one thing I really want. That isn't fair of them.

She wasn't very good company at breakfast. In spite of the bright, cheerful atmosphere in the dining room, which was nearly full, Elizabeth barely touched the grilled ham and tomato omelet her father ordered for her. She slid down in her chair, arms folded across her chest, and watched as he cheerfully relished every bite of his grilled mutton kidneys and bacon. Last night's argument was never mentioned. Instead, her mother asked about Max.

"Your father tells me you were deep in conversation with the Whittaker boy last night. Whatever did you find to talk about for so long?"

Elizabeth seized this opportunity. "He was telling me how hard it was for him, living in Paris with no money, since his parents refused to send him any. It's surprising that he didn't fall ill, living under such desperate conditions. I find it hard to believe his parents really love him," she added pointedly, "if they could let him suffer like that."

"He *chose* to suffer like that," her mother said, and her father added, "He didn't look to me like he'd been suffering unduly. Seems like quite a happy chap, if you ask me. Could use a bit more meat on his bones, that's clear. Probably hasn't been eating sensibly."

"He didn't have enough money for food!" Elizabeth responded.

Her father shrugged. "As your mother pointed out, that was his choice. At any rate, he's seen the light now and is on his way home. I'm sure Jules and Enid will be quite happy to see him."

"Maybe he won't *go* home," Elizabeth said. How could they be so insensitive? "Maybe he'll live on his own in New York, in a garret, just as he did in Paris. And become a world-famous artist with no help from anyone. *Then* his parents will be sorry for the way they treated him!"

Her father laughed as he lifted a scone to his mouth. "Elizabeth, you're not fooling anyone. Your mother and I are not quite as dense as you like to think. It hasn't escaped us that you are not actually talking about the Whittaker boy at all, but yourself." His eyes twinkling with amusement, he added, "I wasn't aware that you aspired to live in a garret and become a world-famous artist."

Elizabeth blinked back tears of frustration. The tables around them were crowded. She couldn't bear it if someone saw her crying. "Please don't laugh at me. I *don't* want to be an artist." Her voice lowered to an insistent whisper. *"I just ... want ... to go ... to college! Why do you want me to be stupid?"*

Her mother daintily forked a bite of baked apple. "What would be stupid," she said calmly, "would be letting a fine, secure gentleman like Alan Reed slip out of your fingers and into someone else's. It's not as though you aren't already educated, Elizabeth. We've spared no expense sending you to the finest schools."

"But there is still so much to learn," Elizabeth cried. Curious glances from people sitting at the tables around them turned her cheeks pink. She lowered her voice again, but the intensity in her words didn't lessen. "I've learned how to do needlepoint, how to entertain forty guests at a time, how to calculate well enough to pay the servants. I know how to write a lovely thank-you note and how to judge the finest fabrics, jewelry, and furniture. I can play the piano adequately, I'm not atrocious at tennis, and I can swim and ride horseback." She stared at her mother, her eyes begging. "Is that *it*? That's all you want me to know throughout my entire lifetime?"

"It seems adequate to me." Nola Farr lifted a coffee cup to her lips. Before sipping, she added, "If you insist upon learning more, you can always take up reading. As long as you employ adequate lighting, and don't overdo. Eyestrain causes forehead wrinkles, dear." She sipped, then added, "But as the wife of a prominent businessman like Alan, I daresay you won't have much time for reading."

Jumping to her feet and leaving, which was what Elizabeth wanted to do, would have created a stir in the dining room. She forced herself to stay in her chair. She couldn't bear the thought of over four hundred pairs of eyes on her as she escaped. But she clamped her lips together and refused to say another word, even when Denver millionairess Mrs. J. J. "Molly" Brown stopped at their table to congratulate her father on his winnings at cards the night before. The woman clapped him on the back and said in a loud voice that she hoped he'd play again that night, "so's I can take another crack at relievin' you of some funds." She smiled a broad grin. "Lighten your wallet a little, give you less to lug around on board."

"Very thoughtful of you," Elizabeth's father said dryly, smiling in return.

When the woman had gone, Elizabeth's mother murmured, "Now, there is a woman who is independently wealthy and completely in charge of her own life. She is also coarse, loud, and vulgar, particularly unattractive qualities in a woman. Is *that* who you would pattern yourself after, Elizabeth?"

"If she is allowed the luxury of making all of her own decisions, yes," Elizabeth answered.

And couldn't resist adding, "So, if Molly Brown were a man, it would be acceptable for her to be coarse, loud, and vulgar? Is that what you're saying, Mother?"

"Vulgarity is not acceptable from anyone," came the stiff reply. Elizabeth's mother, looking offended, touched her lips with the fine linen napkin. "But I do believe it is much more unseemly coming from a woman, and I do not apologize for thinking that. You would do well to think the same."

Elizabeth fell silent again. She was despondent at the turn the discussion had taken. But she was only giving up for now, not for good. She would try again . . . and again . . . and again.

Still, she could hear the clock on the Grand Staircase ticking away the minutes. She willed the great ship to slow down, take its time, give her more hours in which to think up a new strategy, and more hours in which to employ it.

But the *Titanic* continued to speed smoothly across the water, making its way along Saint George's Channel toward Queenstown, Ireland, where more passengers would board.

After breakfast, Elizabeth decided to go up on deck to watch the embarkation. She had never seen Ireland. She had heard that the country was beautiful, and while she might not be able to see that much of it from the ship, which she had been told would be anchored off-shore, it would be foolish to stay inside and see nothing.

When her mother stopped on the way out of the dining room to say hello to the Widener party, Elizabeth's father said quietly, "You might think about apologizing to your mother. Get on her good side. You're not doing yourself any good taking this attitude."

Elizabeth lifted her head to look straight up at him. "I don't want to apologize," she said clearly. "I haven't done anything wrong. It's hard to be polite when someone is arranging your entire life for you." Her father was right about one thing: She wasn't endearing herself to either of them by what they saw as her constant disagreeability. But how can I be agreeable, she asked herself as she left the dining room, when I don't *agree* with what they're doing to me?

When she was on deck, she glanced around for Max, the only other person she knew on board. She was eager to hear more about his adventures in Paris.

But when she found him, he wasn't alone, which both surprised and disturbed her. He was strolling toward the bow along the promenade, and on his arm was a tall, very thin girl wearing clothes that Elizabeth considered odd. Her long, black skirt was much too full by the standards of the day. Her brightly colored jacket of crimson and green in a gaudy flower pattern appeared garish in contrast to the sedate tans and grays and navy blues of other women on deck. Her hair, darker than Max's, hung loose and free around her shoulders, the sea breeze tossing it into a dark cloud around her oval, olive-skinned face.

She looks like a gypsy, Elizabeth thought. But Max was smiling down at the girl as they walked. And she, almost his height, was gazing at him with interest, as if she were hanging on his every word.

If the girl was traveling first class, someone — a mother, an aunt, a close friend?— should have given her lessons in what to wear while at sea. Elizabeth felt a sudden, sharp stab of shame. That was exactly what my mother would think, she thought, disgusted. Am I becoming like her? What difference does it make what that girl is wearing?

Others strolling the deck were not so tolerant. There were many questioning glances sent in the direction of Max and the girl. Neither took any notice.

Finding the sight of the apparently happy couple unsettling, Elizabeth turned away and strode to the rail. Perhaps the girl was someone he'd known in Paris, someone who had boarded with him at Cherbourg.

Just a short while ago, she had willed the ship to slow down, give her more time. Now, as she strained to see the approaching shores of Ireland, she found herself wishing the trip were already over and Max Whittaker had disembarked, out of her life forever.

Elizabeth's blue eyes were bleak as she stood at the rail staring out across the sea.

In Queenstown, waiting at Scott's Quay to board the small tenders that would carry them out to the *Titanic*, Katie Hanrahan was so excited she could hardly contain herself. She strained to get a look at the ship itself, anchored in the distance, but all she saw was a great white lump sitting near the Light Vessel standing guard over Cobh Harbour. It looked enormous, but Brian had already warned her that its size would seem intimidating. "You've never been to sea before, Katie-girl," he'd said as they made their way down the hill to the quay. "I'm warnin' you, if the advertisin' ain't a joke, the size of the *Titanic* is goin' to be a bit of a shock. Don't be frightened of it, girl. 'Tis only a ship, like every other ship."

Rubbing sleep from his eyes, Paddy, whom Brian had had to drag from his nice, warm bed, said hoarsely, "'Tisn't like every other ship, or there wouldn't be all this fuss about it. And 'tisn't its size I'm worried about, 'tis the weight of it, man. Shouldn't be floatin' atall, somethin' that big."

"Hush!" Brian had ordered, his eyes on Katie. "You'll be scarin' the girl to death. It got here from London, didn't it? Didn't sink on the way, did it? I tell you, the *Titanic* is unsinkable. If you really have a need for somethin' to trouble yourself about, trouble yourself about how you plan to support yourself in America."

Brian had a trade. He was an experienced dairy farm worker. Everyone in Ireland knew that America had the largest, grandest farms in all the world. His plan was to travel from New York to Wisconsin, where he would hire out on a dairy farm, save his money, and one day buy his own small farm.

Paddy, on the other hand, had never stuck to any one trade long enough to learn it well. He had tried fishing with his father, farming with Brian at the Hanrahans', where he'd met Katie, and had even waited tables briefly until a customer had aroused his anger to the point where Paddy had deliberately upended a cup of coffee in the man's ample lap.

Now, he claimed that once in America, he was going to become a famous writer. Which worried Brian no end, since he was of the mind that it took many years to become a writer, and what was Paddy to live on during those many years? "Here's the truth of it," he'd told his younger brother in the jaunting cart while Katie listened. "If you had it in your mind to become a writer, why is it that you didn't pay more attention to your grammar lessons from the good nuns?" Paddy's excuse was that he hadn't *known* then that a writer was what he wanted to be.

Although Katie found his grammar deplorable, she had learned during the long trip to Queenstown that Paddy told a good story. Perhaps in America there would be some kind person who would put Paddy's stories to paper for him, doing the spelling and the grammarizing, sparing Paddy the effort.

Brian continued to express his concern throughout the trip. Katie finally decided two things: One, Brian felt responsible for his younger brother in the absence of their parents and two, Brian was the *only* one worried about Paddy's future. Paddy himself seemed a stranger to worry. He remained lighthearted and laughing even when a sudden, chill rain soaked them all to the bone. He seemed to have not a care in the world.

How lovely to not let worry trouble you. However did Paddy manage? They were all facing the unknown, she most of all. Men with strong backs and quick minds, like the brothers Kelleher, could make their way in the world without too much trouble. But it was different for a girl, she knew that. She hadn't even told anyone in Ballyford, except Brian, to whom she told almost everything, what it was she wanted to do with her life. Everyone had assumed she would become a governess, a "nanny" as they called it in England. She "had a way" with the little ones, they'd said.

She had a true fondness for children. But that wasn't what she wanted to do with her life. She wanted to sing. She wanted to go on the American stage, in the city of New York, and have people pay to hear her voice soar through a big old theater. She had been singing all of her life, had even sung on the stage of her school. Still, she had never been paid for it. She wasn't even sure anyone *would* pay. But she was determined to find out. Brian said they would, that she sang "with the voice of an angel." But Brian knew little about music, and himself couldn't carry a tune in a bushel basket. Best not to take his opinions too seriously.

If her ma and da had known what she intended, her ma, at least, would have tied her to the bed to keep her from leaving. "The stage?" she'd have screamed in that voice she used to call the wee ones in for supper. "The stage? With painted ladies and scoundrels? Over me dead body, Kathleen Hanrahan!"

Da wouldn'ta liked the idea, neither. But he

sang, too, in a big, booming bass that shook the rafters of Our Lady of Sorrows Church, and he loved music as she did. If she'd promised him she wasn't aiming to sing in pubs or vaudeville, only the respectable stage, he might have come round. She could get around her da. Her ma was a stone wall no one got around.

The tender pulled up to the dock. As dock-workers heaved the huge sacks of mail in, embarking passengers marched past the doctor who was to inspect them and hand them their health certificates before boarding. When they had their certificates in hand, Brian helped Katie into the tender *America*. There were over one hundred passengers, and the *America* filled so quickly, Paddy, who had lingered to talk to some of the workers, was forced to take a seat in the *Ireland*, the second tender.

The trip from dock to ship took less than half an hour. The last seven or eight minutes of the trip found Katie in a stunned daze, her eyes riveted on the enormous, sparkling ship they were fast approaching. Nothing Brian had said had prepared her for its size. It was bigger than the grandest, finest hotel. And it looked so ... so *new*, everything shiny and spanking clean.

Hoping she would know how to behave properly on such a grand ship, Katie turned to glance over her shoulder one last time at Ireland's shores, wondering with a mixture of excitement and sadness if she would ever see it again.

Seeing the look on her face, Brian put a hand on her shoulder and told her quietly, "Say good-bye now, Katie. Say good-bye to the old life. Sure and once you board the *Titanic*, you say hello to a new one."

Under her breath, so softly she was certain even Brian couldn't hear her, she whispered, "Good-bye, Ireland. Good-bye, Ma and Da. Good-bye, Moira and Sean, Mary and Siobhan." Especially Siobhan, who Katie loved to sing to sleep at night. "Good-bye, Granda." Then, because tears were threatening, pinching at her eyelids, she added in that same whisper, "Maybe I'll be back someday."

Then she blinked twice to clear her eyes, and turned toward the great ship *Titanic*, ready to begin her new life.

Chapter 6

Thursday, April 11, 1912

By the end of that day, Katie's eyes ached fiercely from the effort of taking in so many wondrous sights so quickly.

The most difficult moment came when they first boarded the ship. Eugene Daly, who had been a passenger on one of the tenders, took a moment to stand on the aft third-class promenade and play on his pipes the mournful melody "Erin's Lament." Though Katie was anxious to see where they would be housed during the trip, the sad strains brought her to a halt at the third-class entrance. Tugging on Paddy's sleeve, she said in a hushed voice, "Should we not go and say good-bye to Ireland?"

He shrugged her hand away. "I've said me good-byes." Turning to look at her, he asked, "You're not fixin' to blubber?" Then, to Katie's surprise, he put an arm around her shoulder right there in the middle of a milling, excited crowd and said quietly, "It's okay if you want to, y'know. 'Tis a sore thing, leavin' family behind." He tapped the shoulder of his navy blue peacoat. "Here's the spot. Lay your pretty head right there and blubber all you like."

It was the sort of thing Katie would have expected from Brian, not from his brother. The surprise of it distracted her from the song and her pain, and she found herself laughing. "Now why would I be wantin' to blubber when I'm here on this fine new ship and on my way to America? But," she added hastily, "it was fearful kind of you to offer a shoulder and I'm thankin' you."

She thought for a moment that Paddy's cheeks reddened, but told herself that had to be the way the light was hitting his face. Paddy Kelleher was not a blushing sort of man.

Through open doors flanking the entrance, Katie could see a roomy area with patterned linoleum on the floors, paneling on the walls, and wooden benches, tables and chairs. Everything was new and, to her eyes, beautiful.

Seeing her curiosity, a nearby steward said, "Third-class smoking room. For the gentlemen, you know. That other room" — gesturing with a wave of his hand toward a larger room with white enameled walls framed in pine, furnished

with what Katie regarded as fine furniture —
"is called the general room. Got a piano. You
folks can have yourself some good times in
there."

It was nicer than any of the pubs back home.
Katie would have thought he was mistaken if
he hadn't been wearing a uniform. She would
have thought such fine rooms must be reserved
for the first- and second-class passengers. She
kept the thought to herself, not wanting to appear unsophisticated. Sure and the steward's
word had to be good as gold.

The second painful moment came when, to
Katie's consternation, she learned that an entire ship would separate her from the brothers
Kelleher. Single women were housed near the
stern of the ship, single men near the bow.

"No one told me!" she cried to Brian when
this piece of information was announced. "I
thought you'd be close at hand."

Brian's eyes twinkled. "That wouldn't be
proper, Katie. Not to fret. The gathering room
is just above your quarters. We'll be spendin'
most of our time there. You can't get rid of us
that easy, you'll see."

Paddy hesitated, looking down at Katie with
what looked like concern in his eyes. "You'll be
missin' Brian somethin' sore, I'd say by the look
on your face."

"I'll be missin' both of you," she answered,

touched by his concern. "But Bri is right. We'll just settle ourselves in our cabins and then meet in the gatherin' room. You'll both hurry back here?"

"We will," Paddy assured her, awkwardly patting her shoulder as he turned to follow Brian.

Then Katie had no choice but to follow the stewardess to her quarters. She felt very much alone, a feeling she was not at all accustomed to.

She had expected to be sleeping in one large cabin filled with bunks. Instead, when they got below, she was directed to a group of rooms containing two, four, or six berths each, all with fine, new, red-and-white bedspreads. Some of the rooms, Katie noticed as she passed in a delighted daze, were larger than the tiny bedroom under the eaves she shared at home with Moira and Mary.

"'Tisn't a ship," she told a young woman holding two small children by the hand. "'Tis a grand floating hotel. And a fine one, at that." Seeing the confused look on the woman's face, Katie asked, "Are you lookin' fer your husband, then? Is it himself you've lost?"

"I don't have a husband." The young woman, who looked no older than Katie and had a headful of frothy blond curls, led each of the children to a berth and motioned to them to sit down.

Her dark eyes cleared some then, and she turned back to Katie to extend a hand, saying, "Eileen O'Keefe here. These two" — pointing to the quiet, motionless children — "are Kevin and Bridey Donohue." She lowered her voice. "They've just lost their parents to the influenza. I'm takin' them to America to live with an aunt in Brooklyn. That's in New York City," she added knowingly. She unpinned her wide-brimmed straw hat and dropped it on one of the red-and-white bedspreads. "I've got the willies about goin' to sea on a ship that hasn't never sailed before atall. But the money they're payin' me is fair, and it's a chance to see America."

"You're comin' back then, to Ireland?"

"That I am." Eileen's fair cheeks turned rosy. "Engaged to be married, I am." She held out a hand again, this time to display a gold band boasting a small pearl. "To a fine young lad name of Sean Murphy. An April wedding, though this time of year, rain is almost as sure as the dawn. Me ma wanted me to wait till June. But" — the flush deepened and her eyes twinkled — "Sean says waitin' till June would be the worst kind of torture. So 'tis an April bride I'll be." She turned back to her two charges, still sitting mute on their bunks. "I plan to use the money the aunt is payin' me to buy me trousseau."

"It sounds lovely," Katie said politely, though she couldn't imagine getting married at such a young age. "And it'd please me to give you a hand with these two little ones," she added. "I'm a fair hand with youngsters. It'd give me somethin' to do." And it would be nice, with Brian and Patrick so far away at the far end of the ship, to have a friend right here.

"I could use the help," Eileen admitted. "You might want to help me get their outer garments off now. I was afraid we'd be cold down here, but it's warm as toast."

"Sure, I'd be glad to. Then maybe we could hie ourselves up to the common room," Katie suggested as she untied the string on the little girl's hat. "I've some friends I'd like you to meet. And 'tis my guess," smiling at Bridey, who almost smiled back, "there'll be other children up there for these two to play with." There had been families on board the tenders, and as she helped the little girl slip free of the red coat, she could hear mothers nearby calling to young ones, and fathers' deeper voices echoing the call. Families were permitted to remain together, which she thought must have come as a relief to mothers traveling with a pair or trio of lively little ones.

"Didja catch a glimpse of the common room, Eileen?" she asked. "'Tis lovely. Like a giant pub, only much nicer. I believe there's a piano, even. A sing-along would be nice of an evenin'. Do you sing, then?"

Eileen laughed. "When I sing the hymns at mass on Sunday, Sean says if Saint Patrick hadn't already chased all the snakes out of Ireland, my voice would do it. But," she added cheerfully, "I do love to listen. A musicale might be a treat."

"Well, then," Katie said briskly, "I'll keep the little ones entertained while you change out of your traveling clothes, and then I'll hand them over to you while I do the same." She was anxious to see Brian and Patrick again, and was sure they'd have made their way to the general room by now. Thinking the new white middy with the linen collar her mother had sewn for her for the trip might be nice, Katie opened her satchel.

Elizabeth had watched the tenders disembark their passengers from Ireland. It seemed to her, looking down from above, that most of them were probably destined for third class. She had hoped to find another young companion among these new arrivals. But no one seemed dressed elegantly enough for first class.

Elizabeth was disappointed, and was about to turn away from the rail when someone caught her eye. A young girl ... perhaps her age . . . sat in the tender, her own eyes wide with awe as she looked up at the huge ship. Fiery red hair spilled down her shoulders instead of being confined in a proper do, and her traveling clothes looked wrinkled and dusty. But she had a beautiful face, and there was something about her, an electrical air of excitement that Elizabeth found herself envying. What would it be like to still become so excited about something new? She herself hardly ever did anymore.

Sitting beside the girl was a tall, dark-haired young man in a worn wool jacket. Although he seemed much more restrained than the girl, who was waving wildly at another dark-haired young man arriving in the second tender, Elizabeth was certain the first two were traveling together. Married? They seemed young, but they could be embarking on a honeymoon voyage. But then, who was the second young man? She heard him shout, "Katie!" and saw the red-haired girl wave in response. Katie. Short for Kathleen?

The three held her interest for several moments. She would have continued watching them had not a voice at her elbow said, "Elizabeth, I'd like you to meet someone." Max's voice. Elizabeth sighed in irritation. He was actually going to introduce her to that gypsy person? But she had *no* desire to meet the girl!

Unwilling to let him see her annoyance, she pasted a polite smile on her lips, and turned around. "Oh, hello, Max. I was just watching the Queenstown passengers arrive. It's great fun. They all look so interesting!"

Max gave her a wry smile. "You sound a little like the queen gazing down upon the peasants." The girl at his side, her wild, dark hair windblown, smiled, too.

Elizabeth flushed. "I didn't mean that. I just meant —"

"This is Lily Costello," Max interrupted, smiling at the girl in the brightly flowered jacket. "We met in Paris. She's traveling to New York to go on the stage." The smile broadened. "But she's already an actress. And a very good one. I've seen her in a number of plays."

Elizabeth shook the girl's hand. "Costello doesn't sound French."

"I'm Italian," the girl said, with barely a trace of an accent. "We moved to France when I was eight. When my parents were killed in a train crash, I had already been on the stage for several years, so I decided to stay in France, where I was known in the theater community."

An actress. That explained the odd costuming, the wild hair. Lily Costello wasn't a gypsy at all, she was only an actress. "Your parents allowed you to go on stage as a child?"

Lily's fine, delicately arched brows rose. "Allow me?" She shrugged. "They saw that I had a special talent and that I was determined to use it, and that it would do them no good to stand in my way. I do not understand what you mean by 'allow.' And you? What is it that *you* do in America, Elizabeth?"

Elizabeth was stunned. Within her own circle of friends, no one would have asked such a question. Though she had certainly asked it of herself repeatedly, she had never been asked it by anyone else. And she had never once thought of what the answer might be.

A thick cloud of humiliation enveloped Elizabeth. To answer truthfully, "Nothing. I do nothing," in front of Max Whittaker would have taken far more courage than she had or ever expected to have.

It was Max himself who answered for her, but Elizabeth was unable to see his remark as any kind of rescue. Rather, when Max laughed lightly and said, "Oh, Elizabeth is engaged," she only burned with further humiliation.

To make matters worse, Lily frowned again and asked, "Engaged? Yes, but what does she *do*?" as if being engaged had nothing whatsoever to do with who Elizabeth *was*. The concept was directly the opposite of Elizabeth's mother's belief: that the engagement to Alan Reed had *everything* to do with who Elizabeth was and would be for the rest of her life.

Still, as mortifying as the conversation was, Elizabeth felt a pang of envy. This girl in the strange clothes and wild hair had always done as she wanted, even as a child, and she believed that other people, including Elizabeth, should do the same. "I would like to become a student," she answered stiffly, desperately wanting both Lily and Max to see her as someone with ambition. "But my parents are against it."

To her surprise, instead of Lily's expression going blank, she nodded understandingly. But then she said, "And you are afraid to defy them."

Though that was the truth, Elizabeth was angered. "I can't *afford* to defy them. College is expensive. I have no money of my own."

Below them, the tenders pulled away from the ship. Elizabeth heard the bubbling wash they made and thought again of the red-haired girl and her handsome companion. She wondered if that girl had had to defy her parents to leave Ireland for America. If so, she had clearly done it or she wouldn't be on board the *Titanic* now.

"And do you have great affection for this man to whom you are engaged?" Lily had the effrontery to ask then. She smiled a mischievous grin. "This is a grand passion for you, Elizabeth?"

Elizabeth drew herself up to her full height,

which still left her with the disadvantage of an inch or two below Max and Lily, and said coolly, "I really don't want to talk about it." And she turned and swept away with as much dignity as possible, though she nearly tripped over a deck chair in her haste to escape.

Behind her, she heard Lily say, "I did not mean to offend her." Then, worst of all, Max's deeper voice saying, "I think you struck a nerve with that last question."

Elizabeth took refuge in the glassed-in promenade. How *dare* he? Suggesting to a perfect stranger that Elizabeth didn't love the man she was engaged to! She had never told Max that. Couldn't tell him that. Such an admission would be the most humiliating of all. She would never make it to someone she had just met.

Had she hinted at it, somehow, when they'd first talked? No, she wouldn't have. But she couldn't remember what she *had* said to Max, not exactly.

Even if she had said something, Max had no right to reveal that to Lily Costello.

I hate him, Elizabeth thought, not for the first time. And this time, she meant it.

Chapter 7

Thursday, April 11, 1912

"You look fetching in that middy," Eileen told Katie as, with Bridey and Kevin in tow, they left the cabin to make their way up to the general room. "'Tis a fine collar."

"Me ma made it." A sudden, fierce pang of homesickness assaulted Katie. "She has a knack with the needle. Meself, I'm all thumbs."

"I guess you're not goin' to be a seamstress in America, then? So many of our girls are. Workin' with lace, especially, brings a fine penny, I hear."

Katie laughed. "I'd starve if I ever tried to make me way by sewin'." But she didn't confess what her real goal was. If Eileen disapproved of young women making their way on the stage, they couldn't be friends. That thought was so depressing, Katie added quickly, "I've always liked the little ones." There, she hadn't actually *said* she was intending to become a governess, so it wasn't a true lie. But it would keep Eileen from asking how she planned to earn a living in America.

It did. Eileen nodded and said, "Aye, you have a way with them."

Katie let out a small sigh of relief. The voyage would be much more fun with a companion, especially with Brian and Paddy so far away in the bow.

The brothers were, as she had hoped, already mixing with other third-class passengers in the large, pleasant room filled with lively conversation in a variety of languages. The smell of fresh paint hung in the air. Blue sky showed through the portholes in the white-washed walls, and the feet of playing children clattered noisily across the bare floor.

Brian's dark head towered over the crowd, and Katie heard Patrick's deep, melodious laughter before she actually spied him. He was surrounded by a small cluster of young women, which didn't surprise Katie at all. Back in Cork, Paddy had a reputation as a ladies' man. Brian had once said laughingly of his handsome younger brother, "Slippery as the fish in the cold waters of the Atlantic, that one. The lass who catches him had best hold on for dear life."

Katie had sniffed in disdain. As far as she

was concerned, any man who saw himself as a great "catch" should be cast back into the sea immediately. She knew Paddy had broken more than one young heart in Cork, including the hearts of some of Katie's best friends.

She hadn't been very sympathetic, she remembered now with chagrin. To Mary Frances Molloy, weeping in Katie's bedroom, Katie had said tartly, "Didja think you were so special that he wouldn't be faithless to you like he was with Siobhan and Fiona and Sheila, then?"

"Aye," Mary Frances had sobbed, "I thought he hadn't loved them the way he loved me."

"More the fool you, then." But Katie had gone downstairs to fetch a plate of soda bread and a glass of fresh, cold milk to comfort the distraught girl.

She vowed, not for the first time since she'd met Patrick Thomas Kelleher, to never be taken in, like the other girls, by his dark, snapping eyes and that broad, arrogant grin and thick, dark, curly hair. She hadn't had the chance, as it turned out, because Paddy treated her more like a sister than an available young woman. He was courteous and considerate. He had never once said or done anything flirtatious. When he talked to her, as he often did, it was usually about his brother.

It puzzled Katie sometimes that Paddy expected her to know what was going on in

Brian's head. Why would she? Brian didn't confide in her. She suspected that was because she was a girl. It didn't rile her. She had no need to know Brian's every thought. She also suspected that his thoughts were not nearly so deep as Paddy's. Brian was a bright but uncomplicated fellow. Paddy should know that, being his brother.

Telling herself she felt sorry for the unsuspecting young ladies hanging on Paddy's every word, Katie turned away, intent on meeting some of her fellow travelers.

She was sitting on one of the shiny wooden benches talking with Eileen and a young mother of three small children when there was a slight stir behind them, at the foot of the staircase.

Katie turned to find a small group of elegantly dressed people accompanied by a uniformed steward, gathered on the wide, lower steps. They were gazing around with interest, like visitors touring a museum.

"Why, this is quite nice!" a tall, gray-haired woman with a fur stole draped around her shoulders declared. "Plain, to be sure, but quite comfortable, considering."

"Oh, much better than the usual third class," the steward admitted, adding proudly, "but this is the *Titanic*. Everything on it is grand."

A hush fell over the third-class passengers

gathered in the meeting room. Even the children fell silent. All eyes were turned toward the group gathered on the stairs.

A short, round woman with an unpleasant scowl on her pink, doughy face commented, "I wonder if they appreciate how fortunate they are." A man standing behind her nodded and said, "On any other ship they'd be crammed together like sardines in a can."

Caught off guard by the sudden appearance of the group, it took Katie a few minutes to grasp what was happening. When she did, she became indignant, then furious. She, along with everyone else, was being put on display, like the two-headed calf she'd once seen at a county fair. As if they were a curiosity, something foreign and strange, to be examined carefully by the first-class passengers. 'Twas outrageous! The steward, who must have been conducting a tour of the ship, had no right to invade their privacy like this. Would the third-class passengers ever be permitted to tour first-class facilities, to visit the fancy restaurant, the gymnasium, the Paris-type café she'd read about, the fine staterooms? No, never! There were iron gates barring their way. And no steward eager to unlock them.

Katie rose to her feet. Her cheeks felt hot. Brian and Patrick saw her stand. Both were at her side instantly, flanking her.

As Katie opened her mouth to speak, a tall, very pretty girl in a blue dress, standing in the group of onlookers, said nervously, "I think we should go. We're disturbing these people." She looked directly at Katie as she spoke. For a second, she seemed about to smile. Then, reading the expression on Katie's face, apparently thought better of it.

When the steward said, "Don't worry about offending them by what you say. Most of 'em don't speak English," Katie's temper reached the boiling point.

Her eyes sweeping the room, she shouted to the other third-class passengers, "Do you all understand what's happenin' here, then? Do you see that we're bein' put on show?"

In response, she received only confused glances from those who didn't understand English, and shamed, lowered eyes from those who did. No one said anything.

"Don't give them a show," Brian warned quietly. "You'll just be givin' them somethin' to blather about at supper."

But Katie couldn't repress her anger. Whirling in fury back toward the group on the stairs, she asked the steward heatedly, "Do you charge admission, then, for lettin' the fancy folk get a good look at us common people?"

The pretty girl in blue tugged on her companion's sleeve. "Mother, please! This was a terrible idea. Let's go!" She turned to leave, but no one else did.

Katie felt revulsion as she saw mild amusement in the eyes watching her. Brian had been right. Except for the girl in blue, the onlookers were *entertained* by her display of temper.

Suddenly, Paddy shouted, "If a show is what they want, then that's what they'll get!" And in one swift, sure move he reached out and took Katie into his arms, lifted her chin, and before she could utter a word of protest, kissed her soundly.

She told herself later that if she responded, it was only because she was taken by surprise. No time to raise her defenses.

But she was aware of two other elements of the kiss. One was, she felt a perverse pleasure when she heard shocked gasps from the group on the stairs. And the other, if the truth be told, was that the kiss made her tingle all the way down to her toes. This very pleasant sensation was accompanied by a clear-cut, belated understanding of Mary Frances Molloy's anguished weeping last September.

"Have you lost your mind, man?" Brian demanded of Paddy as the kiss ended.

The steward shrugged.

But the girl in the blue dress, Katie noticed, was openly smiling. The others murmured disapproval among themselves as they retreated up the staircase and disappeared from sight.

Conversation in the room slowly resumed. The children began playing again.

"Sure, and that was a nice display!" Brian told Paddy sharply. It seemed to Katie that his peevishness included her, but she told herself that might just be her guilty conscience. After all, Brian couldn't know how much she'd enjoyed the kiss. Or *could* he? Nothing much got past him. "It pleases you to know you'll be on their tongues tonight when they sit down in their fancy restaurants? They'll be speakin' of you as a common, ignorant lout."

Paddy shrugged. "I care as much for their opinion as I do the cows in the meadow. But I don't mind apologizin' to *you*, Bri. I was so riled up, I wasn't thinkin'."

"No need to apologize to me. But you *might* give some thought to how people on this ship regard Katie!"

That, Katie saw, did give Paddy pause. He reddened, and she realized in awe that she'd been wrong earlier. Paddy Kelleher, ladies' man or no, *did* blush. Amazin'! But why had he seen fit to apologize to Brian for kissing her?

"Sorry, Katie," Paddy muttered. "I should have asked you first if it was fine with you. But they made me so *mad*! Like I told Bri, I wasn't thinkin'...."

"And there's a shock," Brian said sarcastically.

But Katie, remembering how she'd felt when she was being stared at and remarked upon, nodded and said, "I know, Paddy. I was mad, too." The three stood in silence for a few moments. There didn't seem to be anything else to say about the incident. It had happened and it was ugly, but it was over now. Best to forget it. Quickly.

The girls who had been talking with Paddy earlier were, Katie noticed, waiting impatiently for him to rejoin them. They either didn't care that he'd kissed someone else or they were smart enough to realize the kiss had been for show.

"Your adoring fans are waiting," she said, her voice sugary sweet.

When Paddy, with his usual arrogant grin back in place, had sauntered off, Brian said sharply to Katie, "You're not the first girl he's ever kissed, y'know."

"Nor am I the last," she responded blithely, and hurried off to stop Bridey from yanking a fistful of hair off the scalp of her older brother.

Back in their cabin, Elizabeth said in disgust, "I can't believe we *did* that! Staring at those people as if they were mannequins in a department store window! Everyone talking about them as if they were deaf." She wished fervently that she'd stayed with Max and Lily instead of letting her mother talk her into that stupid tour. "They're *people*, Mother! They have feelings! But then," she added, "feelings aren't something you care very much about, are they?"

"You wouldn't dare speak to me that way if your father were here." Nola Farr calmly removed her plumed hat, tossing it carelessly onto the bed, and slipped free of her purple velvet jacket. Because she had neglected until the last minute to see about hiring a maid for the trip and then been unable to find one willing to make the journey, there was no one to pick up after her. The jacket joined the hat on the bed and would remain there until nightfall, when Martin Farr would hang both items in the wardrobe room.

"Well, he *isn't* here." Elizabeth sank into a chair. She kept seeing the furious eyes of that beautiful, red-haired girl. The boy in the second tender had called her "Katie." Katie had been very, very angry. Elizabeth didn't blame her. The steward should never have guided them down there, to gawk and make thoughtless comments. The reverse would never be permitted, she was sure of that. Third-class passengers were barred from entering first-class accommodations. The steward guiding their tour had found it necessary to unlock more than one gate.

"And," Elizabeth added, "I can't believe Father would approve of what just happened. He'd think it was disgusting, just as I do."

Her mother had taken a seat on the velvet bench in front of the mirrored vanity. As if Elizabeth hadn't spoken, she mused aloud, "I wonder if I could hire one of those third-class girls to act as our maid for the rest of the trip." Removing her diamond-and-pearl earrings, she added, "You would think one of them would be delighted with such an opportunity, wouldn't you?"

Though Elizabeth was tired from the guided tour and her legs ached from climbing various staircases in high heels, she jumped to her feet. "Oh, yes, Mother! How generous to allow one of those girls to fetch and carry for us."

Without turning around, her mother said, "Elizabeth, I will not have you speaking to me this way. Please leave. Go to your own cabin. Once there, you might reflect for just a bit on how fortunate *you* are to be traveling first class." A brittle quality Elizabeth knew well crept into her mother's voice. "You might also reflect on just *who* is responsible for your good fortune. Please don't come back here until your attitude has improved."

Glad to be dismissed, Elizabeth left, careful not to slam the door.

But she didn't stay in her own cabin. Instead, she decided to seek out the gymnasium. If unescorted women were permitted to use the equipment, perhaps she could work off some of her anger on one of the exercise machines she'd heard about.

Chapter 8

The gymnasium was uncrowded. In the middle of the afternoon on such a nice day, most passengers seeking fitness preferred to stride briskly around the decks and breathe in the ocean air.

A middle-aged woman in a long, dark skirt and striped blouse was sitting a bit awkwardly on a machine unfamiliar to Elizabeth. It resembled a camel. An older, balding gentleman was using a rowing machine, and a woman with a broad face was pedaling a stationary bicycle, her cheeks red with effort. Elizabeth saw no sign of the instructor she'd been told would be available. The red-faced woman informed her that he had "stepped out" briefly.

Unwilling to sit around doing nothing while she waited, Elizabeth decided to tackle one of the machines on her own. She often rode her own bicycle through Central Park at home. How different could a stationary bicycle be?

Not so different, she decided as she climbed on, and she would have been fine had it not been for the length and fullness of her skirt. Had she been wearing the latest fashion, a hobble skirt that forced a woman to walk as if her ankles were chained together, Elizabeth would have been unable to even think about approaching one of the machines. She believed that her own fuller skirt had enough room for negotiation. It did. But as she swung herself up onto the seat, the hem of her skirt caught on a pedal and stuck there, jerking Elizabeth suddenly sideways and causing her to topple off the seat.

She cried out in surprise as she fell, landing on her left side on the floor, her left leg and ankle still suspended in midair by the imprisoned skirt hem. The ankle twisted viciously as she hit the floor, and she cried out again, this time in pain.

The two women and the man hurried to her side. Before Elizabeth could answer their queries as to her condition, Max and Lily suddenly appeared in the doorway. They, too, rushed over to Elizabeth. Lily swiftly freed the skirt, carefully holding onto Elizabeth's ankle so as not to jolt it unduly, and gently brought it to rest on the floor.

The pain was fierce. Elizabeth had to bite her lower lip to keep from crying out again, something she did not want to do in Max's presence. Lily's, either. She would show both of them that she had some backbone. She wouldn't mouth a word of complaint until she was safely back in her cabin. Then she'd bawl her eyes out if she still felt the need.

Lily and Max knelt by her side. "I do not think it is broken," Lily announced, her fingers gently, carefully probing the injured ankle.

Max said, "I think she'll be just fine. But just in case, I'm going to take her to the doctor. He can check her out." To Elizabeth's astonishment, he bent down and scooped her up off the floor, cradling her in his arms. "Someone go find a steward and ask him where the hospital is."

Shaking her head and murmuring to herself, the red-faced woman hurried off. She was back in only a minute or two, out of breath and saying hurriedly, "Hospital is on D deck, directly below the Café Parisien. You'll have to take the elevator."

"You're not going to carry her all that way?" the balding man asked Max. "Get a steward to do it for you. That's the sort of thing they're supposed to do."

As if I were *baggage*, Elizabeth thought indignantly. Max smiled and said, "Thanks for the suggestion, but I'd rather do it myself." Glancing down at Elizabeth, he ordered, "Will you *relax*? You're as stiff as a board. I'm not going to throw you overboard, if that's what you're worried about." He grinned. "I'm too much of a gentleman for that. Might have you keelhauled, though. Being pulled along behind the boat in those icy Atlantic waters should bring you down off your high horse."

"I already *fell* off my high horse, only it happened to be a bicycle," Elizabeth reminded him. She winced in pain as Max began walking. Every step he took across the room jolted her throbbing ankle, but she was determined not to let it show.

"Max, do not tease her," Lily scolded, striding along beside them.

Why does *she* have to come? Elizabeth thought. She wanted to lay her head on Max's shoulder, which would have been much more comfortable. But she resisted, sitting instead upright and away from him, as if by doing so, she could maintain some measure of independence.

"Lay your head down," he commanded, marching toward the elevator. "It's too hard to carry you when you're fighting me. What are you so afraid of, anyway?"

"Being keelhauled by a callous brute," Elizabeth retorted. But she obeyed. And resting her head against his shoulder did help.

The trip to the hospital seemed to take forever, even with the aid of the elevator. Lily annoyed Elizabeth by persistently asking how she was feeling, until Elizabeth finally snapped, "I feel exactly the same way I felt two seconds ago!"

Max shook his head in disgust. But Lily fell silent.

"It's only a strain," Dr. O'Loughlin announced when he had examined the ankle. "Perhaps a wrench. No sprain, no broken bones. I'll wrap it for you, but I see no need to insist that you stay off it. If it's uncomfortable, you might like to soak it and take an aspirin or two."

Elizabeth felt silly. All this drama, all this effort and she didn't even have a sprained ankle. Max and Lily were probably thinking she was a big baby, the result of too many years of pampering. Which wasn't fair, because she hadn't *asked* to be brought to the hospital. And she hadn't cried out once.

The doctor left to see to a man suffering from a severe case of motion sickness. When he had gone, leaving Elizabeth sitting up on the examination table, there was an awkward silence. Elizabeth broke it by saying stiffly, "I can get back to my cabin by myself. You two run along."

Max arched an eyebrow. "Run along? We're not your household staff, Elizabeth. I brought you down here, I'll take you back up. Whatever the doctor says, that ankle is swollen and it looks sore. You should probably soak it before dinner."

Dinner. With her parents. Arguing again, about Alan. The thought nauseated Elizabeth, and she swayed slightly on the table.

Max reached out to support her, then scooped her off the table and into his arms just as he had lifted her off the gymnasium floor, saying, "There's persistence, which I happen to admire as a character trait, and then there's plain old stubbornness, which I don't."

Elizabeth didn't answer him, and she was only vaguely aware of the trip back up to C deck, to her cabin. Then she heard her mother's voice, followed by her father's, and before she knew it, she was safely ensconced in her own bed. The sore and now-swollen ankle rested on a pillow removed from the chaise lounge in her parents' cabin. She heard voices effusively thanking Max and Lily, heard the door closed, heard her mother's voice saying, "Where on earth does that girl get her clothes? Enid would have a fit if her son ever brought home such a strange creature!"

Elizabeth wanted to shout, "She's an actress, Mother; she's not supposed to dress like you and me!" But her head ached. She felt dizzy. She dreaded another dinner with her parents, and her ankle was throbbing so fiercely, she couldn't imagine having an actual sprain if it was worse than this. Besides, unlike Elizabeth Farr, Lily Costello was a free and independent human being. She could take care of herself, and did. She didn't need Elizabeth to defend her.

Elizabeth closed her eyes and lay perfectly still, waiting for the sharp arrows of pain in her ankle to diminish.

Below, Katie continued to fume. She couldn't dismiss the horrifying feeling of being put on display, of being regarded as a curiosity. Such a thing had never happened to her before, and she prayed that it would never happen again.

Brian, in an effort to calm her down, had said, "But you're goin' to sing on the stage, are you not? You'll be stared at there, Katie-girl."

He didn't understand that it wasn't the same thing, not at all. Being onstage, standing in front of an audience, was so very different. There she had a talent to offer, a gift, and was offering it willingly. She was inviting people to come and see how they liked her singing.

This was different, because she had never

invited those rude first-class passengers in all their fancy finery to stand on the steps and gawk at her and the other steerage passengers.

It was disgusting and made her blood boil.

A small, pretty girl in a plain, brown wool dress came over to Katie and smiled before asking shyly, "So, is that young man your sweetheart?" Her accent wasn't Irish, but Katie wasn't sure what it was. She wasn't that familiar with other languages.

Startled, Katie stared at her. "Beggin' your pardon?"

The girl repeated the question.

"Paddy?" Katie glanced over at the young man in question, surrounded once again by a cluster of giggling girls. "My sweetheart? What makes you think such a thing?"

The girl blushed scarlet. "I did see him kissing you."

Katie felt as if she, too, were blushing and hoped angrily that it wasn't so. "That was just to put on a show for those horrible, rude people. It didn't mean nothin'." Her eyes on Paddy, she added, "Paddy's only real sweetheart is himself, and that's the truth. Brian says when his brother gets up in the mornin', he's at the mirror, first thing, checkin' to make sure he's still as handsome as he was when he went to bed."

The girl laughed. "He is that." She sighed.

"Not that I'd be likely to catch his eye. I think perhaps he would like a bolder type."

"Think of yourself as havin' good fortune, then," Katie said. "He left a trail of broken hearts behind him in Cork. You'd not be wantin' to add yours to it, would you? A pretty girl like you, you could have some fine young man who'd be faithful as the day is long." Her gaze moved to Brian. "Someone like that one over there. Paddy's older brother. True as the sunset and steady as the ocean breeze. Come, I'll give him the pleasure of meetin' you. What's your name?"

"Marta Swensen."

"You're not Irish, are you?"

"No. I'm from Sweden. I'm going to America to live with my aunt and uncle in Minnesota. They have a big farm and can use the help."

Katie hesitated. Brian, too, was a farmworker. The two might fancy each other. It seemed to her, with her limited knowledge of American geography, that Wisconsin, where Brian was going, was somewhere near Minnesota. "I don't suppose you're at least Catholic, then?"

"Oh, no, I belong to the Lutheran church. But," the girl added, seeing the expression on Katie's face, "I'm a good Christian. And I have nothing against the Pope."

Katie laughed. "All right, then, I'll introduce you to Brian, though me ma would say I'm doin' wrong, since you're not of the faith." But then, she told herself quickly, what were the chances that Brian and this Marta would marry? They wouldn't be on the great *Titanic* long enough to become so serious. And it would be nice for Brian to have someone pretty to talk to about farming. She herself hoped she'd seen her last cow for a very long time. "Come along, then, and meet Brian. But," she added hastily, "it might be wise not to mention religion first off, even if you *do* like the Pope."

Once Brian and Marta were engaged in conversation, Katie glanced around for Eileen and her two young charges. In the upset of being interrupted by the first-class tour, Katie had lost sight of the trio. Everyone else seemed to have dismissed the interruption. People were talking loudly again in many different languages, children were chasing each other around the room, a small boy was pounding away on the piano. Katie felt as if she were the only one there whose heart was still sore from the humiliation.

"You take things too much to heart," Paddy said, appearing at her elbow. "Like me. It'll only cause you pain, that I can promise you."

Katie stared up at him, her mouth open. Paddy Kelleher, taking things too much to heart? That wasn't *her* picture of him. Nor, she suspected, was it anyone else's. Brian said Paddy's problem was he didn't take *anything* seriously. How could Brian be wrong about his own brother?

"You're joshin' me," she accused. "I've never known you to take anythin' to heart. Especially not anyone *else's* heart." Wickedly, she added, "Like Mary Frances Molloy's, for instance."

Paddy didn't even blink. "Mary Frances is a nice lass. But she had a mind to marry, I could see it in her fine Irish eyes." He grinned down at Katie. "How could I marry, then, and still become a famous writer? Marryin' takes up a man's time. He's got all he can do to support his family, with no time left over for sittin' and writin'." Then he added more seriously, "But I wasn't speakin' about romance, Katie, when I said that about takin' things too much to heart. I was speakin' about the people standin' on the steps lookin' at all of us like we had two heads on our shoulders."

Exactly what *she'd* thought.

"You can't be gettin' all full of temper when somethin' like that happens," he said soberly. "They don't mind if you get mad, that's the truth of it. It did look like they found it amusin', didn't you think? You gettin' mad, I mean?"

She nodded reluctantly. They *had* looked amused.

Paddy shrugged. "Losin' your temper over

fools like that is like beatin' your pretty head up against the stone wall in Ballyford's town square, Katie."

"You lost your temper, too."

"Aye, I did. And felt more the fool for it."

Was he regretting the kiss? Was that what he was saying? Afraid she'd taken it too seriously, was that what he was fretting over? "Well, I felt foolish, too," she said defiantly, "and you shouldn't have kissed me in front of all those people! I did come close to slappin' your face, Paddy." Not true at all, at all. But she was stung, and needed to convince him that she hadn't enjoyed a moment of that kiss.

"Sorry," he said. "I guess Brian's forgiven me, though." He looked for a moment as if he meant to say something further, but a trio of young women came along just then and, laughing, swept him away.

Katie stood in the center of the room by herself, surrounded by conversation and laughter and the sounds of children playing and squabbling, hearing none of it because she was remembering that Paddy had said "your pretty head."

He thought she was pretty?

Chapter 9

Thursday, April 11, 1912

Depressed and in pain from an ankle that throbbed steadily, Elizabeth slept all afternoon. She was awakened by a knock on the cabin door. It took her several moments to realize where she was and recognize the rapping sounds.

"Who is it?" she called irritably from her bed.

"Max and Lily. We wanted to know how you were doing."

Elizabeth sat up. Max and Lily, Max-and-Lily, MaxandLily, as if they were one person. Did he go *nowhere* without the actress?

The thought brought a sudden cruel stab of pain from her leg. Wincing, Elizabeth got out of bed to test it gingerly. Although she could see when she raised her skirt that the ankle was still swollen, putting her weight on it was not unbearable. She made it to the door with only a slight limp.

Max was wearing the white turtleneck, Lily the wildly flowered jacket. Elizabeth had to smile, imagining the look on her mother's face when she saw them.

"We thought we'd try the à la carte restaurant tonight," Max told her. "We miss French food, and they serve it there. Feel like joining us?"

The "us" annoyed Elizabeth. She had no wish to be a third party. The two of them would probably spend the entire meal sharing their experiences in Paris, assigning her the unpleasant role of polite listener.

But anything had to be better than another uncomfortable meal with her parents.

Acutely conscious of her wrinkled clothing and disheveled hair, Elizabeth accepted the invitation. "I will need at least an hour to make myself presentable. I'll meet you at the entrance to the restaurant" — she glanced down at the watch hanging around her neck — "at eight o'clock."

Max smiled at her. The smile eased the sharpness of his features, making him even more attractive. "You look presentable enough to me." He tilted his head to one side, regarding her carefully, still smiling. "Very fetching, in fact. You should wear your hair loose like that more often. Makes you look more approach-able."

Elizabeth might have been flattered had Max not at that very moment been standing el-bow-to-elbow with someone whose own jacket was wrinkled and whose long, dark hair seemed always to be in disarray. He obviously liked that free-spirited look. But that didn't make it suitable for an appearance in public. Not for Elizabeth Farr, anyway.

"My parents are eating in the restaurant tonight, too," she said, her voice cool. "If my mother saw me walk in looking like this, she would hate it. I'll change and meet you there." Before she closed the door, her eyes swept Lily from head to toe, as if to say, It wouldn't hurt you to tidy up a bit, either.

But she didn't say it aloud because she knew Lily had no intention of changing her outfit or arranging her hair differently. Elizabeth was consumed with envy. How wonderful it must be not to care what other people might think, not to be constantly ruled by rigid standards of what was "proper" and what wasn't.

But then, she told herself as she quickly bathed and changed into a red velvet ankle-length dress with three-quarter-length sleeves and a matching jacket, Lily is on her own and has no parents to fear. She has nothing to lose by flouting convention. While I, on the other hand, she told the mirror as she lightly powdered her face, have everything to lose by alienating my parents just now. If I showed up in the ship's restaurant looking as outlandish as Lily Costello, any chance I ever had of convincing my parents I'm mature enough to lead my own life would vanish like the coast of Ireland when the *Titanic* sailed out of Cobh Harbour.

Elizabeth replaced the watch with a gold locket on a chain and slipped her feet into red satin slippers, wincing again as her weight settled on the sore ankle.

As if summoned by her daughter's thoughts, Nola Farr, resplendent in aquamarine silk, appeared in the doorway. "Oh good, you're up. How is the ankle? The red is stunning on you, Elizabeth. I knew it would be. And it's an excellent choice for tonight. We're dining in the restaurant, and I'm told that it's quite elegant." Whirling before Elizabeth's full-length mirror, her mother added, "I believe we'll do quite nicely, don't you? We shall make a lovely picture when we walk in together. I do hope that Brown woman isn't there. If she's there, my appetite will be ruined."

"I've been invited out to dinner, Mother."

The whirling stopped. "Invited out? By whom? I thought you hadn't met anyone on board. Except, of course, for that wild young son of Enid's —" Nola's jaw dropped. "Oh, no,

Elizabeth! You are *not* dining in the restaurant with him? What will your father say?"

Elizabeth fastened a crystal teardrop earring to each lobe. "Mother, Father is the one who introduced me to Max. If he didn't want me associating with him, he shouldn't have allowed us to meet."

"He was just being polite to the son of an acquaintance. I'm sure he never expected you to actually befriend the boy."

Elizabeth smiled. Yesterday, Mrs. Whittaker had been a close friend. Now she was only a mere "acquaintance"? "Max isn't a boy, Mother. He's almost twenty."

Nola sighed and began fussing with her hair, which was already perfectly arranged. "What can you possibly have in common with someone like that?"

What we have in common, Elizabeth answered silently, is, our parents don't want us making our own decisions. They want us to stay infants forever. Aloud, she said, "He tells interesting stories. He's fun."

Her mother frowned. "Alan isn't fun?"

Elizabeth uttered a short laugh. "Mother, the word 'fun' isn't even in Alan Reed's vocabulary."

"Well," Nola said testily, "fun isn't everything. It certainly won't pay for the kind of clothes you wear, Elizabeth."

Donning the heavily beaded jacket that topped the red dress and painfully aware, in view of her mother's words, that the ensemble must have cost a small fortune, Elizabeth picked up the gold evening bag lying at the foot of the bed. "I know I love nice clothes, Mother. What girl doesn't? But I promise you I could do without them if it meant going to college. And you can tell Father that for me. Anyway, I'm not planning to marry Maxwell Whittaker, whether he's rich or poor. I'm just going to dinner with him."

As Elizabeth left the cabin, her mother's voice followed her. "I'm going to be keeping my eyes on you tonight, Elizabeth. Gossip on a ship runs rampant. I won't have any nasty rumors traveling back to Alan. That could ruin everything."

In the corridor, walking in the midst of other finely dressed couples making their way to dinner, Elizabeth thought that in order to be worried about "ruining everything," you first had to really care about that "everything." And she didn't. It seemed to her, as things stood now, that "everything" could stand a little "ruining." Right now, all she wanted to do was have a nice dinner in the restaurant without tension, without bickering, without unpleasantness. She would be so sweet and agreeable with Max and Lily, they wouldn't need dessert.

If only they didn't make her feel that three was a crowd.

They didn't. To Elizabeth's relief, Lily had made the acquaintance of another young man, a native of France who had been living in the United States for the past seven years. A sophomore at Princeton University, he was returning with his parents from an aunt's funeral in Lourdes. His name was Arthur Duchamps. He seemed nice enough, and he was clearly quite taken with Lily. They conversed in French, which left Max and Elizabeth free to carry on their own conversation.

With Lily otherwise occupied, Elizabeth relaxed. Her parents had not yet arrived. They were probably entertaining themselves in the lounge before settling down to dinner. Elizabeth could only hope they'd take their time. Knowing her mother was watching her like a hawk from across the room would spoil any chance of a good time, no matter how lovely the restaurant.

And it was lovely. The paneling was lighter than other paneling on the ship, a soft, fawn shade. The carpet underfoot was softly shaded in two different rose tones, like a bed of crushed rose petals. While the room was larger than most restaurants, the linens and crystal were as fine as any Elizabeth had seen elsewhere. The room was noisy, but pleasantly so, with the sounds of lively conversation and laughter, of friends greeting friends, the pinging sounds of cutlery against dinnerware, of chairs being swooshed back into place, and with the activities of the bustling waiters, though they seemed to be trying hard to be discreet.

"I like it," she announced when they were seated. "It's really very nice."

"Well, that's grand," Max replied as he unfolded his thick linen napkin and placed it on his lap. "Because if you disapproved, of course we would jump up immediately and leave."

Instead of taking offense, Elizabeth laughed. "Sorry. It's just that since my mother was so enthusiastic about this place, I wasn't sure how I'd feel about it. We so seldom like the same things."

He smiled. "I know exactly what you mean."

Heartened by this sudden show of understanding, Elizabeth felt suddenly ravenous, and picked up the elaborate menu. She settled on filet mignon, medium-rare, a choice Lily commented on with disapproval. Saying that fish was a much more sensible choice, she added, "You wish to keep the good figure, do you not? Food that comes from the sea will do that for you, but never the cows that graze in a field stuffing themselves with grass and hay."

Since Lily herself was as slender as a

sapling, it seemed futile to argue with her. And Elizabeth was in too good a mood to become annoyed. It was very freeing to be eating a meal without her parents present. She felt almost giddy, and laughed again, saying, "I'm sure you're right, Lily. And I do like fish. I just don't feel like eating it tonight."

"Me, either," Max said, laying aside his menu. "Filet mignon sounds just about right. I'll have it, too."

"Are you sure?" Elizabeth asked. She laughed. "I thought you came here for French food."

Max cocked an eyebrow at her. "You're forgetting your French. Filet? Mignon? Both French words, are they not?"

Laughing, Elizabeth replied, "Well, it's an American dish now, and you know it, Max. I think of French food as escargot, pâté de foie gras, peaches in chartreuse jelly, château potatoes." She pointed to the menu. "They're all on here, if you want them."

"I want what you're having." He kept his eyes on hers as he said this. Elizabeth glanced around nervously to see if her parents might have entered the room while she was hidden behind the menu.

They hadn't. But they might, at any second. She should tell Max to sit back in his chair instead of leaning toward her the way he was, with his eyes boring into hers as if he were trying to see into the back of her skull. She should.

But she didn't. She liked the attention. She hadn't failed to notice the admiring glances sent Max's way from other young women in the restaurant, women older than she but still young enough to be interested in a good-looking young man. No one had ever looked envious on the few occasions when she was with Alan in public.

Still, her parents *could* walk in at any moment. Better safe than sorry, Elizabeth told herself, and quickly began listing the restaurant's wonderful qualities: the furnishings, the atmosphere, the beautiful flowers on the table. After just a sentence or two, Max took the hint and sat back in his chair, the expression on his face one of disappointment.

Elizabeth sighed. It would have been fun to flirt with him, at least until they disagreed again, which was sure to happen soon enough. But she didn't dare. Arousing her mother's ire was exactly the wrong thing to do when you wanted something from her. And Elizabeth wanted something from her.

"So," she said to Max with false cheerfulness, "tell me everything you haven't already told me about living in Paris."

"No." He shook his head. "I've told you

enough about me. What about you? Have you always lived in New York? Where else have you traveled, besides Paris and London? I want to know everything." He was leaning toward her again, his chin propped on an elbow improperly resting on the table. "What are your hobbies? What's your favorite color? Does your mother allow you any athletics and if so, what are they? Where do you want to go to college and why do you want to go? And why can't you? Why are you planning to marry a man you don't love?"

Elizabeth gasped, staring at him in horror. The questions had started off innocently enough. She would have answered the first few willingly. But then he'd gone too far. If Lily and Arthur hadn't been deeply engaged in their own conversation, they would have overheard and then Elizabeth would have left the room out of embarrassment.

Because they weren't listening, had not in fact heard a word Max said, Elizabeth's anger faded as quickly as it had come. She needed to talk to someone, someone her own age, someone who might understand what she was feeling. Who better than Max? He was not only her own age, he had defied his parents successfully, at least for a period of time. That was more than she had ever done. Perhaps he could tell her what to do.

Besides, once the trip was over, she need never see Max Whittaker again, so anything she told him now wouldn't matter in the slightest.

Making up her mind to confide in him, Elizabeth glanced once more around the room to make certain her parents hadn't arrived. Thus assured, she leaned slightly toward Max and began, "I want to go to Vassar, because . . ."

While Elizabeth was conversing with Max in the restaurant on B deck, Katie Hanrahan, flanked by two small children and their nanny, Eileen O'Keefe, stood slightly behind Brian and Patrick in the entrance to the third-class dining room on F deck amidships. Katie's eyes were open wide, as was her mouth. "My," she declared softly, her delighted gaze sweeping the room, "isn't it grand, then?"

It was, indeed, quite grand, unlike anything she had ever seen before. She had anticipated a bare-floored room with long, functional wooden tables and uncomfortable benches. The benches would be so crowded, there would hardly be room to lift a fork to one's mouth. But this was not the case in the dining salon. The room was large, its walls enameled a bright, shiny white and decorated with posters of seafaring ships. There were chairs, not benches, and they looked comfortable. The tables were covered with fine white cloths. It was a bright, attractive room.

Katie had expected to stand in line to receive her food. To her amazement, people were already seated at the tables, and waiters in uniform were circulating with trays.

"And are we havin' waiters, too?" Eileen whispered in awe, spotting one of the dark-jacketed gentlemen carrying a tray filled with glasses. "Men waitin' on me, sure and that's a wonder! Wait'll I tell Sean. He'll be green as the grass of Ireland with envy."

Katie noticed Brian peering around the room as if he'd lost something, and guessed instantly who he was looking for. Marta. Katie looked, too, but didn't see her.

"There's another dining room on the other side of the bulkhead," a young waiter said, noticing as he passed them that they seemed to be looking for someone. "Could be whoever you're seeking is in that room."

Without a word, Brian turned on his heels and went to examine the second room. Katie and the others followed, with Paddy complaining that he was hungry and what was Brian looking for, anyway?

It seemed clear to Katie that Brian hadn't shared with his younger brother the news of his new and very pretty shipboard acquaintance. Maybe he was afraid his brother would try to steal her. And Paddy himself had no doubt been too busy fostering his own long list of female acquaintanceships.

Marta was seated at a table near the rear of the room. But when Brian saw that she was surrounded by the friends she was traveling with, he ducked back out of the room. "Let's eat in the first one, then," he said gruffly, and again led the way.

"What was *that* all about?" Paddy queried, but Brian had already chosen a table and was helping the two children with their chairs. Marta's name wasn't mentioned. Paddy took a seat beside Eileen, and seemed surprised when Brian failed to take the empty chair next to Katie's. He frowned, looking confused. After a moment, he got up and slid into the chair. "You shouldn't be sittin' here all alone," he said gruffly, aiming a hostile look at his brother. "What's ditherin' him, anyway? He's not taken a shine to that nanny, has he?"

Katie laughed. "Eileen? She's engaged. To a boy from Cork. And Brian can sit anywhere he wants to." Thinking he had sat down beside her out of a sense of duty, she said archly, "And I can take care of meself, y'know."

He looked at her. "Aye, you can. But you shouldn't have to. 'Tis Brian's job."

Brian wasn't sitting that far away, just two chairs down. "Hush!" Katie remonstrated, putting a finger to her lips. "'Tisn't his job at all, and I don't know where you got such an idea. 'Tis *my* job, now that I've left home, and my job alone."

Paddy looked unconvinced, and might have continued to argue had not the little girl, Bridey, complained loudly that she wanted nothing but bread pudding for dinner and Eileen hadn't better give her anything else or she would throw it on the floor.

Everyone around them laughed.

The food could have tasted like sawdust, and still Katie would have been impressed. She felt as if she were dining in a fine restaurant, and tried very hard not to feel self-conscious. If she was going to spend her life entertaining in public, she really would have to become much more sophisticated, she decided. She would begin practicing now, by behaving in a ladylike, grown-up manner and not exclaiming over every wonderful thing that she saw, as if she had never in her life before seen anything wondrous. Which wasn't exactly true, because she had seen one or two castles in her lifetime, and anyway, the rugged coast of Ireland was a thing of beauty all by itself.

But she couldn't help exclaiming over the food. Not only was there enough of it on her plate to feed herself and two others, but the sausage was wonderfully spicy, the mashed potatoes hot and creamy, the apple-and-rice side dish perfectly seasoned, at least to her palate. She hadn't eaten much during their long trip to Queenstown, and it had been a long day for her. She was starving. It seemed to her as the table became laden that she had come to exactly the right place.

Once or twice during the pleasant meal, she wondered again why Paddy thought it was Brian's job to look out for her, but each time the thought occurred to her, Paddy was deep in an animated conversation with someone else at the table and she didn't want to interrupt.

When she was full, Katie lay down her fork and smiled widely. She felt warm and safe and satisfied. Her da had been right. Traveling on the *Titanic* was a wonderful way to get to America.

Chapter 10

Thursday, April 11, 1912

After dinner, Max insisted they all go next door to the Parisian sidewalk café. "Of course," he added with a smile, "there is no sidewalk and it is not, technically speaking, outdoors. But it is decorated to resemble a café, and the waiters speak French, so we can imagine the rest, can't we?"

Elizabeth protested that it wouldn't be as warm and cozy as the lounge. Lily laughed and tossed her long, dark hair, saying, "Ah, Elizabeth, comfort should not always be the most important thing. Is not fun important to you also?"

"It's hard to have fun when I'm cold," Elizabeth answered, but her tone was pleasant enough. She was determined not to ruin the evening. And the fact that her parents had not yet arrived served to maintain her good mood.

The Farrs appeared in the doorway just as the quartet was leaving. Nola was laughing at something her husband had just said, and her cheeks were high with color, proving that she, too, was having a good time.

She'll be in a pleasant frame of mind later, Elizabeth told herself happily. And because she is, Father will be, too. I would be wise to take advantage of that. I'll have to make a point of getting back to the cabin before they retire.

But Nola's smile disappeared when Max appeared at Elizabeth's elbow. She was barely civil as she greeted them.

"Whew!" Max said under his breath to Elizabeth as they entered the Parisian café. "She really isn't one of my fans, is she? Have I done something to offend her?"

Yes, Elizabeth thought, you defied your parents. She was glad Max had noticed her mother's coolness. Perhaps now he would understand why she was so anxious about her own future. But she didn't want to discuss that now. She was here to have fun, as Lily had said. "I think it was your haircut when she first met you," Elizabeth answered smoothly. "Even though you've had it cut since, she disapproved. It didn't meet her standards. But then, almost nothing does."

"Will she forgive me?"

"Probably not. But it doesn't really matter, does it?"

Max fixed a skeptical eye on Elizabeth as a waiter, conversing in French with Lily and Arthur, ushered them to a table. When Max asked in a low voice, "Why am I getting the feeling that if your mother *did* like me, you wouldn't be here with me now?" Elizabeth just stared at him.

They sat down, Max beside Elizabeth, Arthur's and Lily's barrel-backed rattan chairs side by side. Greenery trailed up white trellises along the walls, a whimsical but attractive detail. The round, heavy tables were crowded with passengers, all of whom seemed to be having a good time. But Elizabeth was focused on Max's strange remark. "You think I'm here to spite my mother? That if she approved of you, I wouldn't? You think I'm that vindictive?"

He shook his head. "No, not vindictive. But the thought crossed my mind that you might be using me to get back at her. I saw you watching the doorway all through dinner. As if you were hoping she'd show up and see you sitting with me."

Elizabeth laughed. "If that's what you thought, you're not nearly as smart as I gave you credit for. It was just the opposite. I was dreading their arrival. I knew she'd be watching me like a hawk every single second. In fact, she said as much when I was leaving the cabin. She's very afraid rumors will get back to Alan. *I'm* not, but she is."

Lily and Arthur stopped talking suddenly, and all Max could say was, "Really? That's the truth of it?"

"That's the truth of it."

He looked satisfied then, and since neither Lily nor Arthur was impolite enough to ask what they'd been talking about, the conversation turned to the delightful atmosphere of the café.

When their pleasant interlude in the Parisian café came to an end, Arthur invited Lily to stroll the promenade with him. Max suggested that he and Elizabeth go up to the boat deck for a last look at the stars before retiring for the evening.

"How do you know there are any stars out tonight?" she teased as they moved on up the staircase to A deck. "It could be cloudy."

"It's not. I promise."

He was right. The sky was clear, the stars sparkling overhead in a vast, velvety sky that seemed endless, as did the flat expanse of sea surrounding the ship like a dark carpet. The sweet strains of a waltz sounded faintly from somewhere below, and although the air was cold, Elizabeth's red-beaded jacket was heavy and lined with silk. She wasn't cold.

But Max must have thought she was because, as they reached the rail and stood there looking out, he put an arm around her shoulders. Elizabeth did not dislike the idea, but her immediate response was, If my mother came upon us now, heads would roll. Mine and Max's. Still, she did not shrug off the arm, or comment on his boldness.

"Look," he said as they both stood gazing out across the dark water, "if I sounded unsympathetic when you first mentioned wanting to go to college, I'm sorry. I guess it's harder for girls to do what they want. I don't really know why that's true, but I think it is. Am I right?"

Elizabeth nodded. "Yes. Do your parents bother you constantly about finding a good wife?"

"No, not really. Just a stable, financially rewarding career."

"That's what I thought. It's different for boys. Your parents *want* you to go out in the world and make your mark. Marriage seems to be the *only* thing my parents ever talk about. Their only child, their daughter, *must* find a good husband. As if that were the only option open to me. As if I weren't capable of anything but marrying."

"Now, why do I think that isn't even close to the truth?"

"I don't know. You don't know me very well. My parents, on the other hand, have known me all my life. Maybe they're right. Maybe I'm *not* suited for anything but marriage."

Max laughed. "You're right about one thing. They *have* known you all your life."

Elizabeth didn't laugh. "What if they *are* right?" She sighed heavily. "What if wanting to get an education is just a silly dream? What if I try it, and fail? That would be so humiliating."

"You won't fail." His voice was firm, allowing no argument. "And if it's what you want, you *should* try it." He slipped his arm off her shoulders and turned toward her. "Elizabeth, look at me."

When she did, the expression on his face was one of earnestness, and his eyes were serious. "If you don't try, you'll wonder for the rest of your life how different things might have been."

"If I were happy in the marriage, I wouldn't." Though she couldn't imagine herself ever being that happy with Alan Reed. When had she ever seen him laughing?

Max shook his head. "I don't see how you can be happy if you're not doing what you want. I just don't see how that's possible."

She lifted her chin. "And what about you? Are you going to do what you want? You're going back home. Doesn't that mean you're giving in? The minute you're back in your parents' Manhattan town house, aren't they going to expect you to do what they want?"

He turned back to the rail. "Oh, I'm not going back there. Did you think I was? I'm getting my own place. It won't be much. I can't afford much, and I'm not taking any more money from my grandmother. But it'll be my own, and that's what I want. I've decided to study art in earnest. That's why I left Paris. Because I know what I want now."

"If you really want to study art, isn't Paris the perfect place to do it?"

"No. The people I met there are already artists. They may not be selling yet; most of them aren't. But they already know how to do what they need to do. Me, I'm just an amateur. I need a lot more study, and there is a man in New York who has agreed to teach me. In return, I'll run errands for him, fix things in his apartment — yes, I *do* know how to fix things, thanks to my grandfather. He knows how to fix everything, and taught me some of what he knows. The man who will be giving me art lessons is a well-known artist who takes on few students." Max smiled. "And he is *not* a friend of my parents, in case you're wondering. He's never met them. He's taking me on because of some work I sent him."

"Max, that's wonderful! You really *are* going to be an artist!"

"We'll see. I don't know that yet. All I know is, I'm going to try my best. I have to." He reached out to place a hand on Elizabeth's cheek. Holding her eyes with his own, he said, "And I think you have to try, too. Whatever it takes, Elizabeth. Or you'll spend your entire life unhappy and wondering."

His touch was warm on her cold cheek, and gentle. He had just lectured her, and she wouldn't have accepted that from anyone else. She was wondering why she was willing to accept it from him, and she was also thinking how close his lips were, just inches away, when her mother's voice cut into the night air like a knife.

"Elizabeth! What do you think you're doing?"

Chapter 11

Thursday, April 11, 1912

"What were you thinking?" Nola Farr cried. "You were practically *kissing* him! In public!"

They were back in the Farrs' stateroom, mother facing daughter, father rising from the desk where he had been penning a note to a friend in New York. He was frowning in irritation at this latest discord. "Kissing whom? What's happening here?"

Elizabeth's face was scarlet. "She embarrassed me in front of Max Whittaker, that's what's going on! Max and I were just talking, that's all." She whirled toward her father. "And the next thing I knew, she was dragging me down the stairs by my sleeve, as if I were a criminal."

"You were acting like one."

"Kissing is not a criminal offense, Mother.

And I wasn't kissing him, anyway. I told you, we were just talking." But I wanted to kiss him, she almost added. She thought better of it at the last moment. As it was, there would be no discussion about her college plans on this night, not with her mother so angry. Unless her father —

"Elizabeth, your mother is right," he said, dashing what little hope she had left. "You know how people on a ship gossip. Alan has friends on this voyage. You don't want to ruin your life over some little shipboard flirtation."

Until that moment, Elizabeth had never intended anything more than that with Max. He was interesting to talk to, he did seem to listen when she talked, and she liked the attention she got from other passengers when he was with her. It would be fun to stroll the promenade with a handsome young man at her side. But Max was planning to defy his parents. That would leave him poor, at least until he became a famous painter, which could take years. How could he be of any help to her if he was struggling himself? He couldn't. So there could be nothing serious between them.

"If he wasn't the son of friends," her mother said, turning toward the mirror to unpin her hat, "I would see to it that you did not spend another moment with young Whittaker again during the remainder of our voyage. But if

Enid heard about it, she would be deeply offended." Dropping the hat on the bed, she turned to face Elizabeth. "I shall be keeping a close watch on you, for your own sake. I only wish to protect you from yourself, Elizabeth. You are headstrong, and I will not stand by and see you ruin your chances of a good, secure life over the likes of Max Whittaker. He is going to be very poor, you know. Biting the hand that feeds him, foolish boy. He will rue the day he turned his back on poor Enid and Jules, and I will not have my daughter suffering along with him."

"Oh, Mother," Elizabeth said, "it should be *my* choice if I wish to suffer, not yours."

Nola Farr laughed, the sound trilling through the room like music. "Darling, do listen to yourself. You do not know the first thing about suffering. Nor do you want to, I promise you that. You would not be good at it." Her voice hardened suddenly. "I mean what I say, Elizabeth. I won't stop you from seeing him, but I had better not come across a scene like the one I witnessed up on deck a few moments ago, do you understand me?"

She didn't add, "If you disobey...," but Elizabeth heard the threat implicit in her words. If you disobey, you have no chance of ever going to college.

Not that the chance was there, anyway. It

probably wasn't. Her mother seemed determined to see her daughter married to Alan Reed.

Do I really want to give up every chance I have, however small, for someone I hardly know? Elizabeth thought.

Max couldn't be *that* interesting.

She made one last try. "That really isn't fair, Mother. Max and I weren't *doing* anything."

But Nola was impervious. "And it is my intention to see that you never do. Go along to bed now, Elizabeth, we're all tired." Removing her diamond earrings and tossing them on the vanity, she cried, "Oh, I *wish* we were getting to New York tomorrow! This trip is not as delightful as I had hoped."

Elizabeth's father looked at her as if to say, Now see what you've done, and went to his wife to comfort her.

In disgust, Elizabeth went into her own cabin and shut the door.

It was all Max's fault. He shouldn't have been looking at her like that, shouldn't have placed his face so close to hers. It was his fault. But she was the one being punished.

Elizabeth sank down on her bed, marveling once again at how steady the ship was. She might have as easily been sitting on a bed in a hotel on solid ground, so smoothly were they sailing. If I had a talent like Lily, she told herself defensively, I could earn my own way in the world, too. I wouldn't have to do what my parents say. But the only thing I seem to have any talent for is shopping.

As if to add to her misery, the injured ankle began to throb again.

Quiet tears slid down Elizabeth's face as she lay down on the bed and pulled the embroidered coverlet over her.

In the third-class general room, Katie shared none of Elizabeth's misery. After the delicious evening meal, when everyone returned to the common area to relax, Brian talked her into taking a seat at the piano. With very little coaxing, Katie launched into some of her favorite songs. She had a rich, full, strong voice that soared out over the room and rendered everyone silent. Even the children stopped playing to listen. The men lit their pipes and leaned forward, elbows on knees, listening intently. The women sat with their hands folded, rapt expressions on their faces.

When she finished, wild applause shook the room. It warmed Katie's heart. She tried not to make too much of it. After all, she told herself, entertainment was limited on the ship, and her "audience" wasn't paying, so they probably weren't expecting too much. It would be different in a theater in New York City. People would not be so quick to applaud an untrained voice such as her own.

Still, it did thrill her to hear people clapping, stamping their feet, and whistling in approval of her singing.

Someone took up the pipes then and people began dancing. Katie, flushed with pride, felt like dancing, too. When Paddy came over to join her at the piano, she hoped he'd ask her.

Instead, he frowned down at her and said in a low voice, "So, what is it that Brian is doin' with that Swedish girl? Did the two of you have a fallin'-out, then?"

Katie glanced over her shoulder to see Brian dancing by with Marta. "A fallin'-out? No. Why would we?"

Paddy sat down on the bench beside her. There was no room to spare, and she found herself sitting close enough to him to feel the warmth of his body. The sensation was not unpleasant. "Then why is he makin' eyes at a strange girl?"

Katie laughed. "Marta's not strange at all. She's very nice. Have you not met her?"

"I haven't had the pleasure." Paddy glanced over at her. "You're not mad, then?"

"No. Why should I be?"

Paddy shrugged. "No reason, I guess. If you're doin' fine, then, I guess I'll find me someone to dance with." He got up from the bench and stood looking down at her. "If you're feelin' so fine, why aren't you dancin'?"

Katie laughed. "No one's asked me."

"Well, I'm askin', then," he said brusquely. "Might as well dance with me as with some other fool."

It wasn't the most gracious invitation she'd ever had. But Katie did feel like dancing, and she happened to know for a fact that Patrick Kelleher cut a fine swath on the dance floor. She'd seen him, more than once, in the church hall, spinning some comely lass around the room.

"Might as well," she said with a wry smile. She slid off the bench and stood up, to find his arms waiting for her. And then the odd thing was, the minute she stepped into those arms, Katie Hanrahan felt like she'd come home. The sensation shocked her. She wasn't prepared for it, had never felt anything like it before. She'd never had a steady suitor, hadn't wanted one, and if she had been looking for one, never would have looked in Paddy's direction. Brian's, maybe, but never Paddy's. Mostly because it was hard to get a good look at Paddy, so surrounded was he by other girls.

The feeling dismayed Katie. She didn't want to feel this way at all, and especially not about a young man who didn't have both feet solidly on the ground.

But there it was, whether she liked it or not, a warm, heady sensation that swept over her from her head to her toes as Paddy, smiling down at her, led her around the floor.

She let herself enjoy the delicious giddiness of it as long as the dance lasted. That much she gave herself. But the minute the pipes stopped playing, she took her emotions in hand, reining them in firmly. Saying a polite, "Thank you, Paddy, that was very nice," she hurried off to find Eileen. Her cheeks felt warm, her hands were shaking slightly, and her knees felt as if they might buckle at any moment. But she kept her head high and repeated to herself under her breath as she walked, "Not Paddy, not Paddy, anyone but Paddy. He's a heartbreaker, that one."

That steadied her, and by the time she located Eileen in a noisy corner, her heart had ceased its fluttering and she was able to speak in a normal voice.

But more than once during the rest of that evening, she found her eyes, against her will, drawn to tall, handsome Patrick Kelleher, and felt the sense of wonder sweeping over her again. *Paddy?* Paddy made her feel as if she'd found something she hadn't even known she was looking for.

No wonder she'd thought she felt something when he kissed her.

Though she danced with him again twice during the course of the evening, she kept her eyes averted from his, made little conversation, and pretended to be relieved when the music stopped.

And when he said, as he led her back to Eileen, "I think you're pinin' for Brian and you're too proud to admit it," she didn't deny it. It seemed best to let him think that. Better than lettin' him know it was *him* she was suddenly pinin' for. She could hardly believe it herself. Had the sea air done something to her brain, then?

She'd be fine once they got to dry land. Paddy would go his way and she'd go hers and she'd forget all about that warm, safe feeling when she'd stepped into his arms. She'd be herself again.

The thought didn't comfort her as much as she'd expected it to.

Chapter 12

Friday, April 12, 1912

"If you eat all of that," Katie commented at breakfast on Friday morning, addressing Paddy, "even this great unsinkable ship will be dragged down beneath the weight of it." She was staring in disbelief at the dishes before him, containing an assortment of foods that included a steaming bowl of oatmeal, a hearty portion of Irish stew, strips of liver and bacon, and chunks of French bread. "The whole Hanrahan clan doesn't eat that much food in a day."

Unperturbed by Katie's comments, Paddy slathered a layer of marmalade on a chunk of bread and popped it into his mouth. When he had finished chewing and swallowed, he grinned at Katie. "I'll not be sinkin' the ship. But I'm mindful that soon as we've landed in New York, food will be a scarcity until I'm earnin' a livin' wage, so I'd best eat while I can."

Katie laughed. "You're stocking up, is that how you're lookin' at it? Like a squirrel storin' nuts for the long winter ahead?"

"Aye. Bri's right about one thing. Could be many a year before I sell any of me writin'. And since I'm not goin' to be on a farm like Bri, I won't be gettin' free food." He was serious now.

Katie had never told Paddy her true ambition in life. She was afraid he'd laugh at her. She had no experience as a paid performer, none at all. He'd think she was reachin' for the moon.

Yet she found herself wanting to tell him. She wanted to share her dream with him. Brian knew, and he hadn't laughed at her. And being free-spirited himself, Paddy should applaud her ambition. Why did she think he wouldn't?

Paddy sent a dark glance in the direction of Brian, sitting further down the table, his head bent in response to a question Marta had asked him. "What is it that he's up to with that Swedish girl?"

Katie kept a straight face. "He's heard there are many Swedish people in Wisconsin, and so he's asked Marta to teach him her native language."

Paddy scowled at her. "That's what he's been tellin' you?"

Laughing, Katie said, "Paddy, I was jokin'.

Anyways, Brian isn't you. He doesn't flit from one female to another, makin' up stories as he goes along."

An expression that on anyone else Katie would have seen as hurt appeared on Paddy's face. But since she hadn't meant anything unkind and was simply speaking the truth, she didn't see any reason why Paddy should be offended. "Marta's very nice," she added. "They're both interested in farming. Maybe that's what they talk about."

She decided not to suggest again that Paddy become acquainted with the Swedish girl. That could be a mistake. Not that Paddy had ever stolen any of Brian's girlfriends. He wouldn't do such a thing. But Marta herself could be drawn to the handsome, charming rascal. Katie knew of at least one instance where that had been true, and Brian had been despondent afterward for weeks. Not Paddy's fault, of course, and Brian hadn't seemed to blame him. What had surprised her was Paddy blamed himself, walking around with his head hanging down in remorse, his eyes full of guilt. He'd bought Brian a book Bri had been wanting, had even done his household chores for him, as if by doing so he could make up for the girl's fickle heart.

Yet he himself broke hearts all over County Cork.

Katie didn't understand. Her ma said, "'Tis the code between brothers. Paddy feels he took somethin' of his brother's, though it was the girl herself who was foolish. And he takes it to heart, as he should. Betrayin' blood leads to a bitterness of the soul that 'tis eternal. There's no forgivin' it."

Katie wondered if Paddy resented the girl because his brother was spending so much time with her instead of keeping his brother company during the voyage. Not that Paddy lacked for companionship. Still, Katie decided it might be a good thing to stay by his side, seeing to it that he wasn't interfering with Brian and Marta. It was the least she could do for Brian, who had been kind enough to help her get to Queenstown and the *Titanic*.

Elizabeth, her ankle swollen, spent most of Friday in bed. Sometime that afternoon, Max, Lily, and Arthur came to extend an invitation. They wanted her to join them in the Parisian Café. Elizabeth let her mother decline on her behalf. She needed to think, and she couldn't do that in the café surrounded by people.

But she kept reaching a point in her "thinking" where there seemed to be no answers, only questions. There was nothing left to do then but doze off. Her long nap made a tangled mess of her hair, which then required washing, finger-curling, and a thorough brushing before dinner. She felt she had wasted most of the day. She had thought to plan, and had planned nothing.

Max came back late in the day to invite her to dinner. He knocked at the door to her cabin rather than her parents', and Elizabeth was forced to answer the door with her hair only half dried and curling wildly around her face.

His response was a delighted laugh. "So you decided to let your hair down, after all? About time. I like it."

Elizabeth couldn't help laughing, too. She knew perfectly well how she looked. "If my mother knew I'd answered the door like this, she'd need smelling salts. You're here early. Anyway, I have to eat with my parents." This was one thing she *had* thought about. She had anticipated Max's invitation and had decided it would be wiser to attempt a peaceful, pleasant meal with her mother and father. Her mother would be delighted that Elizabeth seemed to be avoiding Max. She could always see Max later, after dinner.

He looked disappointed. "You're eating with them? Why?"

She didn't want to tell him the truth: that her mother didn't want her associating with someone so "unsuitable." He might not understand that his money and position weren't worth much to Nola if he wasn't going to follow the path his parents had laid out for him.

"Because I need to talk to them, and dinner is the best time. They're always in a good mood then."

Max looked skeptical. "I hope you've planned some really clever strategy. Because if you haven't, there'll be a scene, and your mother will blame you for it."

Elizabeth bristled. "How do *you* know? You're not exactly an expert on my parents."

Leaning against the door frame, his hands in his pockets, he said, "Sure I am. Because they're just like mine. And I've been where you are now. I know exactly what it's like. If you bring up a serious subject like college at dinner, there *will* be a scene."

Elizabeth knew he was right. Because that annoyed her, she snapped, "Thank you for the advice, but I think I can handle a meal with my parents. I've been doing it for years."

He smiled. "Ah, yes, but the question is, have you done it *well*?" He then added, "Unlike me, I mean. Meals at the Whittaker homestead were often an exercise in indigestion."

Elizabeth laughed. "I could meet you later," she offered, feeling a delicious twinge of satisfaction at behaving so boldly. "On the boat deck. If you want." She could use the sore ankle as an excuse to return to the cabin. Her parents would be out and about, entertaining themselves until late. They wouldn't even know she wasn't in her bed. But she'd have to make sure to return before they did. Her mother would check on her before retiring for the night.

"I want. Nine o'clock?"

Elizabeth nodded. "Unless," she added hastily, suddenly afraid she had been too forward, "Arthur and Lily have other plans."

Max laughed. "I sincerely hope they do." He moved away from the door frame. "I guess you'll have to put your hair up in a proper do again. Too bad. I really do like it like that. Lily wears hers like that and no one's thrown her overboard."

Stung, Elizabeth replied, "I'm not Lily," and closed the door.

When she did arrange her hair, she stabbed the hairpins into place ferociously, as if it were Max — or perhaps Lily — she was pinning into place.

She hoped, as she dressed, that by the time she and her parents arrived in the dining room, Max and his friends would have eaten and left. Just in case Max was right about dinner erupting into a "scene."

He *was* right. And he and his friends were there, sitting only two tables away from Elizabeth and her parents. Thus, she had to suffer the added humiliation of knowing Max was watching as his prediction came true.

Dinner had begun pleasantly enough. Elizabeth was determined to avoid a repeat of their last dinner together. Remembering Max's comments, she initially kept her contribution to the mealtime conversation cheerful and harmless. The food was delicious, she said, and ate heartily. The china pattern was lovely, she commented, and smiled at her mother. The soft rose of her mother's dress matched the carpet in the à la carte restaurant, she pointed out, and got a smile in return. Her father beamed approval.

And just when Elizabeth was congratulating herself, thinking, I can do this, this is not so hard, her father ruined it all by saying, "I'm glad to see you've come to your senses, Elizabeth, and are doing your part to make this a pleasant voyage by not tormenting us with your notion of going off to college instead of marrying Alan." He sipped his wine before adding warmly, "I want you to know your mother and I appreciate it. Perhaps we'll stroll down to a shop later and buy you a lovely souvenir of the trip. I understand they have some exquisite commemorative plates."

Elizabeth darted a sideways glance at Max, to see if he'd heard. He had, in spite of the loud hum of conversation in the dining room. She could tell by the expression on his face. And his eyes warned her . . . Don't, Elizabeth, don't do it.

Too late. She had tried, hadn't she? Tried to be pleasant. Tried to pretend that they were as amiable a family as any in this huge, luxurious, crowded dining room filled with amiable families on this most majestic of all ships. And now her father was talking about buying her a *plate*? Like a good little puppy being given a bone? "I am to be rewarded for behaving properly?" she asked in a strained voice.

Her mother sighed and rolled her eyes toward the embossed ceiling.

Slowly, deliberately, Elizabeth dabbed at her mouth with the white linen napkin. Then she put the napkin down beside her plate and stood up. "If you want to give me a reward," she said distinctly, and knew that Max heard, "give me what I really want. Give me the right to make my own decisions. Forget about marrying me off to Alan Reed, and send me to college. If you will do those things for me, I will never say another unpleasant word again."

Her father did not call after her as she left the room.

She didn't realize that Max was right behind her until she had to stand aside in the corridor to let a waiter with a dining cart pass. As she turned, her back to the wall, she saw him standing there. "If you say I told you so . . ." she said heatedly. She began moving swiftly down the corridor again, limping only slightly on the injured ankle. She did not glance over her shoulder to see if he was following.

"I'm not going to say it." He caught up with her and grabbed her hand. "Slow down, will you? No one's chasing you."

"You think I'm stupid for losing my temper. That I'll never have what I want because I can't control my anger. Why don't you just say so? That's what you're thinking."

"You read minds now?" Tugging on her hand, he stopped her, turned her around to face him. People passing them smiled, perhaps thinking they were one of the honeymooning couples on board. They didn't see the pain in Elizabeth's eyes.

"I wasn't thinking you were stupid. And I wasn't thinking you won't get what you want. I was thinking exactly the opposite." He put a hand under her chin, tilted it upward so that she was forced to meet his eyes with hers. "When I heard what you said and watched you march out of the dining room, your back as straight as the mast on this ship, I *knew* you'd get what you want, no matter what it takes."

Elizabeth relaxed a little, leaning into the wall. "You did? That's really what you were thinking?"

Max nodded. "You bet." He smiled and took a step forward, so there was almost no space between them. "But that's not what I'm thinking now."

"It's not?"

"No, ma'am, it's not. What I'm thinking now is, your parents are still back in that dining room, and there isn't anyone around to stop me from kissing you."

Then Max's lips were on hers, and she couldn't have spoken even if she'd wanted to.

She didn't want to.

Chapter 13

Katie and Paddy were strolling the deck under a black-velvet, star-studded sky when she decided to share her dream with him. She was mindful that he might laugh at her. But her thinking was, if he did, that would cure her forever of her foolish attraction to him and she'd be the better off for it. And if he didn't laugh, she'd have someone to talk to about her high hopes for the new country.

He didn't laugh. "Well, you've a fine voice, that's certain. The people in steerage loved your singin'. But is there much call for stage work in Wisconsin, then?"

Katie stopped walking. The air was chilly, and she was wearing only a shawl around her shoulders. She had worn it partly because it reminded her of her ma, who had knit it for her, but also because the deep blue matched her eyes, or so people told her. Although Patrick Kelleher hadn't seemed to notice. "Wisconsin? I wouldn't know. Brian hasn't said. But there's stage work in New York, and that's where I'll be stayin'. I'm boardin' with me uncle Malachy and his wife, Charlotte. Did you not know that, Paddy?"

He had stopped walking when she did, and now turned to face her. "What are you sayin'? Me brother is leavin' you alone in a big city? For how long?"

Katie leaned against the rail, her back to the sea. Other couples and some families were strolling the deck as, she imagined, people must stroll the sidewalks of New York on a fine summer night, warmer than this one. "I won't be alone. Didn't I just tell you, I'll be with Malachy and Lottie in Brooklyn. They've a fine apartment and I'm welcome there."

He was frowning, as if he were trying to make sense of what she was saying. "Is Brian stayin' with you there in New York, then? He's changed his mind about farmin'?"

"No, acourse not. Farmin' is all Bri ever wanted to do. Why would he change his mind?" Katie didn't understand why Paddy seemed so confused. She had never once said she was on her way to Wisconsin, nor had Brian ever stated any intent to make his way in the city of

New York. "Besides, Marta's goin' to be in Minnesota, and I think that's not so far from Wisconsin."

Paddy snorted in disgust. "Marta! She isn't even Irish! Brian's gone off his head, that's what he's done. I'm goin' to have a talk with him, soon as I get back to our quarters." He moved forward to lean against the railing, facing the sea, the ocean breeze blowing his dark hair back, away from his face.

Katie thought she had never seen anyone so fine-looking. If Paddy wished to be on the stage, as she did, she was certain he could. Women would pay just to look at him. But he wanted to be a writer. Pity. "I don't see why you're goin' on so. Marta's nice. She may not be Irish but she's a lot like Brian. Solid. Dependable. And she wants to do farmwork, like him. I think your ma would take to her, even though she's not of the faith. Me grandmother married out of the faith, and she wasn't struck by lightning." Katie laughed. "She found the only Protestant for miles around and married him. Acourse, the first thing she did was convert him. Quit frettin'. Brian can look out for himself."

"It's not Brian I'm frettin' over," he grumbled, keeping his eyes on the sea. "Seems to me you're the one should be frettin'." He did glance over at her then. "I guess you'll be joinin' him soon enough, but do your ma and da know

Brian's leavin' you alone in the city of New York, even if it's just for a time?"

She turned then to face forward, into the ocean breeze. Her elbow touched his, and a sharp electric tingle shot through her. She moved the elbow. "Of course they do. Me da knows Bri wants to farm until he has enough money to buy his own place. And I'm goin' to be stayin' with Malachy and his family. It's all settled."

Paddy nodded. "Ah, he'll send for you then, when he has his own place? Bri?"

It struck Katie then what was going on. It wasn't herself Paddy was troubling about. 'Twas his brother who was on his mind. Paddy didn't want Brian living alone in a strange country, a strange town, without someone from home. Someone like her. He must have thought all along that the two of them would be together, and that had given him comfort. And with him so dead set against Marta, it wouldn't do to remind him that it looked as if the Swedish girl might be keeping Brian company someday, way up there in Wisconsin. Paddy wouldn't be comforted by the thought.

If it made him feel better to believe that Brian would be sharing any homestead he created in the north country with an Irish lass from home, what would it hurt to let him think it? What did it matter? Once the *Titanic* docked, they would all go their separate ways. Although Paddy, too, would be in New York, she didn't expect to be seeing him there, such a big city it was. He'd have a hundred friends within a week of his arrival. Any remembrance of Katie Hanrahan from Ballyford would be erased like chalk on a blackboard at the end of a school day.

Still, Katie was reluctant to lie. Instead, all she said was, "Hard to say what's goin' to happen in the New World. But you mustn't trouble yourself over Brian, Paddy. He can take care of himself."

He made no response to that. He seemed lost in thought. They stood in silence for a while, listening to the steady swish of the ship as it sliced its way through the dark water and to the faint sounds of music coming from inside. From behind them on the deck came occasional footsteps, voices, and laughter, but their own silence continued. Katie didn't mind. It seemed not an anxious or nervous silence, but a companionable one. The lights cast a pale yellow sheen across the water below them, as if someone had dumped a bucket of melted butter into the sea. She was cold, but not painfully so. If she complained, or shivered, Paddy would take her inside, and she didn't want to go, didn't want to leave, didn't want to move.

But the moment came, as it grew later and

colder, when she couldn't help it, and shivered involuntarily.

Paddy saw the movement, slight though it was, and insisted on taking her to her quarters. "'Tis late, anyway, and I don't want to find Brian asleep when I get back. Can't very well talk to him if he's out cold, can I, then?"

"You're not goin' to pester him about Marta, are you? He won't take kindly to that." Katie didn't want the brothers fighting now, when soon enough they would be separating, probably forever. 'Twould be a sore thing for their last words to be angry ones.

"Don't be tellin' me what to say to me own brother, Katie." His tone was curt, almost brusque, as if he was angry. Katie couldn't believe he was that angry about Marta.

Patrick Kelleher was acting strange, very strange indeed.

Maybe the sea air *did* affect the brain.

He didn't come into the stern area with her. Instead, he told her a quick, curt, "Sleep well, then," and left to seek out his brother.

She had been hoping he'd kiss her again, had known that he wouldn't, what with him acting so strange and all. Still, she'd kept hoping right up until the very last minute. Foolish girl.

The pleasure of her time spent with Paddy evaporated, leaving disappointment in its place.

So when Eileen, already in bed, asked as Katie arrived, "Were you out walkin' with your young man, then?" Katie snapped, "I *haven't* a young man, nor do I want one! They're nothin' but trouble, and that's the truth of it."

"Not my Sean," Eileen said dreamily, and drifted off to sleep.

It was an hour or more before Katie followed suit. When she did, she awoke shortly thereafter soaked in perspiration and shaking. In her dream, the *Titanic* had collided with an equally enormous ship in the middle of the Atlantic Ocean. Both had sunk clear to the bottom of the sea. In Katie's nightmare, only she was aware of the tragedy. The other passengers went right on playing cards, dancing, smoking, and singing, as if they were still sailing along on the surface as they should have been. Brian was dancing with Marta, Paddy with Eileen. All four were laughing, and took no notice of Katie standing on the sidelines screaming at them that the ship was sinking.

It took her another hour to return to sleep. She awakened the following morning with a painful headache.

In his cabin, Max Whittaker mused over the puzzle that was Elizabeth Farr. He lay on his bed, still fully clothed, the porthole over his head partially opened to the chilly night air, his arms behind his head as he studied the ceiling. He had apologized after the kiss, said he was sorry, that he hadn't meant it, that he hoped he hadn't offended her, but the only honest portion of that was the part about hoping he hadn't offended her. He was pretty sure he hadn't. She had kissed him back, that much he was sure of.

He had said the other things because that was what you were supposed to do when you kissed a girl you didn't know all that well. There were rules, rules that he'd had drummed into his head since he was old enough to understand the language. He knew those rules by heart, every one of them. Most of them had to do with "appearances," how what you did or said or wore in public was received by other people. His mother constantly said, "But how would it *look*?"

The friends he'd made in Paris had expressed contempt for those rules, asking him why it was he didn't make his *own* rules.

Max closed his eyes. He didn't have to figure everything out tonight. Elizabeth lived in New York, too. Her parents knew his parents. Their relationship didn't have to end, like most shipboard friendships did, the minute the ship docked. If he was careful not to offend the Farrs he could see her again, in New York, if he wanted to.

He wanted to. There were many things Max

Whittaker didn't know yet, but whether or not he wanted to see more of Elizabeth Farr wasn't one of them.

The question was, would *she* want to see him again, once they'd docked? Especially if he struck out on his own and didn't have two nickles to rub together. How would Elizabeth feel about him then?

That was one of the many things that Max Whittaker *didn't* know. It kept him awake for a long time.

Chapter 14

Saturday, April 13, 1912

On Saturday morning, leaving Eileen still
sound asleep in her berth, Katie went to the
dining room with Kevin and Bridey in tow. She
found Paddy and Brian standing in a corner
near the bulkhead arguing heatedly. They
didn't see her come in, didn't notice her approaching with a child attached to each hand.
And they didn't stop arguing.

". . . ashamed of yourself," she heard Paddy
say in an accusing tone of voice. "Behavin' like
a rogue, you are. What would Ma say?"

They're arguing about Marta, Katie thought,
and stopped walking, holding the children back
as well. She didn't want to overhear this conversation. It was between the brothers and had
nothing to do with her. But if she tried to re-
move the hungry children from the dining room

now, Bridey would pitch a fit. Katie stood perfectly still, trying to shut her ears against their words and hoping they wouldn't notice that she'd arrived.

But since she had to continue holding on to the children, she couldn't very well clap her hands over her ears. With no practical way to keep the heated words from reaching her, she found herself listening in spite of her good intentions.

"What are you blatherin' on about, Paddy? Ma isn't here, is she, then? I'm on me own, and can pick and choose as I see fit. Marta's a fine girl. Strikes me that you might be jealous because 'tisn't you she's fancyin'."

Katie's ears burned. Hadn't she wondered the same thing herself? She strained to catch Paddy's answer. But Bridey picked that moment to begin whining loudly that she was hungry, and all Katie heard was, "can't hold a candle to . . ." She didn't catch the name of the girl Marta couldn't hold a candle to.

". . . don't know what you're talkin' about, Paddy, and that's the truth of it. You never did see things the way they really are, with your head in the clouds all the time. Why don't you ask her how *she* feels? I already know, but you're too thick-headed to see it. *Ask* her!"

Katie frowned. Why was Brian pestering Paddy to ask Marta how she felt, when anyone with two eyes in their head could see for themselves, plain as day?

It was time to end the argument. Katie marched over to the two of them, saying, "Top of the mornin' to you both! Are you not hungry, then? I had thought to see the two of you already sittin' and fillin' your bellies. You could have been savin' us some seats. What good are you?"

Brian laughed and led them all to seats. Paddy followed, looking thoroughly disgruntled.

Chapter 15

Saturday, April 13, 1912

Elizabeth had no intention of spending all day Saturday in her room, as she had Friday. Hiding was for cowards, something she didn't want to be. And with every nautical mile covered by the great, swift ship, which by all accounts was breaking speed records across the north Atlantic, they were drawing ever closer to New York and the end of the voyage. She had little time left and she had accomplished nothing.

It was difficult to find time alone with her parents. They were so busy, gone from their stateroom the majority of the time, having long lunches and dinners with friends, playing cards, walking along the promenade hand in hand as if there were no one else in the world but the two of them. Elizabeth had felt like an outsider in her parents' marriage throughout her life, and this trip was no exception. She had often wished for a sibling or two, just for companionship of her own. She resented their closeness even more now. It was so obvious that they didn't *need* her, why couldn't they just let her *go*? To Poughkeepsie, to Vassar, to a new, exciting life. What difference could it possibly make to them?

She dressed and an hour later took the elevator down to F deck for a quick, refreshing swim. She skipped the Turkish bath, which did not appeal to her at all. She had promised to meet Max for lunch at the à la carte restaurant on B deck at noon. He was playing squash in the morning with her father, but had agreed not to mention the luncheon date to Martin Farr. Elizabeth had been very stern about that. If Max told her father, he would tell her mother, who would surely put her foot down. She had said she wouldn't forbid Elizabeth from seeing Max, but she would never approve an intimate twosome for lunch.

Golden ribbons of light streamed through the huge glass dome over the Grand Staircase when, warmly clad in a long skirt and matching jacket of scarlet wool, Elizabeth went up on deck for a breath of fresh air before making her way to the restaurant.

He was waiting for her just outside the restaurant, as they'd agreed. He looked very handsome in a tweed jacket, and smiled when he saw her approaching. "I was going to invite Lily and Arthur to join us," he said, "but I thought better of it. Do you mind if it's just the two of us?"

Elizabeth laughed as they took their seats. But all she said was, "No, I don't mind at all." She might tell him later that she'd had the same thought. Or maybe not. Admitting that she wanted to be alone with him might be too forward.

There you go again, Elizabeth, she scolded mentally as she picked up a menu. Why are you following silly rules that make no sense to you? Why shouldn't you tell Max you wanted to be alone with him?

But when she spoke, it was to ask him who had won the squash game.

She wasn't surprised by his answer. "Your father, of course." He grinned at her over his menu. "What kind of fool do you think I am?"

"You mean you didn't score points against him because you wanted to score points *with* him," Elizabeth said, smiling. "Isn't that dishonest?" But she was secretly pleased. He had quite a few years on her father, and was thinner and lighter on his feet. He probably could have won. If he'd lost deliberately, it was because of her. She liked that.

Putting his menu aside, Max leaned across

the table, though he didn't attempt to take Elizabeth's hands in his. "I'm not all that sure I could have beaten him. He's good, and he's in great shape. But if you're asking me if I gave it my all, the answer is no." His deep blue eyes were serious as he added, "Do you think I don't know that your parents are only tolerating me because of *my* parents? Elizabeth, I want to keep seeing you after we get back home. Everyone — your parents, my parents — everyone is going to hit the ceiling when I tell my parents I'm moving out to live on my own. Your parents won't even care that I'm a Whittaker then, because I'll be a *poor* Whittaker. So I need all the points in my favor that I can get. Losing a squash game won't get me many, but it's a start." He smiled again. "Your father seemed pretty happy. He actually called me 'Max' instead of 'Whittaker.'"

"He likes winning." But Elizabeth was sobered by the prospect of Max becoming alienated from his parents. Max was right about one thing. The only reason her mother hadn't forbidden Elizabeth to see him was his status as the son of wealthy friends. If Enid and Jules were so angered by Max's defection that they cut him off from the family, he would no longer exist for Nola Farr. He'd never set one foot inside the front door of the Farr mansion. It would be impossible for Elizabeth to ever see him again.

Because that thought was so unpalatable, she tried to persuade him during lunch to reach a compromise with his parents. Even when she realized by the set of his mouth that he was becoming annoyed with the turn the conversation had taken, she persisted.

"You could go to college and paint between classes. That way, you'd be getting what you wanted, but your parents would, too."

"I don't want to finish college. I had two years of it, and I was bored to death. I took business classes, because my father insisted. Have you ever taken an accounting class? The pages of a calendar are more exciting than an accounting textbook. I'm not interested in becoming a businessman, Elizabeth. I thought you understood that."

"I do. But would it be so terrible to take a few classes if it meant keeping peace in your family?"

Max set his glass on the pristine white tablecloth and fixed a level gaze on Elizabeth's face. "Keeping peace? Don't you mean, seeing to it that they don't cut me off without a penny?"

Elizabeth studied the snow-white tablecloth. "It's not the money. It's the *idea*, Max. As long as you're still within the family fold, my parents won't stop me from seeing you. But if you go off on your own entirely, if you make your parents so angry that they disown you, my mother will never tolerate a friendship between the two of us." Her fingers nervously played with her fork. "I wouldn't be allowed to see you again."

"Then I guess you'd have a choice to make, too," he said, his voice firm but gentle. "You would have to decide if you were willing to defy them for my sake, wouldn't you?" He watched her for several seconds, then added quietly, "I'd like to think that you would."

Elizabeth's laugh was harsh, bitter. "Max, I haven't even decided how defiant I'm willing to be for my *own* sake. And if I *do* manage to accomplish what I want, I might not have any energy left to fight for you." Her eyes met his again. "Lily would, I guess. But I'm not as independent as she is."

"Only because you haven't had the opportunities she's had." Max leaned across the table again, and this time he did take Elizabeth's hands in his. "Don't sell yourself short, Elizabeth. You're as strong as Lily any day. All you need is a chance to prove it to yourself."

Elizabeth glanced around nervously, fearful that someone might see Max holding her hands and gazing at her so intently.

Though the restaurant was filled to capacity,

Elizabeth saw no one she recognized as being a shipboard acquaintance of her mother's.

Sudden defiance filled her. Angry with herself for being nervous about being seen with Max, she sat up straighter in her chair, still holding his hands. I like the way he sees me, she told herself, and rewarded him with a brilliant smile. I *want* to be strong and independent like Lily. My parents think I can't be, but Max thinks I can. I'd rather believe him.

If Max were around all the time, maybe after a while she'd see herself the way he saw her.

Then her back stiffened again. No. She wasn't going to get her sense of who she was from someone *else*, not even from someone as nice as Max. It had to come from *her*, or it wouldn't mean anything.

Still, it was nice to have someone encouraging her. That was more than Alan would ever do. He had no wish to see her strong and independent.

She and Max were still mildly arguing about the meaning of compromise when Lily and Arthur arrived and joined them. Because they weren't getting anywhere in their discussion, neither Max nor Elizabeth objected. The lunch interval hadn't turned out quite as they'd planned. If they couldn't spend this time together without discussing family, they might just as well let friends join them.

After lunch, they played shuffleboard on deck. The air was becoming increasingly colder, and someone mentioned the possibility of icebergs in the area. Elizabeth peered off into the distance, but when she saw nothing but the horizon, she dismissed the threat of huge chunks of ice floating in the sea. However, a strange shiver went over her.

Her parents strolled by once, and although Nola failed to smile in Max's direction, she didn't demand that Elizabeth leave the group.

When they had passed by, Lily asked, "She does not like you very much, Max, Elizabeth's mother? What is it that you did to offend her?"

Not wanting to talk about her mother, Elizabeth left the group and went to the rail to stare out across the water. It was as smooth as a black satin comforter. The *Titanic* caused hardly a ripple. Remembering the mention of icebergs, she scanned the sea again, but there were no bulky shapes looming out of the darkness.

Lily joined her at the rail. "You are sad, Elizabeth?"

"No. Not sad. Just . . . frustrated." She glanced down upon the third-class open area, watching as the pretty Irish girl she'd seen loading from the tender at Queenstown, the two brothers who had accompanied her on board, and a laughing girl with blond hair played catch with what looked like a child's rag doll. People sitting on the sidelines cheered them on. Elizabeth envied them. They were third-class passengers, so they had a lot less money than her family or Max's, yet they seemed to be having far more fun than Elizabeth.

Chapter 16

Saturday, April 13, 1912

Kevin and Bridey, contentedly full of rabbit pie and baked potatoes, lay on benches in the general room after dinner, playing with handmade pinwheels given them by a crew member. Katie played the piano and sang, hoping all the while that Paddy would join her on the bench. But each time she glanced around the room in search of him, she found him flanked by a cluster of young women. If he noticed that she was hitting the keys increasingly harder until she was fairly pounding out each note, he gave no sign.

She didn't see Brian and Marta anywhere and assumed they'd gone for a walk. Eileen was ignoring the children and her betrothal to Sean to flirt outrageously with a tall, blond Norwegian.

Katie had her back turned to the general room. Suddenly, she was interrupted in mid-refrain by a child's shriek of terror. When she whirled in alarm on the piano bench, the first thing she saw was Bridey falling, headfirst, from the very top of a tall tower of wooden crates. There was no one standing beneath her to catch her before she crashed to the bare floor.

Voices cried out, shouting a warning. Kevin shouted in panic for Eileen, who was too far away in a dim corner to be of any use. As everyone watched in horror, Bridey continued her headlong dive.

And then Paddy seemed to appear out of nowhere, not so much running as flinging himself forward, his feet barely touching the bare floor, his arms outstretched. There was one terrible, breath-stealing second when it seemed he was too late, when it looked like he was not close enough, and Bridey's headlong descent would continue uninterrupted all the way to the floor.

Making a sound like that of someone punched in the stomach, Paddy stretched his arms up and out, his handsome face scarlet with exertion. Bridey landed in his arms, upside down.

Her sudden weight caused him to lose his balance, and they both toppled forward onto the floor.

But he was careful to swing the child sideways as he fell, so that she landed beside him rather than beneath his weight.

Bridey wailed in rage. Katie rushed over to check her thoroughly. Aside from the humiliation of looking foolish in front of so many people, which Bridey seemed to feel keenly, she was uninjured.

Also unhurt, Paddy scrambled to his feet amid congratulations. Rather than accepting them, he whirled on Eileen, who had abandoned her companion to see what all the fuss was about. "And where, might I ask," he demanded, his face flushed with anger, "was you when this wee one here decided to go climbin'? Is she not in your care? Are you not bein' paid to look after her during this voyage?" He seemed to notice then the blond gentleman standing behind Eileen, and his face flushed a deeper scarlet. "Carryin' on, was you, then? 'Tis a fine thing, an engaged woman like yourself!" He shook his head, adding in disgust, "Is everyone on this grand ship a faithless fool?" Then he turned and stomped out of the room, his boots making a heavy thudding sound as he went.

Eileen's round cheeks flared in anger, but she did stoop then to comfort Bridey, whose wailing had created a runny nose and swollen eyes.

Katie stared after Paddy's departing back in

confusion. She didn't blame him for being upset with Eileen. The girl would win no prizes as a governess. But Paddy's last remark had surprised her. Who else on the ship was a "faithless fool"?

It dawned on her then, in a sudden flash of knowing, that Paddy was referring to his brother. And the person Paddy thought Brian was being "faithless" to was herself, Katie Hanrahan. How dense she had been! Those things Paddy had said about her and Brian going to Wisconsin together, his anger when she told him she was staying in New York, his taking that to mean she'd be only visiting with Malachy and Lottie until Brian sent for her, his angry remarks about faithlessness. . . . Why had it taken so long for the truth to sink in? Did Brian already know what Paddy was thinkin'? If he did, why hadn't he told *her*?

Where *were* Brian and Marta, anyways? She hadn't seen them since supper.

Perhaps she'd best go find them and let Brian know that his brother was pitching a fit.

But she found Paddy before she found his brother and Marta. He was sitting up on the poop deck, chin in his hands, glaring out at the unruffled black canvas that was the sea. She hesitated, thinking that this was a matter between the two brothers. But that wasn't exactly the truth of it. It had to do with her, too.

The notion of Paddy thinking she was pining away of a shattered heart was an unpleasant one to her. Best to set him straight now. It was good that she had come upon him sitting by himself.

"Gettin' colder," he said when he looked up and saw her standing behind him. "There's talk of bergs. Though I guess we needn't fret. It'd take more than an iceberg to stop this great ship, I'm guessin'."

Katie didn't want to talk about icebergs. "What's ailin' you, anyways?" she asked him, plopping down beside him, tucking her brown wool skirt in around her ankles to keep out the cold. "People was wantin' to thank you for savin' Bridey, and next thing we know, you're bitin' our heads off and boltin' from the room like you're goin' off to war. You can't be that mad at Eileen. She's just not very bright, Paddy."

" 'Twasn't her," he muttered.

The noise from the general room directly below them was loud, and he hadn't spoken very clearly. Katie leaned closer. "Pardon? What did you say?"

"I said it wasn't *her*."

"Then what was it?" But of course she knew now. Still, she wanted him to say it.

He was still muttering. "Bri. Him and that Swedish boy. Caught them kissin.' "

Katie heard that and laughed. "You caught them kissin'? You make it sound like a crime. 'Tisn't a crime to kiss, Paddy."

"'Tis if you're supposed to be faithful to someone else."

The sky above them was clear, the stars glittering like jewels. Though they were surrounded by an empty, endless darkness, here on the ship there was ample light. She found herself wishing their conversing were about something nicer, something sweeter. But first, she had to clear his mind of his foolish notions about her and Bri. "Your brother is my friend, Paddy. I couldn'ta come on this trip was it not for Brian." She glanced sideways at Paddy, with a hint of a smile on her face. "Me da likes you, but I'm thinkin' he wouldn'ta trusted me into your care like he did Bri's. You have yourself a reputation in Ballyford, y'know."

Paddy didn't smile.

"We are no more than friends, Bri and me. Never have been. I don't know why 'tis that you think otherwise, but you'd best stop fancifyin' about that and be nice to Marta. You don't want to be partin' from your brother when we dock in New York with bad blood between you. You might not never see him again, and that's the truth of it."

"I'd expect nothin' less from you," he said then. He stood up, looking down at her. "'Tis like you to be brave, Katie. And if it's important to your pride to pretend you're not carin' about his faithlessness, I'll keep me mouth shut."

He wasn't *listening*. Dolt! Katie struggled to hold her temper in check. "I'm not pretending! Are you not hearin' me? Open your ears. I love Brian like a brother, just as you do, and I'm thankful that he helped me get to New York, but that's the limit of my feelin' for him. I never had plans to go to Wisconsin, and I never had plans to marry up with your brother. That was all in your writer's fanciful imagination."

His expression, illuminated for her by the ship's bright lights, was one of doubt. Then his face cleared. "I'm sayin' no more about it. But my thinkin' is, you're protectin' your wounded pride, that's what you're doin'."

Katie jumped to her feet. "Well, even if that were true," she said heatedly, "and it isn't, 'twouldn't be very gentlemanly of you to point that out for me, now, would it?" She wanted fiercely to add, " 'Tisn't Brian in my heart, 'tis you, fool that you are," but then she remembered all those other young girls gathered around Paddy in the general room, and bit her tongue.

"Acourse," he said, nodding, "you're right. Wasn't thinkin', was I?" He sat back down. "It's good that you're not pinin' for him. You wouldn't want to give him the satisfaction." He sounded unconvinced.

"Anyways," he went on doggedly, "I'd bet this is just one of those shipboard things. I've heard it happens. Soon as we've landed in New York, Bri will come to his senses. You'll see."

Katie gave up. He must have stuffed fat wads of cotton into his ears, for all that he heard what she was saying.

"If he don't come to his senses," he went on maddeningly, "you're sure to meet someone better in a city as big as New York. Someone who'll treat you fair."

"That I am." But she didn't want someone from the city of New York. She wanted someone from Ballyford, Ireland, someone named Kelleher.

Elizabeth and Lily didn't return to the restaurant. Instead, Max and Arthur joined them on deck. They strolled in the night air for an hour or so, along with many other couples enjoying the crisp, fresh air and star-studded night sky. It was close to eleven o'clock when Elizabeth stated regretfully that she needed to return to her cabin. She was hoping to see her parents before they called it a night. Time was passing quickly, and while the *Titanic* was making great progress, she was not.

Max knew why she was anxious to return to the stateroom, and wished her good luck at her door. "Staying calm might help," he added matter-of-factly.

"If things get rough in there, just remember this, okay?" and he bent his head and kissed her, a long, slow kiss, warm and tender. She lifted her arms and wrapped them around his neck, completely forgetting that her parents might come along at any moment. Even if she'd remembered, being that close to Max made her feel she could handle anything.

As the kiss ended and they eased apart, he smiled at her and said, "Remember, count to ten."

"I'll try." She watched as he turned and went away down the corridor, a tall, rangy figure so important to her, it was impossible to believe she hadn't even known him when she boarded the *Titanic* on Wednesday.

Chapter 17

Elizabeth fell asleep Saturday night waiting for her parents to return to their stateroom. She was terribly disappointed when she awoke sometime during the night to find herself lying on her bed fully clothed, icy air streaming in through her open porthole, and realized that she had never talked to her parents as she'd planned. The evening had accomplished nothing.

She buried her face in her hands, willing herself not to cry. Buoyed by Max's loving kiss, she had been so prepared for the confrontation with her mother and father. But they were out when she entered their stateroom, and she'd tired of waiting on the chaise lounge. She'd gone into her room thinking only to change into a robe before returning to wait for them, for hours if necessary. But she had made the mistake of sitting down on her bed to slip her aching ankle out of its shoe. Fatigue had overtaken her and she'd sunk back into the comforting pillows, telling herself she would rest just for a few minutes.

And now it was the middle of the night. Her parents would be sound asleep by now.

When she awoke Sunday morning, the air entering through the porthole seemed much colder than on other mornings. Elizabeth remembered yesterday's comments about icebergs in the area. Was it possible? It seemed cold enough. But Captain Smith was an experienced seaman. He would be an expert at steering around any large objects in the sea.

Closing the porthole, Elizabeth dressed hurriedly in a navy blue skirt and jacket, suitable for Sunday services. The service was held at ten-thirty in the first-class dining room. Elizabeth was surprised to see the red-haired girl from third-class there, the girl named Katie, along with a tall, blond girl. Both were gazing around in wide-eyed awe at the furnishings and decor in the salon.

Nola Farr said, "I suppose with Captain Smith conducting the service they felt it was only right to let third- and second-class passengers attend. Makes it rather crowded, doesn't it?" Her tone of voice hinted that she found it more than just crowded, she found it distasteful.

Elizabeth glanced around for Max, found him standing off to her left. He smiled at her and waved, then faced front as the captain began to read from the shipping line's company prayer book.

Her stomach felt queasy. She had no idea what she was going to say to her parents after breakfast. Perhaps they could compromise. She might be willing to endure the debut, if her mother would let her out of the marriage. That seemed fair. But then there was college, too. She wanted that as much as she wanted her engagement broken.

If only Max would face them with her. He could keep her calm, help her count to ten.

But this was her problem, not his. He had his own parents to deal with when he returned to New York. She would have to handle this one alone. And this time, they would *have* to listen.

If she could ever get her family together in one room *to* listen. Throughout the day, Elizabeth was repeatedly thwarted in her efforts to accomplish this.

Max found her in the writing room shortly before dinner. "Where have you been all day? I've been looking all over the ship for you. Lily said she hadn't seen you. There's ice about," he said as he took a seat opposite her. "I was sending my grandmother a Marconigram and saw a few messages warning about ice fields ahead. That probably means icebergs, as well. One of the crewmen said bergs in this area are often as big as houses."

"Big as houses? Who were the messages from?"

"From other ships in the area." Max frowned. "Have you been out on deck? The temperature is diving considerably. So the idea of ice ahead makes a lot of sense."

Elizabeth thought about that for a minute or two. If there really was ice ahead, wouldn't the captain have to slow the ship? Perhaps even stop for a while until morning? It couldn't be sensible to travel through ice at night, could it? If the *Titanic* stopped for the night, she would have more time.

"Have dinner with me," he urged as they got up and prepared to leave the writing room.

Elizabeth shook her head. "I need to eat with my parents. I haven't seen them alone at all. I've already made sure they have no dinner plans with other people. And I can spirit them straight back to the stateroom afterward. I won't let them go into the lounge, and I won't let them out of my sight."

"So you're going to kidnap your own parents?" Max was smiling. "I'd like to see that."

Elizabeth smiled. "I have no choice."

Dinner was a quiet, tense affair, and Elizabeth knew it was her fault. Her parents were both in good spirits, but she was so anxious about confronting them, she barely ate a morsel of food. Which her mother commented upon, which made Elizabeth even more tense. Count to ten, she kept repeating silently, count to ten. One ... two ... three ... four ...

Max was right. It did help.

She almost did have to kidnap her parents to get them back to the stateroom. On the way out of the dining salon, her mother stopped to chat briefly with Madeleine Astor, who was expecting a child, and then her father had to say hello to Mrs. Brown, who clapped him on the back and shouted an invitation to a card game. Elizabeth held her breath until he expressed his regrets and moved on. In the reception room, her parents stopped repeatedly to speak to friends. To Elizabeth, the trip from the table in the dining salon to their stateroom on C deck seemed to take hours.

When the door finally closed behind the three of them, she gave them just time enough to sit before announcing, "I would like to talk to both of you, please."

Her father frowned, and her mother sighed, but they made no move to leave.

Elizabeth, still standing just inside the door

because she was too anxious to sit, began talking. She had said all of these things before, but never so seriously. The time spent in the writing room had proved useful, as her thoughts were now so organized in her head she was able to present them calmly and logically. She explained that she did not wish to enter into a loveless marriage, and she did not love Alan Reed and never would. She added that she would be willing to go through the entire season of debut parties *if* her parents would at least consider sending her to college the following autumn. She kept her voice level and spoke quietly.

It seemed to work. Her parents listened without interruption, though her mother was tapping one foot impatiently against the wood trim on the chaise lounge. Neither got up and moved about, neither got up and left the room. Grateful for that much, she finished her carefully reasoned argument. And waited for their reaction.

Her mother's came first, as she had known it would. "I had no idea you felt so strongly about marrying Alan," she said, smoothing the folds of her pale yellow gown as she spoke. "You might have told us sooner."

Elizabeth held her breath, feeling a kernel of hope spring alive within her. "I'm sorry. I thought I had. I realize it will be embarrassing for both of you when the engagement is canceled, but I'm sure Alan will understand."

"Canceled?" Elizabeth's mother looked up from her position on the chaise. "Oh, my dear, the engagement won't be canceled."

The kernel of hope died a swift but painful death. "But you said —"

"I merely said that you might have told us of your feelings sooner, so that we could have attended to them. We are not heartless, Elizabeth, though you apparently think otherwise. But we won't be canceling anything. Not the engagement, not the debut season. This is why you have parents, darling, to lead you in the proper direction. To stop you from making foolish decisions. We love you very much, and we want the best for you. Seeing that you get it is our job." Glancing at her husband, Nola Farr said, "Wouldn't you say so, darling?"

Elizabeth had one last faint hope left. That her father might take her side, as he occasionally had in the past. If he did, the two of them might be able to sway her mother, just enough to at least cancel the engagement.

That hope lasted while her father seemed to ponder the question for a moment, but it, too, died as he nodded and answered, "Yes, I would say that is our job." To Elizabeth, he said calmly, "Of course, we don't expect you to understand that just now. Children never do. I myself didn't when, at seventeen, I wanted to sign on a ship and travel the world. My father forbade it. I was angry, just as you are now. But he knew what he was doing, and I must say I've been grateful for some time now. My plan was ridiculously foolish. But I was too young to see that."

Elizabeth tried to count. One ... two ... three ... four ... But it was too much. They were allied against her and together they made one formidable foe. "How do you *know* that?" she cried. "How do you know it would have been a foolish thing to do, if you didn't *do* it? Maybe it would have been wonderful. Maybe you were just a coward!"

Elizabeth was sorry immediately. Her father flinched as if she had struck him, and her mother cried out, "Elizabeth, how *could* you!"

But wasn't it true, just a little? He had wanted to go to sea, and he hadn't gone.

She wasn't going to follow his example. She *wasn't*. One ... two ... three ... four ... it was no use. This was much too important to her to back down, and speaking logically and calmly hadn't worked. They weren't giving an inch. "You won't even think about a compromise? I said I would go through the entire debut season. But I won't, I will *not* marry Alan. And you can't make me."

Nola raised an eyebrow at that. She turned

her head to look at her husband. "It's that Whittaker boy," she said, her voice perfectly calm. "I knew it. I should have forbidden her to see him, but I was afraid of offending Enid and Jules." Turning back to Elizabeth, she said, "This is nothing more than a shipboard flirtation. I realize the young man is better-looking than Alan, and closer to your age. But Elizabeth, that boy has no *future*. He wants to be an *artist*, for heaven's sake! You simply cannot be serious about him."

"Oh, but I am. And he feels the same way. And I don't care if he's poor, I really don't."

"Well, now I *am* forbidding you to see him again," Mrs. Farr said. "There will be no more talk of college, and during the remainder of this trip, you will not see or speak to Maxwell Whittaker, do you understand me?"

Tears filled Elizabeth's eyes. But her voice was soft when she spoke. "No, Mother. That's the problem. I *don't* understand you. And I never will." She wanted to keep fighting, not to give up until they had agreed to give her at least something of what she wanted. But it seemed so futile. It *was* futile. They had all the power. She had none.

"I'm not marrying Alan Reed," Elizabeth said, still softly, and then she walked to the door to her room, opened it, went inside, closed the door behind her . . . and locked it.

Chapter 18

At the service on Sunday in the first-class dining room, Katie couldn't believe her eyes. She had thought the dining room in steerage was a sight to behold. But this room, so beauteous, its woodwork so new and shiny, even its ceiling embossed, its long, arched windows made of smoky glass was like nothing she had ever seen before. How fine it all was!

If only Paddy had agreed to come with her and Marta. Father Byles had said it was all right for them to attend the service, though it wasn't Catholic, as long as they also attended his Mass in third class, which Katie had done. But while Marta had eagerly embraced the notion of seeing with her own eyes a first-class facility, Paddy had refused, saying, "Why would I want to be around them people that stared at us like we was freaks?" Brian, too, had refused, saying he had scheduled a game of cards in the smoking room.

So Katie and Marta had joined a small group from third class, mostly women, who thought it a fine idea to get a look at the huge room where the "tony people" ate.

"Not in my wildest dreams," Katie whispered to Marta as the captain began reading, "would I imagine such a room as this. 'Tisn't it fine, then? To think that somethin' so wondrous would be on a *ship*. 'Tis just a ship, after all."

"No," Marta disagreed, also in a whisper, "it is not just a ship. It is the *Titanic*, and everything on it is like nothing ever seen before. I will be so happy to tell my mother and father what I have seen here."

The pretty girl who had argued with her mother on that awful morning in third class was in the crowd, dressed in a navy blue skirt and jacket that looked to Katie to be made of the finest wool. She was standing between her parents. All were so nattily attired and well-groomed, they made Katie think of an advertisement in a magazine. The three made a lovely picture. Any artist who might paint them standing like that would surely title his work "A Happy Family."

When the last hymn had been sung, Katie was reluctant to leave. She wanted to stay a while, sit in one of the fine chairs and try to imagine what it must be like to be surrounded by such luxury. The girl in the blue dress must travel in this way all the time. Fortune had smiled on her. How lovely it must be to never have to trouble yourself about the future.

Reluctantly trailing along behind the other third-class passengers returning to their quarters, Katie wondered if that girl knew how lucky she was. Could be she didn't. If you'd never had troubles, you wouldn't know what they were, and so you wouldn't give them a thought. Or so it seemed to Katie.

Still, when she passed the girl and her family on her way out of the dining room, Katie was struck by the fact that the pretty face didn't seem untroubled. That was a bit of a surprise. There was a frown, there, on her forehead, and was there not a droop to the mouth? Didn't the eyes seem a bit red-rimmed, as if there had been tears recently?

Of course, that couldn't possibly be the truth of it. Why would a girl like that be shedding tears?

I'm imaginin' things, she told herself. I don't need to be thinkin' that someone born into such good fortune could have troubles. She looks that way because she's been concentrating on the service, that's all, and I would have been better off doing the same.

When they returned to steerage, she went straight to the general room in search of Eileen and the two children, to see if Bridey had suffered any ill effects from last night's accident. The little girl seemed fine, which Katie regarded as a good thing since Eileen, dancing in the arms of the Norwegian, was paying no more attention to Bridey than she had before the fall.

Katie took the children out on deck for a breath of fresh air later that afternoon. She was taken aback by how much colder the air had become. Her shawl was woefully inadequate, and Bridey had left her coat folded on a bench inside. They had only been on deck a few minutes when Kevin's teeth began chattering with cold.

"Fresh air ain't goin' to do you any good if you catch pneumonia," Katie said, and took them back inside, thinking that it was a good thing the Atlantic Ocean was saltwater, or it would be frozen solid and then how would they sail on it?

"Might be icebergs about," a crewman commented as a shivering Katie returned to the general room. "Seems cold enough. Seen them around these parts before, on other trips. Big as houses, some o' them."

Big as houses? Alarmed, Katie asked, "There's no danger, is there?"

The crewman laughed. "No, ma'am, I don't guess so. It'd take a lot more than an old berg to do damage to the *Titanic*."

But Katie was picturing a chunk of ice the size of a house floating toward them on the open sea. The thought made her stomach begin to churn. Was it really true, as the crewman had said, that an object so large could collide with the *Titanic* and cause no harm?

She would ask Paddy and Brian what they thought.

But she had to wait all afternoon, as they didn't return from their card games until just before supper. She didn't want to ruin the meal, so she kept her worries to herself until afterward, when they were all back in the general room. A party had already begun, and Brian went off to dance with Marta, leaving Katie alone with Paddy.

"There's talk of ice," she said abruptly over the sound of the accordion and the pipes. "Bergs as big as houses. Do you think that's likely, Paddy?"

He nodded. "Of course. I was out on deck a while ago. It's turned cold as an icehouse out there. Could be bergs. Why? You're not troublin' yourself about it, are you? You don't trust the captain to steer the ship through an ice field?"

Katie thought about that for a minute. "I

don't even know the captain," she answered then. "You haven't seen him walkin' around down here talkin' to all us third-class passengers, have you, now? How would I be knowin' whether or not I should trust him?"

"Well, he's got us this far. I guess he can take us the rest of the way. Anyways, the shipping line wouldn't trust a ship as fine as this one to just any old captain, would they? Don't you think they'd hire the best? The one with the most experience?" Then Paddy said the words Katie had been hoping to hear. "Quit troublin' yourself about icebergs and come dance with me."

Whirling in his arms, Katie forgot about the crewman's words and let the music lift her feet off the floor.

Elizabeth had agreed to meet Max on the boat deck at nine o'clock. She almost changed her mind and went to bed instead, wanting nothing more than to huddle deep beneath the coverlet and wallow in her misery. Besides, he'd be disappointed again that she'd failed to talk herself out of a loveless marriage. She didn't want to see the look on his face when she shared that depressing bit of news with him.

She went, after all, only because she needed to see him. Not that seeing him would change anything. But it would make her feel better.

She listened at the door of her parents' cabin before she left her own. Silence. She hadn't heard their door closing, but that was probably because she'd been lost in her own thoughts. They wouldn't have gone to bed this early, so the silence meant they'd gone out.

Elizabeth threw on the gray cloak, left her room, and hurried down the corridor and up the stairs to meet Max.

He was very understanding at first. It was too cold to stay outside, so he led her into the warmer gymnasium, which was nearly empty. Many people were attending a concert being performed by the ship's orchestra; others were playing cards or eating in the restaurant. Max and Elizabeth sat on side-by-side stationary bicycles to talk.

"It's not your fault," he said sympathetically. "Maybe a sea voyage isn't the place to discuss such serious matters. When you get home, it'll be different."

"When I get home," Elizabeth said bitterly, "my debut will begin immediately. There won't be any *time* to talk. I was counting on this trip. It seemed to me the ideal time to talk to them, since the only way they could avoid me would be to jump overboard."

Max laughed.

Elizabeth did not. "I didn't realize they'd be so busy all the time, or that even when they weren't, they wouldn't really listen." She would almost certainly have to endure the debut season, and it looked very much as if college was out of the question, at least for a while. It could take her years to wear them down. All of which meant life was going to be pretty dismal when she returned to New York in three days. The only bright spot she could think of was having Max Whittaker in that life. Without him . . .

Elizabeth shuddered at the thought of life without Max.

"Max, if you agree to take just one or two college courses, your parents will let you study painting at the same time. You won't be disowned, and my parents won't have any reason to keep me from seeing you."

"We've already had this discussion, Elizabeth," Max said firmly. "I haven't changed my mind. Pigheaded or not, it's time for me to go out on my own. When you think about it, leaving home is the only way to grow up, right?"

Every girl Elizabeth knew expected to go straight from her parents' home to her husband's home. Young women did not leave their parents until they married. Even Monica Beaumont, who was attending Vassar, still lived at home when she wasn't attending classes. Young women did *not* live on their own.

"Just because a person never lives in a garret somewhere in New York City," she said indignantly, sliding off the bicycle seat to stand up, "doesn't mean that person never grows up. Marrying and raising children is very maturing, I'm sure. *My* mother's not a child." The minute the words were out of her mouth, she regretted them. Everything she had ever told Max about her mother had made Nola sound like a spoiled child. If he laughed now, she would never speak to him again.

He laughed. Then, seeing the look of fury on Elizabeth's face, he sobered and said seriously, "Well, *my* mother is very childlike. My father caters to her every whim, but he also treats her like she doesn't have a brain in her head. She knows that's not true, and I know it's not true, and I'm pretty sure he knows it. But they pretend. When she gets unhappy or restless because she isn't doing anything very interesting, he brings home a new fur from the store, and she pretends it's what she wanted all along. They play this game, and it keeps peace in the family, so . . ." Completely serious now, he added, "I would never treat you like that, Elizabeth, whether or not you ever go to college. I know you have a brain, and I know you're not a child. But you have to prove that to your parents by not acting like one. By insisting on having what you need."

Elizabeth stared at him. He was *lecturing* her! Talking to her as if she couldn't figure that much out for herself. And saying at the same time that he knew she had a brain! He certainly wasn't treating her as if he believed that.

"Compromising is part of being grown-up, too," she said coldly, turning away from him. "Since you're not willing to do that, not even so we can see each other in New York, I guess you're not any more mature than I am, even though you're older and have lived in Paris. So why should I take advice from you?" She began walking away.

Behind her, she heard, "Elizabeth, don't storm off like this. Wait."

Elizabeth was becoming very weary of walking away from arguments. She seemed always to be storming out of a room: her parents' stateroom, the dining room, the restaurant, and now the gymnasium. But what else was there to do when people refused to listen to her? To take her seriously?

She kept walking. When she exited the gymnasium and the frigid air outside took her breath away, she remembered Max's earlier remarks about ice in the area. Though she had wished then for an ice field, to slow down the *Titanic* and give her more time, now she wanted nothing more than to race straight to New York and put an end to this useless, disappointing voyage.

Max did not follow her.

Hurt and angry, Elizabeth locked her cabin door and threw herself across her bed, too furious to cry, too despondent to sit up and close the porthole, which someone, probably her mother, had opened again. The air streaming in through the opening was so bitterly cold, she wouldn't have been surprised to find frost on the coverlet.

She buried herself in the bedding for warmth and as she fell asleep, she made up her mind to stay exactly where she was until they arrived in New York Harbor on Wednesday.

Chapter 19

At eleven-thirty on Sunday night, Elizabeth awoke suddenly. She couldn't have said what had disturbed her sleep. The sound of her parents' door slamming shut? A sudden, abrupt motion of the ship? Whatever it was, it yanked her out of a deep, disturbed sleep, and it took her several moments to clear her head.

She lay in bed listening to the distant vibration of the engines far below. The sound was like the steady beating of a heart. Without the rhythmic vibrations, she would have forgotten she was at sea.

It was icy cold in the cabin. Wrapping the coverlet around her shoulders, Elizabeth rose to a kneeling position to close the porthole over her bed.

The bed moved.

197

No, the bed couldn't have moved. The bed was stationary, firmly affixed to the floor.

But there had been something. She'd felt it. Nothing alarming. No sound of a collision, no warning whistles shrilling. The lights were still on. The brass antique lamp on her nightstand was still in place, and the crystal pitcher of water beside it had jiggled only slightly.

Nothing in the cabin looked any different.

To Elizabeth, lying in bed on C deck, it felt as if the great ship had briefly stumbled in its smooth, easy glide across the water, the way someone trips over a small stone in the path while strolling in the woods. The person doesn't fall, quickly regains his balance, and is on his way again, no harm done.

She expected the same thing to happen now. She expected the smooth glide to continue as before.

But before it could, Elizabeth heard what sounded like a giant, sharp fingernail being slowly scraped along the side of the ship. It reminded her of the way that annoying girl, Nina Chevalier, had tormented them at summer camp during the lectures on hiking safety held in the dining hall. Nina had long, pointed, scarlet nails and loved to drag them along the menu blackboard as they were leaving. The noise Elizabeth heard now was like that.

When that sound faded, there was a brief moment or two when Elizabeth listened and waited, with more curiosity than uneasiness.

And then the throbbing heartbeat far below died. Completely.

The porthole closed, Elizabeth sank back to a sitting position, the comforter still wrapped around her. Her first instinct was to rush into her parents' room and ask them what had happened. But along with the sudden silence from the depths of the *Titanic*, there was also silence from her parents' stateroom. She glanced at her locket-clock, lying on her bedside table. Not yet midnight. Her parents were still out, possibly having too much fun wherever they were to even notice that the engines had stopped.

Elizabeth remembered then what Max had said about the possibility of running into an ice field in the North Atlantic. "We'd have to stop for the night," he had told her. "Too hard to negotiate icebergs in the dark."

If the reason for the silent engines was an ice obstacle of some kind, Elizabeth wanted to see it. She was curious about what a field of ice large enough to halt a massive ship like the *Titanic* would look like.

In her anger at Max she had gotten into bed without undressing. All she needed to do now was don her gray woolen hooded cape and slip into shoes. She didn't bother to smooth her hair or put on a hat. She cared little who saw her.

Thus attired, she left the cabin, her spirits rising. She was venturing out alone at night. The idea appealed to her.

A stewardess in uniform was descending the staircase as Elizabeth approached. All she said as she passed was a cryptic, "Iceberg, miss," as if Elizabeth had asked. Then she hurried on her way.

Elizabeth turned to stare after her. Iceberg? What *about* an iceberg?

Perhaps the stewardess was simply saying an iceberg was the reason they'd stopped.

Wouldn't it have to be an enormous berg to stop a ship this large? Were the icebergs of such a size in North Atlantic waters?

Elizabeth didn't know. She had never studied such things. Maybe I would know, she thought as she climbed the deserted staircase, if I were better educated.

When she emerged from the glass-enclosed promenade on A deck, the icy cold took her breath away. Wishing she had borrowed one of her mother's furs, she climbed to the boat deck and moved swiftly to the starboard rail, where a handful of people had already gathered. Some were wearing nightwear under their coats. One woman, Elizabeth noticed, had the silliest white satin mules on her feet, leaving her bare toes exposed to the cold. The ship's lights turned her toes a garish green-yellow.

"What is it?" Elizabeth asked as she joined the small group at the rail. "What's happened?"

"I heard we hit an iceberg," a woman answered. A man's voice corrected, "I heard *it* hit *us*."

No one seemed anxious or frightened. Everyone's eyes were focused on the third-class recreation deck below, where a makeshift, gleeful game of "catch" was being conducted, with ungloved hands tossing varying sizes of ice chunks back and forth.

There seemed to be fragments and shavings and chunks of ice everywhere.

"How big was it?" Elizabeth wanted to know. "The iceberg." Judging from the considerable amount of ice sliced from it as it passed, it must have been enormous.

No one at the railing had seen it. One man, reading in an easy chair in his B-deck cabin, had heard the scraping noise. He had glanced up, he said, to see a large, dark object passing his open porthole. "Looked like a building was passing by," he joked. But by the time he reached the opening, the object was gone, leaving a pile of ice shavings on his carpet.

"You had the porthole open on such a cold night?" the woman wearing mules asked him incredulously.

"I came on this voyage for the sea air, and the sea air is what I'm going to get."

Elizabeth thought the woman was a fine one to talk about the cold, with her own feet practically bare. "Is there any damage to the ship?" she asked, thinking it a silly question even as she asked it. Surely even a very large iceberg could do no real harm to the unsinkable *Titanic*.

"There wouldn't be any damage to *this* ship," one of the men answered her. "The captain probably just stopped for a minute to check things out. We'll be on our way again in no time."

Elizabeth had spotted on the deck below the two young men from third class whom she had seen boarding in two different tenders at Queenstown, along with that lovely red-haired girl. There was no sign of the girl. But it was late, nearly midnight, and their tour guide had said single women in third class were berthed in the ship's stern, young men in the bow. The girl addressed as "Katie" by one of the boys would have had a long trek, the length of the ship, just to toss a few chunks of ice.

They are brothers, Elizabeth thought with certainty, continuing to watch the two laughing young men. They're brothers, and that "Katie" is trying to make up her mind which one she likes best, which one would be the better choice.

She's like me, she told herself, feeling a sudden strong kinship with the red-haired girl. Her head knows the older brother, the one with the quiet smile, is a better choice for her . . . as Alan might be for me. But her feelings are pulling her toward the younger one, the one with the heart-tugging grin, just as I'm being pulled toward Max.

One of the women at the rail mused aloud. "I wonder if I shouldn't see the purser about my jewelry? If anything *were* to go wrong, my husband would never forgive me if I lost his aunt Winifred's ruby brooch."

Elizabeth fought the urge to laugh. Ruby brooch? If anything *did* go wrong, which of course it wouldn't because the *Titanic* was impervious to disaster, it seemed to her a piece of jewelry would hardly be of great concern. Of much greater concern would be the freezing cold water and the utter isolation of the area.

Not that there really was anything to worry about. How could there be?

Nevertheless, Elizabeth decided to go in search of her parents. They might know how soon the engines would start up again. *If* her mother or father were speaking to her. She shouldn't have said the things she had.

The ruby brooch's owner left to seek out the purser's office. The woman in mules declared she was "freezing to death" and left, too, presumably in search of more sensible footgear. Elizabeth, hoping her parents would be in their stateroom so she wouldn't have to go looking for them, followed the two women down the stairs.

As she went, she wondered where Max and Lily were.

Katie had not had a good night's sleep since she boarded the *Titanic*. Ever mindful that she had never learned to swim, she found herself sleeping fitfully, waking with a start intermittently, always convinced the ship was sinking.

But on this night, she had been exhausted from hours of dancing and merriment combined with the task of seeing to Bridey and Kevin, which Eileen did only in fits and starts. And so, Katie had fallen asleep within five minutes after she climbed into her berth.

When she awoke an hour later, it was with a rude jolt that nearly sent her tumbling to the floor. Only the fact that she was tangled, cocoonlike, in her bedclothes, kept her in the berth.

Eileen had not been so lucky. Although the two children slept on, Eileen, looking stunned, had been tossed out of bed. She was sitting up, her hair tousled around her face, her eyes frightened as she stared up at Katie. She cried, "We've hit something!"

Katie sat up, rubbing sleep from her eyes. The jolt had knocked her sideways, into the wall. Her right elbow hurt. "How can that be, then? I was meself on deck earlier. There wasn't nothin' out there to hit. Nothin' but empty black sea as far as the eyes could see."

"I don't care!" Eileen cried, scrambling to her feet. "I wasn't knocked out of me bed by nothin'! I'm goin' to see what's happenin'." And, still in her flannel flowered nightgown, the red-and-white quilt wrapped around her like a large shawl, she was out of the cabin before Katie could stop her.

Bridey and Kevin slept on.

Chapter 20

Sunday, April 14, 1912

When Elizabeth reached the foot of the stairs on B deck, she found Max pacing back and forth. People swirled around him, some looking confused, as if they'd gone to a party and discovered they'd arrived on the wrong night, while others were laughing and joking, as if they'd had better luck, showing up at the appointed place and time. Some were wearing pastel-colored nightclothes under winter coats. Hems of nightgowns and pajamas trailed out from beneath heavy black or brown or gray wool. But there were tuxedos in the crowd, too, and silk, beaded evening gowns.

"Where have you been?" Max demanded, rushing over to Elizabeth. "I've been looking all over for you."

"I wanted to see what was going on," Elizabeth told Max. She glanced around for some sign of her parents, but didn't see them. "I guess an iceberg bumped up against us or something. There's ice everywhere outside. Why were you looking for me? I thought you were mad. Have you seen my parents?"

"It was an iceberg, all right. But I'm not so sure it just bumped us," Max said tersely, taking her elbow to lead her down the stairs to C deck. "I think something's going on. On my way here, I saw the captain talking to Ismay, the fellow from the White Star Line. They both looked upset. Something has to be up, but no one's saying anything yet."

Elizabeth's heart pounded suddenly with dread. Max wouldn't be worried for no reason.

They hurried down the stairs to Elizabeth's cabin. Many of the people passing them in the opposite direction were dressed in the same bizarre fashion as those they'd seen on B deck. Elizabeth passed two women wearing peach or pink nightgowns under fur stoles. Both had taken the time to don multiple golden chains and necklaces. The jewelry jangled as they made their way up the stairs.

No one seemed unduly alarmed. Elizabeth overheard a woman complain mildly, "Well, it seems an odd time of night to have a lifeboat drill, if you ask me. I was just getting to sleep."

Elizabeth gasped at the idea of a drill. She

glanced over at Max. "A lifeboat drill? Do you think that's what's going on?"

He shrugged. "I don't know. Maybe your parents know something."

It became clear the minute Elizabeth opened the door to her parents' cabin that they did indeed know something. Her father was assisting her mother in donning a white life vest, a cumbersome arrangement that involved straps about the waist. He was already wearing his. They had changed out of their evening wear into warm wool garments. Elizabeth's mother said frantically, "I wondered where you were. You must change your clothes quickly, Elizabeth. Put on something warm. The suit that matches that cape would be best, I think. And then you must put on your life vest. Quickly." Her tone of voice was anxious, the expression on her face strained.

"And you, young man," Martin Farr addressed Max, "would be well-advised to hurry to your cabin and put on your own vest. We don't have an extra one here. We have all been ordered up to the boat deck. Quickly, now! I don't want to have to tell your parents you disobeyed the captain's instructions."

Max nodded, looking thoughtful. "Be right back," he told Elizabeth, and left.

When the door had closed after him, Elizabeth said to her parents, "We heard that it was only a lifeboat drill." She heard the hope in her voice. Reaching out to take the vest her father handed her, she added, "We've had them on ships before, remember?"

"Never at this hour of night," her mother answered grimly, and continued fastening her vest. Elizabeth noticed that her hands were shaking.

It was true that on other ships, lifeboat drills had taken place in mid-morning sunshine or perhaps early afternoon. "Maybe this captain," she said, hoping to reassure her mother, "just wants to catch the passengers off-guard, as we would be in a real emergency."

"I don't believe this is just a drill," her father said, though he said it calmly. "Do as your mother says. Go and change."

Her heart fluttering anxiously, Elizabeth did so, wishing Max hadn't left. His cabin was on D deck. If something really was amiss, he might not be able to get back to her. She wouldn't know where he was or if he was all right.

Her earlier anger at Max was completely forgotten.

When she had changed into the gray wool suit and a pair of warm boots and taken a pair of black pigskin gloves from the bureau, she went to the large, square porthole and opened it. There was nothing outside that looked at all abnormal. The stars gleamed in a quiet sky of black velvet, the sea was calm, and she heard no cries of alarm. It is a drill, she told herself firmly, it is only a drill. Father is wrong. Max will come back, we'll all go up to the boat deck, and when the boat drill is finished, we'll go to bed and the ship will be on its way again.

She was unable to manage the life vest alone and returned to her parents' cabin for assistance. Her mother's face was pale. Elizabeth felt a deep pang of sympathy. Why wasn't her father reassuring her mother?

A deep sense of unease seized her. If there was nothing to worry about, her father would be saying so. He knew his wife often worried about trivial things, exaggerating them until they became monumental in her mind. "Making a mountain out of a molehill," he called it. And he knew exactly how to calm her down. There had to be a reason why he wasn't doing that now.

Elizabeth's hands felt clammy and cold.

While her mother adjusted her wide-brimmed black hat in the dresser mirror, Elizabeth asked her father in a low voice, "Have you heard something, Father?"

"We have hit an iceberg, my dear." His voice was as quiet as hers. "Or perhaps I should say it has hit us. Captain Smith himself informed me. But I'm sure they'll repair the problem quickly. In the meantime, we must follow instructions."

Elizabeth was stunned. The iceberg had *hit* them? It hadn't just brushed by, leaving shavings on the decks? What kind of problem was it that required "repairs"? And how could her father be sure the damage, if there truly was any, could even *be* repaired?

If Max didn't return soon, they would have to go up to the boat deck without him. She didn't want to. If all of the passengers were up there, as her father had said they'd been instructed, she would never find Max in such a large crowd.

What was taking him so long?

In her third-class cabin in the stern, Katie sat quietly for fifteen minutes or so, waiting for Eileen to return. When she didn't, Katie wasn't sure what to do. Out in the corridor, she heard someone open a cabin door and ask a steward what was happening. "Not to worry, Mum," came the reply. "There's no danger. We'll be gettin' on soon."

But when Katie stepped out into the hallway, she found many of the third-class passengers heading for the open deck. Men, women, and children, all carrying boxes and packages and worn suitcases.

"Where are you goin', then?" Katie called. At first no one answered. But then Mrs. Toomey, with whom Katie had chatted at dinner, passed by with her three young ones in tow, and called out, "You'd best be gettin' on up above, Katie. We've hit somethin', and the ship is ailin'!"

When the crowd had passed, the hallway fell silent again.

Katie went back inside, her stomach churning with fear. The great ship *Titanic* had hit something? How could that be? What was there to hit on such a vast, empty sea? It couldn't be true. Why hadn't Brian and Paddy come for her? They would know what was going on. They could tell her.

And if Eileen ever came back, she'd be given a piece of Kathleen Hanrahan's mind, that was for certain! Shame on her, runnin' off like that, leavin' the two wee ones behind.

Uncertain of what to do, and fighting unsuccessfully the fear that had overtaken her, Katie sank down on a berth beside the sleeping Bridey to wait, although she wasn't at all sure what she was waiting for.

To Elizabeth's profound relief, Max returned just as Martin Farr was locking the cabin door behind them. "No point in having anything stolen while we're above-decks," he said as he turned the key.

"There's talk we've hit an iceberg," Max said. His life vest was on, and he was breathing fast, so Elizabeth knew he'd hurried to return to her. "Is it true, sir?"

"Never mind," Elizabeth's father said crisply, darting a concerned glance at his wife. "I'm sure Captain Smith knows how to deal with the problem. Let us just do as we've been asked for now. To the boat deck, then."

They were climbing the stairs to B deck when Mrs. Farr, walking with her husband ahead of Max and Elizabeth, stopped suddenly. Her face had gone bone-white. Elizabeth heard her say in a whisper, "Martin, the stairs . . ."

He nodded, his expression sober, but said nothing. Taking her elbow, he urged her to continue climbing. Behind them, Elizabeth took a step up and understood what her mother meant. Her stomach rolled over, and she caught her breath in fear.

The stairs were no longer precisely level.

The difference was almost imperceptible, and had they been standing at the foot of the stairs looking up or at the top looking down, they would have noticed nothing out of the ordinary. But looking at something was very different from feeling, and now that she was *on* the stairs, Elizabeth could *feel* the slight slant, as if a giant hand beneath the ship was tipping it gently toward the bow, perhaps as a prank.

"Oh, God, Max," she murmured as they all began moving again, "something *is* wrong."

He reached out and took her hand, squeezing it reassuringly. "Don't forget, this ship is unsinkable. That's precisely why my grandmother booked passage for me. Unsinkable. Keep that in mind, okay?"

Elizabeth felt a little better. If the people who had built this amazing ship had built it not to sink, then it wouldn't, would it? They knew what they were doing. Building ships was their business.

But when they reached the boat deck, the first thing she saw was a group of people gathered around two of the lifeboats. The canvas cover was being peeled off one boat like the skin of an orange, while the other boat was being lowered until it hung level with the deck.

All of the comfort she'd taken in Max's words evaporated like the little clouds of breath that hung in the air whenever anyone spoke on this coldest of all nights. Elizabeth already felt the chill, and was amazed to see passengers on deck still wearing nightclothes under their coats. Why had they not taken the time to don warmer clothing? Did they expect to return quickly to the warmth and safety of their own beds?

One woman, standing alone near the entrance holding what looked to be a giant wad of cotton in her arms that turned out to be a fluffy white dog, was in her stocking feet.

The sight of those unshod feet chilled Elizabeth further. Was the danger so imminent that the woman was afraid to take an extra moment to slip into a pair of shoes? What did she know that Elizabeth didn't?

"Have you seen Lily or Arthur?" Max asked. He was still holding Elizabeth's gloved hand. His own fingers were bare, and she felt a sudden flash of irritation that he hadn't dressed more warmly. He should have listened more carefully to her father's instructions.

"No." Elizabeth glanced around. More and more passengers were arriving on the boat deck. The rapidly increasing crowd was quiet and orderly for the most part, though there were those who continued to joke and laugh among themselves. They were the people Elizabeth focused on, because watching them lifted her spirits. She wanted to believe, as they seemed to, that this was a lark. Nothing to worry about, nothing to take seriously.

But then why were the lifeboats being uncovered?

It wasn't just the bitter cold that was chilling the blood in her veins. The thought of perhaps having to enter one of the lifeboats and leave the security of the huge, safe ship for that vast, black emptiness surrounding the *Titanic* was terrifying.

"I think," her father said, turning toward Elizabeth and Max, "that what they intend to do is have us leave the ship just long enough for the repairs to be made. Then they'll bring us back on board and we'll be underway again."

"Oh, Martin," his wife complained, "I'm not going out there on that cold, dark sea while they fix the ship! Why can't I just go back to our stateroom and lie down until they're done? That seems much more sensible."

"I don't think they'll allow that, dear. Perhaps they need everyone off the ship before they can make the repairs. Why don't we just wait and see?"

The waiting was difficult. It was so cold on the boat deck, Elizabeth's toes began to feel numb, in spite of her warm boots. The woman in the doorway was still there, still shoeless. How numb her toes must be by now! She wore a bewildered expression on her face. She clutched her dog to her chest as if the small ball of white fur might somehow save her from whatever was happening.

She looks, Elizabeth thought, the way I feel. Is that same expression on *my* face? Just a few short hours ago, the worst thing in my life was disagreeing with my parents and with Max.

Now I would give anything just to go back to my stateroom and crawl into my nice, warm bed, with no bigger worry on my mind than whether or not Max would forgive me. Which he certainly seems to have done.

No one was mad at her anymore. It was as if the iceberg had swept away everyone's anger at Elizabeth Farr as it brushed by the ship.

Below, Katie could wait no longer. It was far too quiet out in the hallway. Something was very amiss. A second noisy group of people had passed her cabin, and she had wanted to go along. But the children were still asleep, so she had stayed with them.

Why hadn't Eileen come back? She wasn't even dressed properly!

Katie was afraid that if she waited much longer for someone to tell her what to do, she and the two children would be left all alone. The thought was so frightening, it made her eyes water with unshed tears.

If there was something wrong, why hadn't Brian or Paddy come for her?

You said you could take care of yourself, she scolded silently, remember? 'Tisn't that what you told Paddy whilst you were up on your high horse?

But she couldn't take care of herself and two wee ones. Not without some help.

"Wake up, Bridey, Kevin!" she cried, tossing their coverlets aside and shaking them gently. "We're goin' up on top to see what's happenin'. Hurry now, we're goin' to go find Eileen."

Bridey cried the whole time Katie was dressing her in warm clothing.

Chapter 21

Somehow, Katie managed to get the two sleepy, protesting children dressed in coats, caps, and gloves. She threw her own worn, dark coat on over her woolen navy blue dress, and was about to leave the cabin when a crewman dashed by, calling out, "Life preservers on, everyone, get your life preservers on!"

Katie froze. "Jesus, Mary, and Joseph," she murmured, her face drained of all color, "we're sinkin', then!"

Young Kevin roused himself from his sleep-induced stupor long enough to say, "Aw, Katie, wasn't you listenin' when Brian told us about this ship? The *Titanic* can't sink, Brian said so."

Bridey began crying again, and Katie was forced to swallow her panic enough to comfort the child.

But her heart was beating fiercely, her hands trembling. If Brian and her da were right about the ship being unsinkable, why the order to put on life preservers? What reason other than disaster could there be for such an order? Unless — hope sprang alive in her chest — unless this was a practice of some kind. Hadn't Brian said they had such things on long voyages? Could that be?

The first thing was, she must do as she'd been told. Telling the children to sit down on their berths, she began searching for life vests. She found them on top of a cupboard.

But there were only two.

Katie held them by their straps, staring at them in dismay. Two! She needed three, and if Eileen came back, a fourth.

Perhaps there would be extra ones up on deck.

It took her a good ten minutes to figure out how the vests worked and then fasten two impatient, squirming children into them. When she had finished, she stood up and took each of them by a hand, saying, "Come along, then, we'll be goin' up on deck now with the others."

There was no one in the hallway. Katie was frightened by the complete and utter silence. The steady *dum-dum* of the engines had stopped. There was no shouting, no laughter, no voices coming from the cabins as there had been ever since she came on board, except for those hours when everyone was asleep. Was she walkin' on a ghost ship, then? Was there no one left down here then but them? The thought so terrified her, she stopped in the hallway and stared wide-eyed around her, desperate for the sight of another human face, the sound of a voice.

"Katie?" Kevin was staring up at her, his own eyes wide and frightened. "Katie, what's ailin' you?"

Katie roused herself. The children — she must take care of the children. There was no one else to do it.

She shook her head to clear it, and began walking in the direction that seemed right to her. Up a corridor, around a corner ... still no people, no crew, no one to tell her which way to go to get up on top ... down another hallway, around another corner ... it was like a maze. And there were no voices leading her onward, no signs giving her instructions. What if she was leading them in the wrong direction? What if they got lost down here in the belly of the ship and never did find their way up on top? If the ship really was sinking, they would all three disappear into the deep, dark ocean, never to be seen again. And it would be her fault. Ma and Da would be so disappointed in her.

When she saw, ahead of her, a steward hurrying along the passageway, she thought at first that she was fancifying, that he couldn't really be there. But she shouted to him, anyway, and to her heartfelt relief, he turned. And waited until Katie and her charges caught up with him.

"I only have two life preservers," she said breathily, "and as you can see, there are three of us. Might you have another one with you, then?"

He shook his head. "Could be more up top, though. You'd best get up there, miss, quick as you can. Make your way to the boat deck if you can. There's people gatherin' on the well deck, but it's my opinion that they might find themselves stuck there. The gates, y'know. They'll be locked, as they always is. You'll be wantin' to be closer to the lifeboats, so the boat deck is the place to be. Don't let no one stop you."

Katie lowered her voice. Her hands were trembling. "Is there real danger, then?"

He looked away, then looked back at her, and kept his own voice low as he answered, "Yes, miss, I'm afraid there is."

Before that could sink in and render her completely incapable of making any more sensible decisions, Katie asked quickly, "Can you tell us how to get up top, please?"

He gave her directions, and hurried off, perhaps to find his own life preserver.

Katie had only one thought now, and that was to get herself and the two children out of the depths of the ship and up on deck, where there would be air and light and people ... people who would know what to do. She felt she would suffocate if she didn't get out of these narrow passageways soon. "We'll be hurryin' now," she told the children, "now that we know which way to go. We'll find Brian and Paddy. They'll know what to do. We'll be right as rain in no time." But her words sounded hollow even to her own ears.

Still, she heaved another sigh of relief when they reached the gate mentioned by the steward as a way out.

And gasped in horror when she tried to open it and found it locked.

Katie glanced around frantically. He hadn't told her any other way to go, only this way, and how could she go this way if the gate was locked to her?

She pulled and tugged and kicked, but to no avail. Tears of frustration gathered in her eyes. Responsibility for the safety of the children weighed on her heavily. She was painfully aware of their questioning eyes on her, knew they were expecting her to save them from whatever horror was taking place.

Taking a deep breath, she turned to say to them in as even a voice as she could manage,

"Well, we shan't be goin' this way, after all. We'll have to do a bit of explorin' now, on our own. Won't that be an adventure, then?"

She could see by the look on Kevin's face that he knew the truth, but Bridey seemed to perk up just a bit. "Can I lead the way, Katie?" she asked, and since there seemed to be no reason to deny her request, Katie let her take the lead.

So it was Bridey who first turned a corner and cried out, "Paddy! You found us!"

Her shout sent Katie's heart leaping for joy even before Paddy's tall, strong figure appeared. "God, I've been lookin' all over creation for the lot of you," he shouted when he saw her. "Where in the name of all that's holy have you been? I went to your cabin, had a devil of a time gettin' through, what with everyone goin' the other way, bag and baggage, and none of you was there. Some of the girls was cryin'. They said they hadn't seen you. What are you doin', wanderin' around down here like this when orders are to get up on top?"

But when he reached her, he stopped shouting and pulled her roughly into his arms. She thought she felt him trembling, just as she was. "Oh, Katie-girl," he murmured into her hair, "I thought I wasn't goin' to find you." He held her so tight, she could scarcely breathe, but she didn't mind. Her body felt like warm water, so glad was she to be safe against his chest. All of her terror melted under his touch.

"The gate ... it was locked," she told him. "The steward said to go that way, but the gate was locked."

"There's another way, the way I came. There's a door connecting E deck to a second-class staircase, goes to the boat deck. Everyone was passin' it right by as if it was locked, but 'twasn't. I checked. I'll show you. Then I've got to go find Brian. He was helpin' some old people with their things, and I lost sight of him."

As she walked beside him down the passageway, Katie wanted to shout, No, don't go! Don't leave us! But she didn't. It was enough that he was leading them above-decks, taking them out of the dark, lonely depths of the ship. She couldn't ask for more than that. And she could understand why he needed to find his brother. "Are we really sinkin', then?" she asked him softly so the children wouldn't hear.

His expression became grim. "Looks like it. But there's lifeboats above. I'll see that you and the wee ones get into one before I hunt for Bri."

"No! I have to know Brian's all right before I go sailin' off in some lifeboat. We'll wait. Surely there's time?"

Paddy looked doubtful. "Bri can take care of

himself, but I know you'd be frettin' over him. I'll find him for you, Katie."

And who will find *you* for me, then? Katie wondered, her heart racing with fear for both brothers. She didn't want to lose either of them. But she knew her heart would never mend if she lost Paddy. Never.

They hurried in silence, Paddy moving with a certainty that reassured Katie. He knew where he was going, which was more than she could say for herself. Still, pride forced her to say, "I could have found a way out, you know. I'm grateful to you for showin' up, but I could have found a way. I wouldn't have let the wee ones drown."

He turned his head to grin down at her. "Aye, I know you would have. Even if you had to shinny the jibs, the way some of the fellows are doin'. When they found locked gates, like you did, they took to crawlin' along the jibs of the cargo cranes into second class, then from there to the boat deck. I pressed Bri to go with them, but he was busy helpin' the Molloys and that Swedish girl and her friends."

Alarm seized Katie. "We won't have to do that, will we? Crawl on the jibs?" She hated heights. And the children would never be able to manage.

"No, ma'am. Like I said, I found us an open door."

Still, it seemed to Katie to take hours, up one passageway and down another, through a giant labyrinth that she was certain she could never have navigated by herself. Up a metal staircase that clanged noisily under their feet, into still another narrow corridor, then another. Paddy seemed to know where he was going. She was grateful for that.

She was aware the whole time of an odd sensation under her feet. They had come from the stern area and were moving toward the bow. And it was as if they were going, ever so slightly, downhill. She noticed it most when they began climbing the metal staircase. She would lift her foot to place it on a higher step, but then the step seemed lower than it should have been, as if the treads hadn't been placed correctly.

Katie tried to figure out what that meant. Did it not mean that the stern was higher than the bow already? Even just a little? If the stern was higher than the bow, that would mean the ship was sinking by the bow. And yet they seemed to be moving toward the bow. Perhaps they were making a terrible mistake. Wouldn't it be safer to seek refuge in the stern, which would be higher in the water?

She asked Paddy as much.

"We have to go where the lifeboats are," he answered. "And we're not headed for the bow, Katie, just amidships. From there, someone will direct us to the boats. Anyways, I've been thinkin'. Remember how we said when we was boardin' the ship that it sat so high out of the water because it was so tall? Seems to me, even any part of it that's sinkin' will still be high up out of the water for hours and hours."

Katie could only hope he was right.

Which part of the ship was Brian in? Was he safe? And the others, the Molloys, the Dono-hues, the Norwegian family she'd spoken with at dinner, and Marta and Eileen, where were they all now?

When they finally reached the boat deck, they were shocked by how frigid the air had become. Last night they had sat on the poop deck together, and though it had been cold, it had not been unbearably so. It was now.

Paddy asked the first crewman they encoun-tered how much time they had. The answer was an unhelpful "Dunno."

Katie couldn't help noticing that the major-ity of people on the deck were dressed ele-gantly. Even those in nightwear had topped it with fur. Some of the women were laden with jewels. Where, then, were all the other third-class women? Why weren't Marta and Eileen in this crowd?

There was a more perceptible tilt to the deck now. Katie could feel the tension in the air. Fear was beginning to sweep over the ship like a thick cloak of fog. Some people spoke quietly, their anxious eyes searching the deck for an answer to their predicament. Others, more impatient, called out sharply to crew members for answers to their questions, though none seemed to be forthcoming. Jaws were clenched tightly, faces pale, eyes wide with anxiety. Mothers clung fiercely to the hands of their small children.

Katie's own anxious eyes moved to the people beginning to gather at the lifeboats and thought sickeningly, We are all terrified of having to leave the ship. We are all terrified of having to descend into that black, icy emptiness. But the *Titanic* was tilting! Who could deny that? It was no longer the safe, secure fortress it had seemed to be.

There was raw anguish in Paddy's dark eyes when he glanced at her and said, "I don't want to leave you. But 'tis up to me to find Brian. Will you get into a boat, then, so I'll know you're safe enough before I go?"

"No. I will not. We'll be waitin' right here for you. But I'd be grateful if you'd hurry back, you and Bri."

He looked so torn, she stepped forward impulsively and stood on tiptoe to kiss him on the cheek. She was never sure afterward exactly how it happened, but at the last moment he turned his head and suddenly she was kissing his lips instead.

It was a very thorough, heartfelt kiss.

The children giggled.

When Paddy lifted his head, he looked chagrined. "Sorry," he muttered, stepping away from Katie. "Looks like I done it again. Wasn't thinkin', and that's the truth of it."

He was leaving and Katie didn't know what was going to happen. The thought of not knowing where he was on the huge ship filled her with panic. Hiding her feelings, she said softly, "Don't fret." She reached up to touch his cheek with an icy but gentle hand. "And thanks to you for bringing us up on top. Make haste now, will you?"

"I will." Then he was gone, disappearing into the crowd milling about the deck.

His sudden absence left her feeling forlorn and lost.

But she still had the children to think of. "You'd best be gettin' into a boat, miss," a steward said. His face was ruddy with cold, although drops of perspiration beaded his forehead. "I'll show you the way."

"No!" Katie glanced around for some sign of Brian or Eileen. Though the boat deck was crowded, she saw no familiar faces. The clothing worn by the milling passengers spoke to her only of first class. She recognized no one from third class. Where were the families, and the young girls and men with whom she'd been traveling? "I don't want to go yet. There's time, isn't there?"

He shook his head. "I don't know, miss. Doesn't seem like there is. They're sayin' it's time to get into the boats, that's all I know."

Katie debated. She had to think of the children. But how could she leave the ship without knowing that Brian and Paddy were safe?

Still, she couldn't deny the sense of urgency spreading among the passengers on deck. Though some had been joking when they first arrived up top, that had ended as the tilt of the ship became more noticeable. Even the most optimistic among them could no longer pretend this was just a routine drill. And those who had been calm, as if they might be waiting for the arrival of a train, were now pressing closer to the lifeboats, intent on finding a place in one. The words of those who spoke now and again were tense, high-pitched with fear.

"I'll wait just a bit," Katie told the steward. "But I won't risk the children, I promise you that."

Nodding, he hurried off to deal with more cooperative passengers.

Tightly clutching the hands of Bridey and Kevin, and terrified that she had just made a terrible mistake, Katie waited for Brian and Paddy.

Chapter 22

Monday, April 15, 1912

Elizabeth's mother refused to stand out in the cold. She insisted that Elizabeth come with her into the gymnasium, where many people had gathered to wait for instructions. "It's warm in there," Nola Farr said, her voice breathless with agitation. As she spoke, she tugged on Elizabeth's sleeve. "I have no idea what's happening, but it is foolish to stay out here and freeze to death."

Elizabeth's father didn't go with them, saying he needed to talk to the captain or Bruce Ismay, the head of the White Star Line, to find out exactly "what the situation is." Max went with him.

No one inside the warm, brightly lit gymnasium seemed to know what the "situation" was. Elizabeth knew the fear she saw in most of the faces and felt within herself was fear of the unknown. No one was aware of exactly what was happening, they only knew that *something* was. And it frightened them. Hands holding coffee cups or glasses trembled, high-pitched voices quavered as they discussed what might be taking place. Occasional laughter sounded false and forced.

Elizabeth saw people deep in intense conversation. Others were standing silent and white-faced, and still others wore the same look of bewilderment she had seen on the shoeless woman. All were wearing the bulky white life vests over their clothing. Although many women were wearing furs, there were others dressed far less sensibly. A beautiful blonde woman in a vivid blue evening gown and matching satin heeled slippers had for warmth only a silk, long-sleeved jacket in the same bright blue. She was visibly shivering with cold and, Elizabeth realized, fear. Another woman had taken the time to don a wide-brimmed, veiled black hat, though she was wearing thin nightclothes under a pink chenille bathrobe. A bald man in pajamas and overcoat had forgotten his eyeglasses and was complaining that he couldn't see well. His lack of clear vision seemed to be adding to his barely restrained panic as he wandered from group to group, asking querulously if anyone had yet spoken to the captain about this "annoying delay."

In spite of the tangible anxiety in the gymnasium, as Nola led the way to a warm corner, Elizabeth picked up bits and fragments of conversation meant to reassure.

"... only take a few minutes to fix it. Then we'll be on our way again. Hardly lose any time at all. The ship's been breaking speed records, anyway, so we won't be more than a little late into New York."

"... might put us off on the lifeboats, but it'll only be till they've seen to the problem. A nuisance, no one's arguing that, but apparently it's necessary. Something about weight, I gather. We'll be back on board before breakfast."

"... not leaving the ship to get into some flimsy old lifeboat, I can tell you. Damn cold out there, catch our death, die of pneumonia before we get to New York."

"... sue the White Star Line, that's what I say. I paid a pretty penny for my first-class ticket, and I have a right to better service than this. Speaking to my attorneys, I am, the minute we get back to civilization. They'll have something to say about all of this nonsense."

Elizabeth wished she could believe that it was all "nonsense." But she didn't, not for a second. Although no one had come right out and said the ship was sinking, she could *feel* that something was very wrong. They wouldn't be holding a drill this late at night, not when it was so unbearably cold outside. Captain Smith wouldn't be that inconsiderate. She still held out hope that the first person she had overheard was correct, that if they left the ship at all, it would only be briefly. Then they'd get back on and continue with their trip.

Still, in spite of the reassuring statements, the air of anxiety in the room continued unabated.

A crewman passed through the crowd then, shouting an inquiry as to who still needed a life vest. No one did. "This is only a precaution," he added, still in a shout as he left the gymnasium. "You will all be returning to your staterooms before long." Before anyone could press him for details, he was gone.

Elizabeth couldn't have said why she didn't believe him. She wanted to. He was a crew member, after all, and should know better than they what was taking place. But there was something in his voice . . .

She didn't believe him. She didn't think anyone else did, either. She could almost smell the fear in the room.

Nola, however, chose to believe. The lines of tension in her face eased, and she expressed annoyance at the inconvenience. "You know I need my sleep, Elizabeth," she complained as she perched uncertainly on the seat of a mechanical camel. "I'm not the young girl I once was. Not like you. You could go without sleep for days on end and still look fresh and beautiful. But I need my rest if my eyes are not to look like dark, fat pillows in the morning. I must say, they've picked a most inconvenient time to take their precautions. And *where* is your father?"

When he returned, pressing through the crowd with Max at his side, Elizabeth could tell from the expession on both their faces that the crewman had indeed been mistaken. Her heart sank. Her father's brow was furrowed, Max's face a study in concern. Max moved to Elizabeth's side and took her hand. Martin Farr did the same with his wife.

"Nola," he said quietly, calmly, "you are going to have to leave the ship. They're readying the lifeboats. I would like you to come with me now, so that I may see you and Elizabeth safely off."

Elizabeth drew in her breath in alarm. "Safely off?" They had to leave the comfort and warmth of the ship and venture out into that black, icy void? She couldn't. She couldn't do it. The thought was simply too terrifying. What would happen to them out there?

"Oh, heavens, Martin," her mother responded with a wave of dismissal from her free hand. "I'm not going anywhere. I'm staying right here where it's nice and warm." In spite of the casual tone of her voice, her face had gone very pale. "And what do you mean, see us off? You can't possibly think I would leave here without you."

"Oh, I'll be along." He helped her dismount the camel. "Young Whittaker here and I shall follow in another boat." His tone of voice was as casual as hers, but Elizabeth knew the tone was forced. "But it's women and children first, Nola. You've sailed often enough to know that. The men go last, that's the way of it."

"Martin." Mrs. Farr stood very straight, her back stiff with resistance, though her voice shook. "I am not leaving this ship without you. That's final."

Her husband's hazel eyes narrowed. "And what of our daughter? You are not concerned with her welfare?"

"Of course I am! She'll be fine right here with me until this silliness is over." She turned toward Elizabeth and spoke in her sweetest, most persuasive voice, though it was still unsteady. Elizabeth knew that tone well. "You'll be fine, won't you, dear? You wouldn't want to leave the ship without your father, would you?"

"Darling, please don't do that," Elizabeth's father said sharply. "Don't force her to align herself with you in such foolish recklessness."

His voice hardened. "You are both getting into lifeboats, and that's final. I don't want to hear another word about it. Come along, then." His voice softened again as he put an arm around his wife's shoulders and began gently but firmly leading her forward before she could protest further. "I am telling you, dear heart, I shall be along later. You must trust me."

As they walked, Max and Elizabeth followed. Her knees felt like warm porridge. Was she really going to have to get into one of those dangling lifeboats? No, she couldn't. She couldn't do it. "They say there are ships in the immediate area," Max told her. "I expect that we'll be rescued as soon as the lifeboats are in the water. So you needn't worry about freezing out there, Elizabeth. You won't be out there long enough to freeze."

They had to walk very close together to get through the mass of people milling about on the boat deck. The earlier calmness had dissipated. Realizing the seriousness of the situation, people were chattering loudly, demanding assistance, calling out the names of friends and relatives they'd become separated from, pushing anxiously toward the lifeboats. "Then the *Titanic* really is in trouble?" Elizabeth asked. "Is it going to sink?"

He nodded. "Yes, I think so. I know they said it couldn't, but it looks like they were wrong. I heard someone say just now that we have perhaps no more than two hours, if even that. Your father's right. You've got to get into a boat."

Elizabeth fought back tears. "You have to come, too, Max. With us." She wanted him with her. The thought of leaving him behind on a ship that might be sinking was unbearable.

He shook his head. "Can't do that, Elizabeth. I'm not a child, and I'm not a woman. I'll wait with your father until the boats for the men have been readied. And I'll catch up with you on whichever ship picks us up. If it's a really big ship, it may take a while, but we'll find each other."

Just ahead of her, Elizabeth could see the lifeboats being uncovered and lowered slowly on the davits to deck level. The sight stopped the flow of blood in her veins. It was really going to happen. They were all going to have to leave the ship in the pathetically small lifeboats and sail off into that cold, black emptiness out there. And if something happened that prevented them from reboarding the *Titanic*, they could only hope to be plucked off the water by a rescuing ship.

What if that didn't happen? What if there were no ships out there?

Elizabeth wanted more than anything to be brave and strong, to impress Max with her fortitude. But sheer, raw terror at the sight of the lifeboats being lowered, and the certain knowledge that she was about to be sent off the warm, beautiful ship that still seemed so safe in spite of everything and out into the dark, frigid night without her father and without Max, sent her spinning around to throw herself into his arms and whisper intently, "Oh, Max, I don't want to leave you here! I'm so frightened!"

He let her stay there, holding her close, his chin resting on the top of her head. He didn't tell her she was being silly, that she was a coward, didn't even try to reassure her. Instead, he whispered back, "I'm afraid, too, Elizabeth."

At first she thought she'd heard him wrong. "You? You're afraid?"

He laughed ruefully. "Wouldn't I be stupid not to be afraid? The ship is going down, we know that much now. Anyone who's not afraid isn't thinking clearly."

And indeed, the people milling around them were pushing more forcefully now, anxious to find a place in the boats. The crewmen stationed near the lifeboats spoke firmly, clearly intent on maintaining order. "Women and children first," one of them called out emphatically. "Women and children first!"

Max put his hands on Elizabeth's elbows and looked directly into her eyes. "Listen, Elizabeth, that last argument we had —"

She reached up to put a trembling finger

over his lips. "Shh! Not now, Max. Please. What's the difference now? It all seems so silly."

"I just want to say ... I need to tell you —"

"Elizabeth!" her father called from a few feet away. "You must come now!"

Desperation in his eyes, Max said quickly, "Elizabeth, I think I'm in love with you."

She had to struggle against tears. Why make it worse for him by crying? She smiled instead. "I think you are, too." Her smile widened. "But that works out quite well, don't you think? Because I feel the same way about you."

Her father's voice rang out again. "Elizabeth! *Now!*"

There was time then for only one brief kiss, not nearly long enough, but filled with all of the emotion they couldn't put into words. When they moved apart, they joined Elizabeth's parents on the lifeboat line.

Katie, waiting with the children in hand, had been watching the sad tableau. She recognized the girl in gray as the one with the happy family. The girl who hadn't wanted to gawk in third class. Katie needed no interpreter to tell her what was happening between the girl and the handsome, sandy-haired young man talking to her. They were saying their good-byes, and it was so clearly painful for both that it brought tears to Katie's eyes, though she didn't know either of them.

She didn't understand why they were parting. Why wasn't the young man going with the girl? She was with her parents, instead, but it seemed the father wasn't disembarking, either. His wife was clinging to him as if she might never see him again. Why wasn't he going along? There was plenty of room in the lifeboat. Families should always stay together, no matter what was happening.

Small wonder the girl was upset. Leaving both her beau, for he was clearly that, and her father behind, on a ship that was in trouble.

It wasn't right. It wasn't right at all.

When Brian and Paddy returned, she would insist that they all leave the ship in the same lifeboat. She wouldn't let them argue with her. Brian was a man of his word, and he had promised her da he would see to it that she got to America safely. She would hold him to that promise, shame him if he refused to get into the lifeboat.

But first, they both had to return. The moments were ticking away, and people were leaving in the lifeboats, and still there was no sign of Paddy or Brian.

Chapter 23

Standing on the ship's starboard side near lifeboat number five as it was being lowered, Elizabeth could see, far below her, one boat already sitting on the flat black sea, bobbing like a bathtub toy. "Why are both boats nearly empty?" she asked Max, now standing at her elbow. The ear-splitting roar of steam from the huge funnels above them made it necessary to shout. "Shouldn't they be full? There are so many people on board."

"They've probably assigned those boats the task of picking up —" he stopped abruptly, as if regretting his words.

But Elizabeth knew what he'd been about to say. "Picking up survivors." And he'd stopped in midsentence because he didn't want her thinking about survivors. He didn't want her picturing people flailing around in those icy waters, shouting for help.

But if the ship went down before every passenger and crew member had been removed by lifeboat, that ugly image would become reality.

No wonder Max had stopped speaking. It was too horrible a possibility to even think about.

Her only response was a shocked "Oh." She was having trouble regulating her breathing. Impossible to tell herself there was no cause for alarm. How could she, when there were now two lifeboats pulling away from the ship?

But then, pointing, Max said, "There's a steamer in the distance. See the lights? They're probably on their way here right now to take on passengers."

That thought was somewhat reassuring.

Elizabeth wondered nervously if that was why there was not much of a crowd waiting to board the next lifeboat. Because people believed they'd be safer staying on board, waiting for the steamer to arrive? Perhaps they all thought it would take hours for the *Titanic* to sink, and long before that happened, the steamer would have pulled alongside.

Or had the word not gone round yet that the ship was sinking? Had no one made the announcement in the gymnasium, or in the smoking rooms or the lounges?

She asked her father what time it was.

"A little after twelve-thirty," he answered.

Forty-five minutes since the engines had stopped. Yet, except for that almost imperceptible tilt to the deck, the ship still seemed as stable and as safe as ever.

But Elizabeth knew it wasn't.

"Father," she called, touching his sleeve to get his attention over the roar of the steam, "there are ships on their way to rescue us. Couldn't we just wait here with everyone else until they arrive? It seems so much safer than the lifeboats. And you can see mother is frightened about leaving the ship. So am I."

The expression on his face told her he was as reluctant to separate the family as she was. "We shall stay together as long as it is safe," he consented. "There seems to be no urgency just yet. But when I say the word, Elizabeth, I want no argument. None, do you hear me?"

"Yes, Father." Satisfied with that, Elizabeth grasped Max's hand and held it tightly as the Farrs moved slightly backward, away from the line preparing to board boat number three. Perhaps there would be no need to leave the *Titanic* at all . . . if the rescue ship arrived soon.

Her mother looked so pale. How frightened she must be, not just at the thought of the lifeboat's terrifyingly long drop from the deck to the water below, but at the possibility of having to leave her husband behind, not really knowing when she would see him again.

As if reading Elizabeth's thoughts, Nola turned suddenly and embraced her husband. "I'm not going to leave you," she said, tears filling her eyes. "I'm not. The boats are leaving only half full. Other men are boarding. No one will mind if you come with us. Please, Martin, you must!"

His handsome face filled with pain. But he shook his head, and although he put his arms around his wife to comfort her, he said, "Oh, Nola, you know I can't do that." He held her silently for a few moments, then gently pulled away, saying in a firm but gentle voice, "We will wait for a bit, together. I feel no immediate danger. But as I told Elizabeth, when I say you must go, that will be that. Understood?"

Relief in her face, his wife said, "Yes, Martin."

It was clear to Elizabeth that her mother believed, as she herself wanted to, that if they waited long enough, a rescue ship would save them from being lowered out into that cold, dark sea in a small boat.

As boat number five began to drop the last few feet to the sea, a voice shouted from the deck, "See to the plug, see to the plug!"

"What plug?" Elizabeth asked Max.

He began shouting his answer, which Elizabeth couldn't really hear. But halfway through his explanation, the funnel noise stopped abruptly — "letting rainwater drain out while the boats are hanging in place, unused," Max was saying. His shout sounded odd in the sudden silence. He lowered his voice. "If they don't put the plug back in before they hit the sea, they'll be swamped. I hope they thought to put a lantern on the boats, or they'll have a devil of a time finding the plug in the dark."

They must have found the plug and inserted it, because they began rowing aft. As they did, Elizabeth could see an officer in the boat giving orders. He seemed to be looking for something, but eventually gave up on whatever it was, and began pulling out to sea, away from the *Titanic*. The boat seemed so small, the ocean so vast, Elizabeth wondered in dread how a rescue ship would ever spot such a small blot on the endless seascape, especially in the dark of night.

Her father had turned away for a moment to talk to a crewman. Elizabeth couldn't hear what they were saying, but her father's expression turned grim. His glance went from one lifeboat to the next, as if he were mentally counting them, and when he had finished, his eyes looked bleak.

What terrible truth had he been told? Something about the boats.

Elizabeth knew there were more lifeboats on

the port side. But she didn't know how many. Her alarm deepened. Exactly how many lifeboats were there? How many passengers? Why had her father looked so grim after he'd done his mental counting?

"Max?" she asked, turning back to him. Fear made her voice husky. "Are there enough lifeboats?"

"Oh, sure," he said. Too easily, Elizabeth thought. It didn't sound genuine, and she wondered uneasily if he had heard the fear in her voice and was addressing it. As if she were a child who needed placating. "On a ship like this? Bound to be. Why?"

Elizabeth spoke insistently. "Because if everyone really believed the ship was unsinkable, they might not have installed as many lifeboats as on other ships. Because no one thought they'd be needed."

"Oh, I don't think that would make any difference. There are maritime laws about that sort of thing. They'd have to install the correct number of lifeboats whether they thought the ship was unsinkable or not."

Elizabeth fought to accept that. Max sounded like he knew what he was talking about. There were laws about such things. If he was right, her father and Max would have a lifeboat, after all. They would leave the sinking ship just a bit later than Elizabeth and her mother, but they would all meet again later on the rescue ship that saved them.

Though she fought to believe that, something stopped her. It was the understanding that the builders of the *Titanic*, declaring their ship unsinkable, must have sounded like *they* knew what they were talking about, too. If they, experts that they were, could be wrong, as it certainly seemed they had been, Max could be wrong, too.

And didn't it seem now that more of the faces around her were registering alarm? Were not the voices turning more strident and shrill as they shouted questions at the crewmen? Weren't there more people pushing forward toward the lifeboats? Mothers gripping the hands of their children. Husbands with a protective arm wrapped around a wife's shoulders. Honeymooners clutching each other with new desperation.

Or was she imagining these things because of her own fear?

No, she was not. There was fear in the air as thick as the morning fog.

Elizabeth turned to her father, who kept an arm around his wife's shoulders as they waited. Her lips white with anxiety, she said, "Father? I'm sorry I made you angry earlier. I didn't mean what I said. Of course you're no coward. I hope you can forgive me."

His eyes looked incredibly sad as he smiled down at her and reached out with his free arm to pull her in against him. "Ah, Elizabeth, how much time have we wasted arguing? Such a pity!" Softly, so that his wife wouldn't hear him, he whispered into Elizabeth's ear, "You'll take care of your mother for me, yes? She's not strong, like you, Elizabeth. From the moment you both leave this ship, you must do as she says. Promise me."

Elizabeth knew then that Max was wrong. Knew it for certain. The blood in her veins chilled as if she'd been dropped into the icy sea. Her father was certain there weren't enough lifeboats for everyone. That was what he'd learned from the crewman. He no longer expected to leave the *Titanic* later, as he'd promised earlier. Maybe he had believed it then. But he didn't now. Or he wouldn't have that despairing look in his eyes. It spoke of no hope.

But she needed him to say it. Aloud. With a direct gaze that said she would tolerate nothing less than the absolute truth, and keeping an unsteady voice as low as his, she asked, "There aren't enough lifeboats, are there, Father?"

For just a moment, she could see that he silently questioned the wisdom of telling her the truth. Then he must have decided she could handle it, because he shook his head no. Continuing to whisper, he said, "You must promise me, Elizabeth. You and your mother will be taken care of financially, but she will need much more than that. She is not accustomed to handling life alone. This might well shatter her. You must stay with her and care for her, and if you marry, you must take her to live with you."

There flashed through Elizabeth's mind then a picture of her mother running the town house in Manhattan and the country house with an iron hand. Things ran smoothly in both Farr households because her mother saw to it that they did. Nola Farr was not as helpless as her husband seemed to think she was. And look how she had refused to give in to Elizabeth's pleas for college. It was as if she were two separate and distinct people: the organized, efficient matron who handled home and family brilliantly when her husband was away at work, and the sweeter, dependent woman who appeared the minute he walked in the door. "She'll be fine, Father." Elizabeth's voice broke, and tears spilled from her eyes. "Mother will be fine. We will both be fine." But she didn't believe it for a second. How could they be, without him?

"Promise me!"

"I promise." If Elizabeth had chosen to dwell on what she had just contracted to do, she would have been horrified. To stay by her mother's side forever? To never go out on her own and live her own life? At least her father had said, "*If* you marry," not "*When you marry Alan.*" He had seen how things were between her and Max, then, and was no longer taking for granted her marriage to Alan Reed. If only he'd reached that conclusion sooner.

But what did any of that matter now? It all seemed so trivial, in view of the crisis taking place on board the ship. What she wanted now, more than she had ever wanted anything, was for everyone on board the *Titanic* to survive this long, terrible night at sea.

Now that her father had shared with her the shortage of lifeboats, it was impossible to keep her hopes up. A cold, black despair welled up within her, as if the ocean had already claimed her.

At least he wasn't rushing them off the boat, separating all of them sooner than necessary. But she could see by the anxiety in his eyes that it wouldn't be long before he insisted they leave the ship. How she dreaded that moment! How could she say good-bye to her own father, or to Max, knowing she might never see them again?

Elizabeth, already despairing, remembered something else then, and almost wept. Her father didn't swim. He had never learned. When they went to the country house on Long Island

Sound, he was always careful to don a life vest before they took the boat out. And although he had talked periodically about taking swimming lessons, he'd never gotten around to it.

Feeling sick, Elizabeth was incapable of doing anything more than clutching her father on one side, Max on the other, for as long as she would be allowed.

She didn't even try to stop the tears that slid quietly down her face. It would have seemed to her an abomination not to be crying.

She saw then that there were other tears on deck besides her own. Women who had begun to realize the true horror of what was happening had begun to weep openly. Those who weren't already crying were pleading for reassurance from husbands and crew members. Everyone, it seemed to Elizabeth, was clinging to someone else, a husband, a child, a companion, a friend, as if by holding on to another human being, they could be saved from the waiting sea.

The distant sounds of sudden laughter from inside the gymnasium shocked her. The sound was so contradictory to the atmosphere on deck. Then she realized that those inside wouldn't be aware of the shortage of lifeboats. And the people still inside, playing cards in the smoking room or the lounge or sitting in the gymnasium, still hadn't accepted that the *Ti-*

tanic was actually sinking, or they would be out here, milling about on the boat deck, clambering for a position in one of the boats.

They didn't know what was happening.

But they would, soon enough.

And they, too, would weep with terror.

Chapter 24

Monday, April 15, 1912

In the quiet corner where she waited with Bridey and Kevin, Katie surveyed the crowd for some sign of Eileen. If she would arrive to take over the care of the children, Katie would be free to search for Brian and Paddy. Eileen had to be here somewhere ... unless she had left the ship in the first lifeboat. She might have done that. She'd been gone from the cabin a long time.

"Keep your eyes peeled for Eileen," she told the children. Bridey complained that she had to go to the bathroom, and Kevin had begun a childish chant, "We're goin' ta sink, we're goin' ta sink, to the bottom of the deep blue sea," sing-songing it over and over again until a shivering Katie thought she would lose her mind. What did he know, the wee thing, about drowning? How the black, icy water would close over your head and freeze your limbs so that even if you knew how to swim it would do you no good at all, how the frigid, salty water would fill your lungs until your chest exploded? He was only six. He knew nothing of such horrors.

And she didn't want him to. He didn't have to. He was wearing a life vest and there were lifeboats. She would see to it that he got into one, and Bridey, too. They'd be saved.

A crewman approached, a life vest in hand. He thrust it at Katie. "Here," he said, "take this!"

She took it. Noticing that he wasn't wearing one, she asked, "Is it yours, then, that you're givin' me?"

"Doesn't matter," he said, and disappeared into the crowd.

She put it on with trembling hands.

When she finally spotted Eileen, it was purely accidental. She was looking not for Eileen at that moment, but for the girl who had worn the blue dress, the one who was being forced to leave her love and her father at the same time. Such a sad, tragic thing.

But when her gaze moved to the group waiting for lifeboat number three as it was being lowered to deck level, she spotted a froth of blond curls, a red-and-white coverlet wrapped around thin shoulders, and realized what she was looking at. Eileen, preparing to abandon the ship without a thought for her two young charges!

Before Katie could shout, Eileen, with the help of an officer, stretched her legs to step across and into the boat. It was flush with the boat deck, but hanging several feet away from the side of the ship. From where she stood, Katie could see the gap and wondered in dread how, even if Brian and Paddy suddenly appeared so they could all leave the ship together, she would ever have the courage to bridge that gap. Her legs were much shorter than Eileen's. 'Twould be impossible for me to leap across, she told herself with sickening certainty. What if I fell? Even if I knew how to swim, I would certainly bash me brains out when I hit the water, fallin' from such a great distance.

Never mind, she wasn't ready to leave the ship yet, anyway. There were other boats. She and Paddy and Brian would leave later. Perhaps there'd be no gap then.

Eileen could not be allowed to desert the two wee ones.

Grabbing each child by the hand, Katie shouted, "Come, now, we've found her! There's Eileen, in one of them boats. You run with me and we'll put you in with her."

"No!" Bridey screamed, pulling back. "I gotta go to the bathroom. And I don't like Eileen! She's mean."

Tightening her lips, Katie reached down and lifted the child. Bridey was heavy, and the distance across the deck to the lifeboat seemed interminable. When she got there, she hoped the pretty girl would be getting into the boat, too. Then if Eileen would have nothing to do with the children, perhaps the girl would see to them. She had a kind face, and she hadn't wanted to be in third class that morning poking fun at them. She had to be a good-hearted person.

When Katie pushed her way through the line standing at the rail, Elizabeth recognized her as the girl who had boarded on the tender in Queenstown. But she hadn't had any young children with her when she arrived. Elizabeth's own terrors were momentarily put aside as she watched to see what the red-haired girl, who looked out of place in her simple, dark wool clothing in the midst of so many first-class passengers, was about to do.

"Eileen!" Katie shouted angrily, holding Bridey up in her arms. "Are you leavin' without the children, then? And what kind of fine person does that make you? Are you ashamed of yourself, as you should be?"

Startled, Eileen slunk down in her seat.

Elizabeth thought "Eileen" looked too young to be the mother of the boy, who could be as old as five or six.

But then, a woman in the boat turned to Eileen to ask, "Are you the mother of those children?"

"No!" Eileen shouted, clutching the coverlet around her more tightly. "I'm nobody's mother! And I never promised to care for them wee ones on a sinkin' ship! I've got meself to think about."

The words "a sinkin' ship" shouted aloud brought shocked gasps from the crowd surrounding Elizabeth. She realized that although everyone on deck had to know by now what was happening, many had stubbornly clung to some small shred of denial. No more. The young Irish woman in the lifeboat had slapped each and every one of them in the face with the harsh, bitter truth. Some women burst into terrified tears, while others whispered softly, as if they were praying, and still others, their mouths set determinedly, began to push forward in line.

Her own mouth set with purpose, Katie turned to a crewman preparing to enter the boat. "Hand these children over to her," she commanded. "They are in her care, and she's the only one who knows where they belong when they get to America. 'Tis her they must be goin' with."

But the boat, though only half full, had already begun lowering again. The gap between the lifeboat and the *Titanic* was now not only wide, but deep.

"You *must* get these wee ones in that boat!" Katie shouted, leaning forward as far as she dared with Bridey still in her arms.

Suddenly, the tall, handsome young man who had kissed the pretty girl good-bye and was still standing with her at the rail reached out for Bridey. "Here, give her to me. I'll put her in."

And he did. As Elizabeth watched in horror, Max swung his long legs over the rail so that he was hanging on the outside of the ship, clinging to the rail with his left arm only. With his right hand, he reached out for the child.

A crewman standing by warned, "Hey, you oughtn't to be doin' that, mister. That ain't safe."

Max ignored him. When his free right arm was around the child's waist, he bent down as far as possible in an effort to deposit the little girl, now shrieking wildly, into the lifeboat.

Elizabeth pleaded, "Max, be careful!" The drop from ship to sea was a long one, and he was only holding on with one arm. The tips of his feet had found a precarious support on the edge of the deck. Not enough, Elizabeth thought, to keep him from falling if he lost his one-armed grip.

Katie understood the fear in the girl's voice.

The woman who had asked Eileen if she was a mother jumped to her feet in the lifeboat and, standing unsteadily, reached up and out with both arms to take the child. She caught her, and Bridey's weight sent them both slamming back down onto the wooden seat.

But the child was now safe in the lifeboat, no thanks to Eileen. Katie glared at her, but Eileen refused to meet her eyes.

Elizabeth heaved a sigh of relief and called to Max to climb back over the rail.

But Katie was unrelenting. "Now the boy!" she begged, pushing Kevin forward. He was too heavy for her. She was terrified that if she couldn't lift him, the young man called Max wouldn't be able to, either.

"I can do it meself!" Kevin shouted, and tried to hoist himself up on the rail, prepared to jump.

But there was that gap.

Katie gasped.

"No!" Max shouted, and reached out to grasp the boy's hand. "I'll swing you down. Hold on!"

Elizabeth, watching from the rail, held her breath. She was terrified for Max as he used his free arm to swing the boy out and down, until Kevin's feet were only inches from the seats in the boat. Then he dropped him.

But he had misjudged the boy's weight and the tremendous pull it would create. His arm began to slip from the rail. He realized instantly what was happening, and Elizabeth, watching, saw his eyes fill with dread.

Katie saw it, too, and gasped, her hands flying to her mouth.

Elizabeth reached out to grab for Max's coat, crying out, "No, Max, no —"

And then her father was at her side, and a crewman on the other side, and all three were reaching, reaching, trying to grasp a collar, a sleeve, anything that would keep Maxwell Whittaker from falling to his death.

There was then one small, dark moment, the blackest of Elizabeth's life, when her own hands, reaching, clutching, grasping, touched nothing but air and in her mind's eye, she saw Max falling . . . falling into that deep, dark sea below.

So terrified was she that it took her another moment to realize that what she had missed, her father and the crewman had not. There were strong, determined hands gripping first Max's coat collar, then his shoulders, holding on tightly as they pulled him backwards up, up, and over the rail.

He landed on the deck on his back.

People cheered and clapped.

Elizabeth fell to her knees beside him, unmindful of the coldness of the deck. "You're all right?" she gasped. "You're not hurt?"

Although his face was as gray as her coat, he managed a weak grin. "Why would I be hurt? It's not like I fell off a stationary bicycle, like some people I could mention."

Beginning to shake, Elizabeth sank back on her heels, while Katie sagged against the rail, her hands folded in thankful prayer. She would never have forgiven herself if the young man had fallen to his death. She leaned forward to call out to Max, "'Tis grateful to you I am, mister. And the wee ones, too. Saved them, you did. We're all grateful."

Nodding, he climbed shakily to his feet, helped Elizabeth to hers, and they hugged. Her parents, standing nearby, made no objection. Not that it would have mattered to Elizabeth.

The orchestra, standing near the first-class entrance, began playing "Alexander's Ragtime Band."

As if he saw that as a cue, one of the crewmen shouted, "All right, everybody, let's get on with it, then! Lower away!"

Boat number three began creaking down the falls.

Elizabeth continued to hold onto Max as if

she would never let him go. He was alive. Had he fallen, had he missed the lifeboat because of that wide gap and gone straight down to the sea, the black water would have closed over his head and she would never have seen him again.

Her relief was short-lived. Max had been saved this time. But she still had to leave him soon.

And when she did, he would be standing on the deck of a ship that was sinking into the sea.

Chapter 25

Katie waited only long enough to make sure the young man who had saved Bridey and Kevin was safe and sound. Then she located a stewardess standing on deck with a pile of blankets in her arms and asked her, "How is it that I can get to the aft well deck? Tell me, quickly!"

"Oh, miss," the stewardess answered, "you don't be wantin' to go all the way aft. The lifeboats is up here, both port and starboard." She lowered her voice, adding, "I hear we're sinkin' fast. They haven't told no one 'cause they're feared of a panic. But it's true. You'd best be gettin' in a boat, not runnin' around the ship. I'm to be puttin' these blankets in the lifeboats but," her voice dropping almost to a whisper, "these here blankets won't help much out there on the sea, and that's the truth of it."

265

Although the horror of what the woman had said chilled Katie to the core, she argued, "I can't go yet. There's somethin' I must do first. I canna leave without my friends."

The girl shrugged. "Suit yourself. Just go down to A deck by the stairs over there." She pointed. "Then go aft until you find a door that'll take you outside so's you can look down upon the well deck. But" — she shook her head as she turned to leave — "it's foolish you're bein'. If I wasn't a stewardess, I'd be in one of them boats this very minute."

Katie was startled. "What's that you're sayin'? Stewardesses don't get to go in a lifeboat? But I saw one, in a uniform, in one of the boats already on the sea. Number five, the officer said it was."

The girl shrugged. "'Twasn't me, that's all I know. Passengers get first crack at the boats, especially first- and second-class passengers. That's the way of it. But it don't matter. There's a coupla ships comin' to get us. Won't be as grand as the *Titanic*, of course, but beggars can't be choosers. Good luck finding your friends."

Katie nodded and hurried away. The ship really was sinking. Still, the stewardess had said there were rescue ships on the way. And at least she knew the wee ones were already safe in a boat. If Eileen didn't take care of them, one of the other women would.

The tilt as Katie made her way aft was more noticeable, except that now it was uphill. Like when she was walking to church in Ballyford on a Sunday morning. A strong ache of homesickness seized her. The stewardess had to be right about the rescue ships comin' along quickly, because she couldn't bear thinking of the pain her family would suffer if she drowned in the Atlantic Ocean.

In spite of the now obvious tilt to the ship, Katie passed people in the corridors who showed not a trace of alarm. A pair of young men who had clearly had too much to drink and were leaning on each other for support called out as she passed, "Hello, there, pretty thing, what's your hurry?" A handsomely dressed couple holding hands passed by, glancing in disdain at the young men's drunken behavior. But the couple, too, gave no sign of alarm, and seemed in no hurry. An elderly man in a tuxedo ambled along the hallway with the help of a cane. He smiled at Katie as if they were both simply out for a leisurely stroll.

They're only like that, Katie thought as she hurried along looking for an exit, 'cause they don't know yet. When they do, they'll be as afeared as everyone else.

The first two doors she found provided no view of the well deck, so she kept going. When she finally found an open door that was far enough aft, she was once again repelled by sudden, icy cold as she stepped outside. Inside the ship, where it was warm, she'd forgotten how low the temperature outside had dropped.

Clutching her coat around her, Katie stepped to the rail with a sense of urgency and looked down. People were milling about below her, their belongings piled at their feet. Some sat on their baggage, as if to protect it, while others stood in small clusters, conversing anxiously. While most of the younger children were playing, shouting and laughing as if they were in a park on a warm summer's day, there was a perceptible air of bewilderment about the adults. If they knew what was happening, it seemed clear to Katie that they didn't know what to do about it. And she saw no sign of anyone in authority telling them what course of action to take.

She saw no lifeboats. She saw no crewmen. She saw no sign that anything was being done to direct these people to safety.

Aware of the moments racing by, she leaned over the rail to shout, "Brian?" as loud as she could. "Paddy?" She didn't see them, but there were so many people crowding the deck. If a Kelleher heard her voice, he'd come to the rail, look up and see her. Then the brothers would join her, and they could hurry to safety. If there was such a thing available to them.

"Paddy? Brian?"

A few people heard her and glanced up, but none of the faces staring up at Katie belonged to Paddy or Brian. She didn't know what to do. She had come here to find them and she wasn't leaving until she'd done so. She would have to go down there and look for herself.

She turned and hurried back to the door. She opened it to find Brian standing there. His thick, dark, curly hair, so like his brother's, was windblown and tousled, and there were streaks of dirt on his cheeks. His eyes looked tired, but he smiled when she threw herself into his arms, shouting his name.

"Come inside," he ordered, pulling her in and closing the door. "You'll freeze to death out there."

"Where's Paddy?" was the first thing she asked him.

"He's below. He's fine, no need to fret about him. We're tryin' to talk people into comin' up to the boats. But the women won't go. Won't leave their men. I'm not sure they know what's really happenin'. One of the stewards, a fellow named Cox, he's been helpin', too, leadin' both men and women up to the boat deck. But some o' them won't even put a life vest on." Brian shrugged. "They say there's no damage, when any fool can see that's not so."

"You'll come with me, will you not?" Katie asked with hope in her voice. "To the lifeboats? But you'll go down and get Paddy first?"

He shook his head. "Can't do that, Katie. The women below got to be talked into goin' up top. Paddy's doin' some good work down there." He laughed. "You know yourself, Paddy's got the gift of gab. He's better at persuadin' folks to leave the well deck than me." Brian thought for a minute, then continued. "Still and all, Steward Cox asked if anyone knew anything about boats, sayin' they might need people to man the lifeboats. I spoke up and said Paddy'd tried his hand at fishin'. If they could use him in a boat, he should go. He might if I told him he was needed up here. And," he added, smiling, "if he knew you was waitin' on him."

Katie's heart leaped with hope. She didn't want to leave Brian behind, not at all. But if she could at least get Paddy to come with her . . .

Brian surprised her then by saying earnestly, "You need to be tellin' him what's in your heart, Katie."

When, stunned, she said nothing, he went on, "Now's the time. He don't know it's him. He's thinkin' it's me. That's why he's been frettin' so over Marta. He thinks I'm betrayin' you."

"But . . . but it's *not* you I love!" Katie burst out bluntly. " 'Tis himself!"

Brian laughed. "I know that. But Paddy don't. And it ain't my place to tell him different. That's for you to do, Katie." His smile disappeared, his eyes turned bleak. "And you'd best be doin' it now, tonight."

Katie looked doubtful. "And what makes you think 'twould mean anything to him? With him havin' all them other girls, I mean."

It was Brian's turn to look surprised. "You don't know he's frettin' over you? Lordy, Katie, are you not as keen as I was thinkin' you are? The boy is achin' with worry over you. Only he wasn't about to reach for somethin' he thought was his big brother's. It's on you to set him straight."

Any other time, Katie would have protested that she didn't want to seem too bold, too forward. But on this night, when no one knew what would happen but knew it was most likely going to be fearsome, she couldn't fret about seeming bold.

She nodded. "I'll do it, then. If he'll come up here, I'll tell him."

"I'll tell him you're needin' to see him. But I can't promise that he'll come. There's still a lot of people in the public room and in their cabins, and Paddy's makin' it his business to pass the word to them to get out." His expression grew very serious. "Steward Cox says there ain't a whole lot of time, Katie. You wait here just five minutes. If Paddy ain't up here by that time, you got to go and find yourself a boat. Promise me? I told your da I'd take care of you, and I mean to keep me word. It's just about all I got. Don't take that from me, Katie. Don't stay out there at the rail waitin' for Paddy when you should be gettin' into a lifeboat. You promise?"

"I promise." She wasn't sure she meant it, but she wanted that look of anxiety out of Brian's eyes.

It didn't disappear, but it eased somewhat when she had given him her word.

He drew her to his chest and hugged her tightly, saying, "It'll be all right, Katie-girl, it'll be all right." Then he stepped back. Repeating, "Five minutes, remember?" he turned and hurried away.

It was the longest five minutes of Katie's life. She went back outside and stood at the rail, shivering with cold and studying the well deck for some sign of Paddy. She finally decided he must have gone below to get more people out, because while there were other young men on the well deck, he wasn't among them.

And then, just as she was about to give up and go inside, not because she wanted to but because she had promised Brian, there Paddy was, stepping out of the doorway to say to her, "I was thinkin' I'd not be seein' you again. The thought gave me a fierce pain, like someone was steppin' on me chest."

Because he had confessed that his heart hurt thinking he wouldn't be seeing her again, it was easy for Katie to blurt out, "I'd die if I wasn't to see you again, Patrick Kelleher. And that's the truth of it. Me own heart was hurtin', not knowin' where you'd got to, not knowin' if you was safe." There, she'd said it. Let him do with it whatever he wanted.

She watched as the look on his handsome face changed from confusion to disbelief, and back to confusion again. His jaw dropped, and he asked, "What are you sayin'? Say it again, so I don't get it wrong."

"I love you, Paddy."

Then he was at her side and she was in his arms. It was as if the great ship were in no trouble, disaster wasn't looming, everything was fine and in its proper place, as it should be. And this time when Paddy kissed her, he didn't draw back, fearful that he'd stepped into his brother's territory.

When he finally lifted his head, she asked tremulously, "Brian's not with you, then?"

"Wouldn't come. They're only lettin' the women and children up top just now. They said the men can come along later." His expression grew somber, just as Brian's had. "Look here, Katie, I've got to be gettin' back down there. There's a lot of people won't come up to the boats. They need to be talked into it, and I got to help do that."

"I'll be comin' with you." She spoke firmly, though her teeth were chattering from the cold.

He looked at her with alarm. "Oh, no, you don't! You're gettin' into a boat. I promised Bri I'd see to you before I came back down. He wanted me to offer to help in one of the boats, but we got to get the people up on deck first. But you're not comin' with me. I'll take you to the boat, then I'll go back down, and I'll meet up with you later on the rescue ship."

"I'm comin' with you."

"Katie!"

"There's no rush for the lifeboats, Paddy. It's bound to take the *Titanic* hours and hours before it sinks." She believed that only because she had to. There was no choice, not really. "I'll come with you, help you bring the people up, and then we'll both find a lifeboat together. And Bri, too. That way, we won't have to be separated at all."

Paddy looked doubtful. Katie could see that he was torn. "Bri'll have me head."

"I'll tell him it was my fault. He knows I can be just as pigheaded as the both of you. It'll

come as no shock to him that I wouldn't do what
you said. Come on, then. Sooner started, sooner
finished." Without waiting for any more argument, Katie took Paddy's hand and pulled him
to the door.

Chapter 26

Monday, April 15, 1912

The ragtime music the orchestra continued to play did nothing to lift Elizabeth's spirits. She stood on deck with her arms around Max, her parents just behind them, dreading the moment when her father would say, "It's time."

Boat number three had settled on the sea. From where she stood, it looked as if the crewman was having trouble propelling the boat away from the *Titanic*.

"That man doesn't know what he's doing," her father said in disgust. "I'm glad we waited. I wouldn't want you and your mother in that boat." He took her hand. "Perhaps we'd best try port side. I haven't seen the captain these past few minutes. He could be over there. If he is, I'll make sure he gives your boat an experienced crewman. Come along, then."

They were making their way along the deck to port side when there was an explosion above them and a brilliant white light appeared in the sky, spilling out a shower of stars.

"Rockets!" her father declared. Shaking his head, he urged them to hurry. "Everyone knows the meaning of rockets fired off at sea. Even people who have been clinging to a shred of hope will finally understand now what's going on. They might rush the lifeboats. We've got to get you settled before that happens."

Martin Farr hurried them over to the portside rail and boat number six, which was just loading forward of the first-class Grand Staircase. Captain Smith, as Elizabeth's father had hoped, was indeed there. He was standing near the officer's quarters, calling out, "Women and children first!" A second officer in uniform stood near the boat, repeating the captain's words. Elizabeth, her face white and drawn, assumed he was responsible for keeping order. But how much order could he keep, now that a rocket had been sent up? Fear would sweep over the ship like a tidal wave. People would panic. It would surely take more than one lone officer to calm them.

Five minutes later, as they stood in line, another rocket exploded with a startling bang. The sky lit up again.

"That's to lead the steamer to us," Max explained to Elizabeth. "They can use the rocket to fix our position. Of course, the captain probably already sent any ship in the area a distress message when the iceberg first struck. But it's pretty dark out here, and the rockets will help."

Elizabeth glanced up at the sky. She had never seen so many stars, shining down upon them as if eager to lend their light to the disaster scene. They failed to reassure her, nor did Max's calm, matter-of-fact words ease her terror. He seemed so certain a ship would come to their aid quickly. She felt no such certainty. The lights in the distance seemed to her fixed exactly as they had been the last time she looked. If it was indeed a ship, it was moving very slowly, if at all.

The rockets continued to light up the sky at five-minute intervals. Elizabeth found their explosive noise and bright glare painful, and shuddered with each new blast. If there were ships out there, as Max believed there were, how could they fail to see the telling rocket display? Why wasn't one of them rushing to their aid? They should know exactly where to look for the wounded *Titanic*.

Please, please, please, Elizabeth prayed, please come and save us so we don't have to go out onto that cold, black sea in the dark of night! Please!

But she could see no lights approaching.

Other women were praying, too, many of them aloud. New brides cried and clung to their husbands. Elizabeth thought she saw tears in the eyes of more than one man, as well. She was surrounded by people of wealth, totally unaccustomed to showing any emotion in public and yet, in this darkest of hours, many had given up trying to hide their agony at being separated from those they loved, with no knowledge of when, if ever, they would meet again. Tears flowed freely as wives were wrenched from their husbands by well-meaning stewardesses, or pushed forcibly away and into boats by equally well-intentioned husbands. Elizabeth took in the sight of hands visibly shaking, faces stone-white with fear, mouths set in desperation, and knew that she was looking at mirror images of herself and her family.

We all look like that, she thought, her heart pounding fiercely as her father pushed them forward toward the lifeboat, every one of us. We are all more frightened than we have ever been before.

When a woman screamed hysterically that she was not leaving the ship, Elizabeth was not surprised. She wouldn't have been surprised if every passenger on deck had begun screaming hysterically. The barely restrained panic emanating from the crowd had thickened to the point where Elizabeth felt she could reach out into the air and grasp a handful of it.

If only I could stop trembling, Elizabeth thought as they pressed forward, other bodies pressing more urgently now behind them, seeking escape. If I could stop shaking, perhaps I wouldn't feel so frightened.

Before Nola Farr and her daughter boarded the lifeboat, her father boldly asked the second officer, whom he addressed as "Officer Lightoller," if the crewmen in the boat would be experienced seamen. "You can understand the question," he added. "I am entrusting my wife and daughter to them."

"I have two men," the officer replied as he ushered two more women into the boat. "Mr. Fleet here is a lookout, and Quartermaster Hichens was at the wheel of this ship when the iceberg hit. He's a senior crew member, and he'll be in charge. You can trust him."

"I hope so." Turning to Elizabeth and her mother, Martin Farr said with no apparent show of emotion, though his eyes were bleak, "It's time. Get in, dears, and I shall meet you on board the steamer."

He sounded so convincing that Elizabeth tried desperately to believe him. There were still lifeboats suspended in the davits. Couldn't he have been wrong about a shortage? On the forward port deck, she could see women, most of them weeping openly or protesting loudly, being loaded into boat number eight. Perhaps there weren't as many women on board as men. The remaining women might all fit into boats six and eight. Then her father and Max and any other men could leave in the boats that were left. And they would all meet again on the rescue ship Max kept mentioning, though Elizabeth still saw no approaching lights in the distance.

Telling herself that, Elizabeth was able to hug her father tightly and tell him she would look for him, first thing, on the rescue ship. She hadn't forgotten that he didn't know how to swim. Still, she was hardly crying at all. Then she let him go so that her mother could say her good-bye.

But when Elizabeth hugged Max good-bye, a sense of foreboding swooped down upon her. It was so overpowering, her knees felt like seawater. She could barely whisper, "I'll see you soon. I *will*, Max." Even with the sense of dread filling her, she refused to say the word "Goodbye." It was too final.

He kissed her, just once, but the kiss lasted a long time, because neither of them wanted it to end.

The worst moment came when they had to leave the solid, sturdy, though tilted, deck of the great liner and step out over the churning black water and into the lifeboat. Icy fingers of terror clutched at Elizabeth, telling her this was a terrible mistake. *Stay on the ship*, a voice in her head warned. *Do not go out into the unknown.*

But she had no choice.

Other women seemed to be having the same reaction. Even the bravest among them quailed at the moment of getting into the lifeboat. Some had to be physically lifted by a crewman across the slight span from ship to boat and dropped to a wooden seat. One woman tried desperately to climb back out, shaking violently with terror, only to be restrained by two women on either side of her. Even as she gave in and took her place, she wept desperately.

Elizabeth and her mother climbed in and sat down. Both kept their eyes fastened on the face of Martin Farr as long as they could.

Officer Lightoller told Quartermaster Hichens to row toward the lights of the approaching steamer, drop off the women, and come back to the *Titanic* to pick up more passengers. He sounded so certain that this plan would work, Elizabeth was heartened again. "More passengers" meant Max and her father.

Then Lightoller ordered the crew to lower away.

As they prepared to do so, a beautifully

dressed woman on deck, speaking with a heavy
French accent, was exclaiming anxiously about
her jewels, which were apparently still in the
care of the purser. Mrs. Brown, the millionairess from Colorado so disliked by Elizabeth's
mother, was trying to persuade the woman to
enter the boat. At the very last moment, the
woman gave in and was helped to a seat beside
Elizabeth.

The boat began to descend. The sound of
quiet, frightened weeping accompanied the
creak of the davits.

Above them, Elizabeth heard an authorita-
tive voice say, "*You* are going, too." She lifted
her head, hoping to see Max and her father
jumping into the boat. Instead, there was a cry
of protest, and Mrs. Molly Brown dropped four
feet from above and into the boat with a heavy
thud, her hat tilting sideways on her head as
she landed.

Elizabeth wondered if Max and her father
were still at the rail watching the descent.
When she looked up, her vision was clouded, as
if she were looking through a thick, black veil,
and she realized her eyes were filled with tears.
Because she didn't want to do this. Not only did
she not want to leave Max and her father, she
was frozen with fear at having to leave the
safety and security of the huge *Titanic* to venture out into the vast unknown, even if, as the

second officer had said, it would only be for a short while.

She wished she could believe him.

Her hands were trembling, and not from cold.

When they came even with B deck, the quartermaster suddenly cried up to Lightoller, "I can't manage this boat with only one seaman!"

The boat stopped its descent.

Maybe they'll pull us back up, Elizabeth thought in her distress, and we can climb out of the boat and back onto the ship and wait with Father and Max for the rescue ship, as I wanted to do all along.

But they weren't pulled back up. They hung instead, suspended alongside the *Titanic*, while the second officer above tried to decide the best way to respond to the quartermaster's complaint.

"Even if there's another crew member up there," a woman whose voice seemed remarkably calm said aloud to no one in particular, "we're two decks down. How's he going to get down here? Can't jump, it's too far. Break his neck, he would. Not something *I* care to see."

But Elizabeth's mother said nervously, "If the quartermaster thinks we need more men, we should have more men. We don't want to get out on that open sea and be unable to handle this boat."

Elizabeth heard a noise above them. When she looked up, she saw to her astonishment a man who looked to be older than her father swing hand over hand out onto the davit and begin climbing down the ropes toward them.

Her mother gasped, Molly Brown uttered an oath under her breath, and the first woman who had spoken added, "Lost his mind, he has. Going to fall, for sure."

But he didn't fall.

When the man landed in the boat, the quartermaster ordered him to put the boat's plug in place. The new arrival, a nice-looking older man with a neatly trimmed beard, who said his name was Major Peuchen, was unable to find the plug in the dark. Giving up, he went back to where Hichens was sitting. They spoke for a moment, and Elizabeth saw the senior officer pick something up and insert it into the boat. When the plug was in place, the quartermaster returned to the stern. He took his place, then declared to the major that *he* was in charge of the boat and would give the orders.

Elizabeth thought it very rude of him. But with no argument, Major Peuchen sat down beside the lookout named Fleet. When the boat hit the flat, calm water, both men began rowing.

The cold was unbearable from the moment they hit the sea. Elizabeth's toes felt frozen though she was wearing warm boots. There were women in the boat who had only evening slippers on their feet, and one woman had no shoes at all, only hose.

Her mother, though warmly dressed, was shivering uncontrollably. Elizabeth put an arm around her. As the boat began pulling away from the *Titanic*, she said quietly, "Mother, we'll be all right. That steamer out there will pick us up, and then Father and Max will meet us later. Really, we're going to be fine." Her father had said she must take care of her mother, and so that was what she would do. Even if she didn't really believe the things she was saying.

Her mother's face, bone-white under the wide-brimmed black hat, turned toward her. "Well, yes, of course, dear. We shall see your father shortly. And I must admit, I misjudged Enid's son. I had no idea it was in him to be a hero. That was a very brave act, hoisting those two children into the lifeboat. I really must tell Enid what a chance he took." There was no emotion in her voice. It was as if someone had written lines for her and she was reciting them. But then, she was a Langston, and Langstons did not show emotion in public. It just wasn't done. And it seemed totally in character for Nola to then add, "I do hope that Brown woman minds her manners. It's unpleasant enough in this horrid boat without listening to her vulgarities." Then she sounded more like herself.

Elizabeth stifled hysterical laughter. Only her mother would insist that people mind their manners under these conditions.

She silently counted the number of people in the boat. Twenty-eight, including the crew. Bitterness surged through her. There was so much room. Fifty or sixty people could fit in this boat! Yet her father and Max were still on board the sinking ship. It seemed criminal to her, and she failed to see the reasoning behind it. Why shouldn't the men have come along if the boat was going to leave only half full? To leave them on a sinking ship was indeed a crime of the worst sort.

And from where they were sitting on the water, well away from the *Titanic*, it was now painfully clear that the ship was indeed sinking. Its lights still glowing brightly, it sat at a slight but obvious tilt, its bow down, its stern raised, while rockets continued to shower it with white-hot stars from eight hundred feet above its decks. As more and more passengers in the lifeboat lifted their heads to take a good look, and understood, there were smothered sobs, open weeping, and gasps of horror.

Elizabeth forced herself to think calmly for a moment, wondering if the approaching steamer, its own lights wavering faintly in the distance, had a view of the ailing *Titanic* yet and could see what was taking place. Probably not. Its own outline was not yet visible, only the pale glow of its lights.

Shouldn't it be in sight by now? Max had said that Captain Smith would have sent it a distress message. How slow it must be traveling to have made so little progress by this time. Hadn't the message made the urgency of their situation clear to the ship's captain? Why wasn't he rushing toward them?

Panic rose within her again. If it really *was* a ship, it had to hurry. It *had* to! There couldn't be much time left for those still aboard the *Titanic*. Her heart was breaking for her father and Max, and for all the others who were still standing at the rails. What must they be thinking and feeling? They had to be filled with terror as the lifeboats continued to pull away. Or could they still not believe this nightmare was actually taking place?

Remembering what Max had told her, Elizabeth waited for Hichens to announce that if it came to that, they would be returning to the *Titanic* to pick up survivors. Then she would hope with everything in her that Max and her father would be among them.

On the aft well deck, Katie was using all of her powers of persuasion to move people out of that area and up to the boat deck. Though her da had once told her with a twinkle in his eye,

"Katie-girl, you could talk the stars right down out of the sky if you'd a mind to," she wasn't having much luck. Women refused to leave their husbands. Their husbands refused to leave the aft well deck, insisting there was no serious problem. Even if they'd been willing, by the time Katie and Paddy returned to that area, crewmen had locked the gates again and were allowing only women and children abovedecks.

Some of the passengers had moved to the smoking room aft of the well deck. Katie could hear the piano being played and wondered if people were actually dancing. Did they really not know what was happening, or were they just playacting, pretending this was any other night on the sea to hide their fears?

At the gate, Brian was arguing with the crewmen. She thought he was probably asking that families be allowed to leave intact, but she could see one of the crewmen shaking his head no. She could almost hear him saying, "No men, and that's final."

"Can you not see," she pleaded with the mother of six young children, "that the ship has a noticeable list to it now? Think of the children! You must be savin' them!"

The woman's lips tightened. Her English was not good, but she understood what Katie was saying. "Karl come, too," she said firmly, referring to her husband, a tall, blond-haired man standing behind her talking to another man.

"The men will come later, in other boats," Katie argued. "But you and the children must go now." She was so cold, her voice trembled. She pointed to the crewmen standing at the gate letting only women and children through. "There, you must go there. Someone will direct you to the boats."

The woman didn't budge. Pulling her black shawl tighter around her shoulders, she announced stubbornly, "Karl don't go, I don't go."

In frustration, Katie glanced around for Paddy. He might be able to do what she couldn't. But she didn't see him. Belowdecks he was, making certain there were no stragglers left behind. Then she scanned the crowd for Father Byles, who had been circulating among them earlier. Perhaps the priest could convince this woman that her children must be saved.

She didn't see Father Byles, either.

Giving up, Katie moved across the well deck to another family, hoping she would have better luck this time.

Chapter 27

Monday, April 15, 1912

Rockets continued to light up the sky as Quartermaster Hichens directed lifeboat number six away from the *Titanic*. The sudden incandescence, brief though it was, warmed the dark sky with dozens of tiny silver lanterns. Someone in the boat remarked in a robotlike voice that they were "pretty," which struck Elizabeth as odd until she realized that the woman was in shock and not thinking clearly.

They seemed to be making little progress in rowing away from the ship. Elizabeth was glad. She didn't *want* to leave the ship. The closer they stayed, the safer she would feel. Max and her father would not seem so far away. But there was something else, too, something she thought about in spite of her barely controlled terror. Addressing her mother, she said, "I think we should stay right where we are. We have plenty of room to take on more passengers. We must stay close by in case we're needed." She meant in case the ship actually sank, but she didn't want to say that aloud. She sensed that the reason no one in the boat was visibly hysterical or screaming in fear was a belief that either the ship wouldn't sink, or rescue ships would come along at any moment to save those still on board. She also doubted that any of the other women realized there were not enough lifeboats on board the *Titanic*. If they did, they would surely lose control completely instead of simply weeping quietly for those they'd left behind.

She was not about to tell them about the lifeboat shortage. And she was very grateful that her mother didn't know.

Nola, who had been silent since her remark about Mrs. Molly Brown, made no response to Elizabeth's comment about staying close by. She sat slumped on the seat, staring silently and intently at the sinking ship, as if her eyes were still fastened on her husband's face. It was as if she had no interest in anything that might take place on the lifeboat. She seemed lifeless.

The shrill sound of a whistle fought with the explosion of the latest rocket. The whistle, a longer, thinner sound, won. Quartermaster

Hichens ordered Lookout Fleet and Major Peuchen to stop rowing, so he could hear. They stopped, and he listened.

Elizabeth heard a voice that sounded like Captain Smith's shout, "Come alongside!"

"What does he want?" one of the women asked another. "They told us to row toward the lights of the rescue ship, and now they're telling us to come back?"

A second, terror-stricken voice cried, "No, no, it's not safe! We can't go back!"

Elizabeth could see the quartermaster debating. He was supposed to obey the captain's orders, but he clearly didn't want to. She wasn't sure why. Shouldn't he at least find out what Captain Smith wanted?

She wouldn't have minded returning to the *Titanic*. Maybe they'd be allowed back on. To see Max and her father ... to be on board again, where they could all take refuge in the warm, brightly lit gymnasium or the lounge, to be out of this dark and lonely cold, would that be so bad? Still, the ship was listing more noticeably now toward the bow. Her heart sank again, realizing that it wasn't likely anyone would be allowed back on board.

Hichens shook his head. "Pull away," he said defiantly, motioning to the two men to begin rowing again. "We are not going back. It is our lives now, not theirs."

But they weren't making much progress with only two men rowing. Apparently impatient with this state of affairs, Mrs. Brown suddenly hoisted an oar, slipped it into an oarlock, then asked one of the women to hold a second oar while it was placed into a lock on the other side. The woman assisted without complaint. The two began rowing in tandem. Other women also took up oars, and soon boat number six was able to pull away from the *Titanic*. Elizabeth would have liked to help, but she was worried about her mother. She seemed completely withdrawn. Elizabeth suspected that Nola had finally realized that nothing in their lives would ever be the same again, and she wondered if her mother might be in shock. Perhaps she needed a doctor. But there were none on board.

As the women rowed, they were subjected to a dismaying outburst from Quartermaster Hichens about the dangers of the *Titanic*'s suction, when it sank, pulling their lifeboat down with it. "When it goes down," he added, "the boilers will explode. It'll take everything down with it for miles around."

The thought terrified Elizabeth. She could see that it shocked the other women in the boat. None had yet accepted that the *Titanic* was actually sinking, and Hichens mentioning it as fact startled them.

As for Elizabeth, she was truly agonizing over their desertion of the ship. If there really were not enough lifeboats on board, what would happen to the people still awaiting rescue? If the steamer, whose lights still seemed as far away as they had from the rail of the *Titanic*, didn't arrive fast enough, scores of people would be spilled into the icy water when the ship plunged into the sea. There should be lifeboats standing by to pluck those victims from the dark sea.

But Hichens was immovable. Whenever Elizabeth said aloud that they should remain close to the ship in case they were needed, he repeated his warning about being dragged down along with the *Titanic* when it went.

And although several women, most notably Mrs. Molly Brown, argued with him, he remained immovable.

On the boat deck, Max shared Elizabeth's thoughts. Hands in his coat pockets, he watched as one lifeboat after another withdrew from the vicinity of the ship, and he remembered his confident words to Elizabeth as to why they weren't full. "To pick up survivors," he had said, as if he knew what he was talking about. She had believed him. Judging from the distance most of the boats were creating between themselves and the *Titanic*, their crewmen had no intention of picking up anyone. Captain Smith periodically called out to them through a megaphone, ordering the boats that weren't full to return, but no one so far had responded.

Black, cloying fear overtook Max, catching him off guard and taking his breath away.

"Afraid they'll swamp," Martin Farr, standing beside Max, said. "Can't say that I blame them."

Max swallowed the thick, overwhelming fear to say staunchly, "You'd return, sir. If you were in one of those boats, like Major Peuchen, you'd come back to pick up survivors."

Elizabeth's father didn't even turn his head. "Now, how could you possibly know that?"

"I know it from everything Elizabeth told me about you. It didn't sound to me like you were someone who'd save his own neck while other people were drowning, sir. And I know I'm right because you didn't get in a boat when you could have. No one would have stopped you, not in the beginning. The boats weren't full, and other men were leaving the ship."

Puffing on his pipe, Mr. Farr replied, "I might say the same for you, Whittaker. I thought all young people were only concerned with saving their own necks. Yet you saved those two children, at great risk to yourself, I might add. I owe you an apology."

"No need, sir." The last of the boats had descended from the starboard side. There had been some frightening moments when it had looked as if boat thirteen was about to land on top of fifteen, but quick thinking had solved that problem with no injury to anyone. Both boats were now on their way.

A terrible, aching sense of isolation descended upon Max. The *Titanic*, once a safe, secure, floating hotel, had become a floating death trap. Max knew it as surely as he knew that out on the flat, black sea, Elizabeth was terror-stricken . . . for *him*. He wished he could reassure her that he would be okay. Impossible to do when he couldn't even tell himself that and believe it.

"No point in waiting out here," he told Martin Farr. "Why don't we go inside where it's warm? I noticed a few people playing cards in the lounge. We might be more comfortable in there." He knew that Elizabeth couldn't possibly still see them standing on deck. Her boat was too far away, though it had gone slowly, as if dragging an anchor. But *he* could see which boat was hers, could picture her sitting in it, frightened and shivering with cold. He didn't think he could bear to watch for another minute. And he didn't think it was good for Elizabeth's father to keep watch, either.

"Good idea. Lead the way."

They passed the bandsmen, standing at the entrance to the first-class staircase, on the way. Wearing life jackets over their tuxedos, they had switched from ragtime to quieter strains. A waltz, Max thought, and felt a deep pang of disappointment. It was as if the musicians, like some of the people still on board, had finally lost hope.

As had most of the passengers. Max could tell by the anxious faces, the frightened eyes even in the faces of men he knew to be brave, by the resignation apparent in the way men leaned against the rail, sharply tilted now.

There were a few people who clung stubbornly to denial. As Max and Mr. Farr passed a group of people standing just inside the lounge, a woman complained, "Did you hear Thomas Andrews shouting at the women to get into the two remaining port-side boats? It was positively embarrassing. You'd think the builder of this ship would have more dignity than to be yelling at women in such a common manner. As far as I'm concerned, if we're going to be back on board the ship by breakfast, as one of the crewmen told me, it is just plain silly to go out on the open sea in such bitterly cold weather. Don't you agree, Mattie?"

Although Max didn't hear whether or not Mattie agreed, his heart went out to the two women. We won't be back on board for breakfast or any other meal, he argued mentally. Still he clung to one tiny shred of hope. The ship *was* going down, no doubt about that. But another could still arrive in time to get the remaining passengers off, just as he had told Elizabeth.

Elizabeth . . . was she all right out there on the water? She'd been dressed warmly. But the cold was so harsh, so bitter. He was glad her boat hadn't returned. There probably *was* a danger of being swamped if . . . when . . . the *Titanic* went down.

He felt, suddenly, very angry. Angry at the White Star Line, angry at the ship's captain, angry at the iceberg that had struck them, and especially angry at the great ship, *Titanic*, for not being unsinkable as everyone had said it was. He knew even as he felt the fury within him that he was being unreasonable, even childish, that the anger he felt was simply a way of disguising his very real terror at the thought of the endless dark depths of the ocean awaiting him.

He wanted very much to live.

The thought made his chest feel as if someone were squeezing it with cruel fingers.

On the aft well deck, Brian, his face red with cold, came up behind Katie as she was tying a little girl's bonnet strings. "You'll be needin' to go now, Katie. The ship is listin' intolerably to the bow. Find Paddy and take him with you."

She stood up. "And you? You'll be comin', too?"

He looked away. "Not just yet. Soon, though. There's still some things to be done down here."

"Brian, any of the women who haven't left yet aren't goin' to. They will not leave their husbands, and nothin' you say will be changin' their minds. Come with Paddy and me. Father Byles is here, he'll give comfort to the ones remainin'."

Brian shook his head. "In a bit, I'll be up top. You go along now and find Paddy. But you'll be givin' me a hug first, won't you?"

Katie swallowed hard. Tears stung her eyelids. She didn't believe Brian. He wasn't going to come along soon. He was going to stay with the families who'd refused to leave. "Has Marta gone up top, then?" she asked, realizing she hadn't seen the girl in some time.

"She has. Didn't want to, but her friends persuaded her. Go now, Katie, and tell Paddy I said he's to offer his services as a crewman in one of the boats. That way, he'll be sure and get a place."

Nodding, Katie said quietly, "Aye, I'll do that." Then she threw herself at Brian for the second time that night, and held on for dear life for several moments. What a cruel, bitter night this was! Not trusting herself to utter the word "Good-bye," she said nothing as she pulled away, turned, and rushed off to find Paddy.

He was standing in a corner trying to convince an old woman that she needed to go up to the boat deck. She seemed completely uncomprehending, and Katie realized she didn't speak the language.

"Is she traveling alone?" Katie asked Paddy as she arrived at his side.

"That she is. Give it a try, will you?"

Without saying a word, Katie reached out and took the gnarled old hand in her own. "We're leaving now," she told Paddy, "and we'll just take her with us. Brian says to get up on deck. You're to offer your services as a crewman. He says that way you'll be sure to get a place in the boats."

Paddy planted his feet firmly on the decking. "And where is he, might I ask? You can't think I'm goin' without me brother."

"That surely is what I think," Katie replied hotly. "Brian's the older of you two, and he's given the order. You're to do what he says, and you're to do it now! Unless," she added in desperation, "you want to go over there and make him feel guilty for not comin'. You could always do that, I suppose, if it'd make you feel better.

It'll make him feel worse, of course, but maybe you don't care. Anyways, you're not goin' to change his mind. I tried. He's stayin'."

When Paddy still didn't move, she took his hand and pulled him along, tugging hard until he finally relented and came willingly. A few other women and children joined them as they left the aft well deck.

But when they reached the gate leading to second class, the crewman told them Paddy couldn't come through.

Katie was prepared for that. "Ah, but he's a seaman," she said confidently. "I heard there was need of good crewmen for the boats. Best to let him through."

The man, too disheartened to argue, nodded and let Paddy pass.

When they were out of earshot, he bent his head to Katie's and said, "A seaman? Are you not stretchin' the truth just a bit? I tried me hand at fishin', is all it was. And I wasn't good at it."

"Never mind." Katie helped the old woman up a step. "You're strong, healthy, and smart. You'll be a big help, I know you will."

They arrived on the promenade deck to find a group of women and children gathered at a window, and a boat hanging just beyond the sill. The window was open, and crew members were pulling the boat closer to erase any danger of a gap as people began to board through the window.

Katie was surprised to hear someone say it was nearly two o'clock in the morning. She'd been too busy to pay attention to time passing, but it seemed to her only moments ago when Brian had found her looking down upon the aft well deck. More than an hour had passed since then.

It seemed strange to be boarding a boat through a window. But Katie heard one woman tell another that there were almost no boats left, and if they didn't board this one, they might not get off the ship at all.

The thought of going down with the ship took Katie's breath away. Down, down, into that bottomless black pit? No, she couldn't! She couldn't die that way. No way of dyin' was good, but drownin' had to be one of the worst.

She was so terrified, she had to swallow hard to keep from vomiting up her dinner.

And she was not at all prepared when one of the officers helping the women board pushed Paddy back, saying, "Sorry, women and children only."

Katie gasped in horror. But she recovered quickly out of desperation. "He's got sea experience," she said hastily. "He can help with the boat."

But Paddy was shaking his head at her. "I

can't do this," he whispered in her ear. "I'm not takin' a seat that rightfully belongs to a woman or her child. I'm no seaman, and I'm no coward, neither." He pushed her forward. "You go on, though."

Shocked to the core, Katie begged and pleaded, fighting tears. When she had first learned they might have to leave the ship, she had never for a moment expected to leave it without Brian and Paddy at her side. Then, though she hadn't wanted to, she'd had to accept that Brian wasn't willing to leave. But now Paddy, too, had to stay behind? How could she bear to go without him? No, no, she couldn't. Never!

But she couldn't change his mind, and he wouldn't hear of her staying with him. "If you don't step into that boat right now, I'll throw you in, I promise you that."

She didn't even have any privacy in which to tell him a proper good-bye.

They managed only a hasty embrace and a quick, unsatisfactory kiss before Katie, trembling so violently with fright that she stumbled twice and nearly fell, was directed through the window and into the boat. Her legs like water, she sank down onto a seat beside the old woman who spoke no English. She looked as fear-stricken as Katie felt, and Katie had no choice but to rouse herself enough to reach out and hold the woman's wrinkled hand in her own. Both hands shook.

Her tears spilled over as lifeboat number four began to lower in a series of unsteady, bone-jarring jerks. Katie was shocked to see the C-deck portholes disappearing beneath the surface. Some of the portholes were open, water gushing through them as if from a giant faucet and into the ship. It saddened her to picture the beautiful furnishings inside lost to a torrent of salt water and seaweed, but more than that, the sight of the rushing water swallowing up the great *Titanic* like a hungry giant made her heart tremble with fear for Brian and Paddy.

When the boat landed, one of the crew shouted up to Second Officer Lightoller on deck that there were not enough seamen to man the boat properly.

"I'm sending Quartermaster Perkis," Lightoller called down, and moments later, the seaman scrambled down the falls. The ship had sunk so low, there was not that great a distance from the promenade to the lifeboat. A moment later, three more men dropped into the boat to help man it.

One of those men was Paddy Kelleher. He landed on his back only a foot from where Katie sat, crying quietly.

When she saw him, she shrieked with joy

and scrambled over to throw her arms around his neck. "They told me to come," he mumbled, though he hugged her back before sitting up. "Didn't even ask if I had sea experience, just told me to jump down here and help. So I did."

Katie was weak with relief and joy. If only Brian could have come with Paddy . . .

Perkis told the crewmen to row toward the *Titanic*'s stern, toward an open gangway. The water their oars dipped into was littered with deck chairs being tossed overboard. Katie wondered if the chairs were meant to be used as floats, or if someone inside hoped to lighten the weight of the great ship. She thought sadly that deck chairs would not do the job.

From inside, they could hear cracking sounds. "'Tis the water sending the furniture smashing about," a woman announced grimly. "That lovely walnut table in our stateroom, with the mother-of-pearl engravings . . . ruined. Such a shame!" Another woman mourned the loss of a grand piano, while still another mentioned being quite taken with the china pattern in the à la carte restaurant and regretted the smashing of it.

And while Katie found it distressing that they were mourning the loss of objects rather than people, she understood that they were in shock. She also understood that their remarks meant they had accepted, as well, the loss of the *Titanic*. They no longer expected it to right itself and be saved. They couldn't bear to think about the people still on board, so they distracted themselves by thinking of objects instead. She didn't blame them.

She thought again, her heart breaking so sharply it seemed she could hear the sound it made, *Brian*.

When they were directly below the stern boat deck, a group of firemen waiting on board either worked their way down the falls and dropped into the lifeboat, or fell into the water. Those who landed in the sea were quickly hauled aboard by the women. The rescued men were shaking violently from exposure to the icy water. Katie thought they looked half dead lying there gray in color and motionless.

As they gave up on the gangway they couldn't locate and pulled away from the tilting, brilliantly lit *Titanic*, Katie said a quiet prayer of thanks that Paddy was safely beside her, then another of mourning for his brother.

Chapter 28

Monday, April 15, 1912

There had been, after all, no steamer approaching the *Titanic* to pick up survivors. This heartbreaking news spread slowly throughout lifeboat number six, stunning all of them. The lights seen from the ship's deck had been nothing more than the glow of the northern lights, the aurora borealis. The realization was a serious blow. They had clung desperately to the belief that help was on the way.

No rescue ship? What would happen to them now, adrift on a blank, black canvas of salt water?

The boat's passengers fell into a depressed silence. There was some subdued weeping, but most were too frozen and too shocked to protest loudly.

Elizabeth felt she couldn't bear the penetrating cold another second. Her feet in the bottom of the boat were already wet in spite of her boots, her toes aching with cold. The fingers on her left hand were too numb to bend. Yet to complain about such things when people were still on board the *Titanic* seemed childish and petulant. Surely she was not so pampered and spoiled that she couldn't deal with this hardship.

She must think of Max. He would want her to be brave, as he had been when he had risked his own life to save those two children. She mustn't disappoint him.

But in her heart, Elizabeth didn't really think she could deal with the pain and horror of what was happening. She felt as if, at any moment, her heart would shatter into a thousand pieces, terror at the darkness and the icy cold and the sense of isolation would render her completely helpless, and the sight of what was happening to the ship would numb her mind so that she could no longer think or feel.

Of what use to her mother would she be then?

The *Titanic*'s lights were still shining brightly. Elizabeth strained her eyes for some sign of Max standing at the rail, but could make out nothing more than shapes.

"If it were really sinking," a woman sitting near the stern declared, "its lights wouldn't still be on, would they? I think we came out here for nothing, and now we're frozen. We'll probably all die of pneumonia."

"That's better than drowning," another woman said caustically.

One of the newlyweds, a young woman with pale blonde hair, cried out, "I want to go back! Please, I don't want to be out here! Let me go back to my husband!"

No one answered her, and after a few moments, she fell to silent, heartbroken weeping.

They could still hear music floating faintly out from the *Titanic*. When, in an effort to elicit a response from her silent mother, Elizabeth asked Nola to identify a waltz, she received in return nothing but silence. Remembering her promise to her father, Elizabeth wondered if he might have been right, after all. Was this terrible night going to shatter her mother forever?

What would save Nola, Elizabeth knew, was the rescue of Martin Farr. She looked again for some sign of a rescue ship, but saw only an empty horizon.

The list of the *Titanic* was becoming more dramatic by the moment.

Elizabeth, heartsick, groaned softly under her breath. How much time did they have left, those people still on board? Her father, and Max, and hundreds of others?

She couldn't bear this. How could she? How could anyone?

"We should go back," she said for a second time. "Closer to the ship. If it really is going down, we should be there to help pick up survivors."

And although Molly Brown and Margaret Martin nodded in agreement, Quartermaster Hichens launched once again into his tirade on the dangers of being swamped. After his first half-dozen words, Elizabeth stopped listening.

On board the *Titanic*, Max, along with Martin Farr, left the lounge and went to the warmer gymnasium. There was a sharp tilt to the deck now, and the atmosphere had changed. There was no longer anyone sitting on the mechanical animals. Instead, as the two men entered, a swarm of people moved toward them, heading for the doors. Those who had until now seemed to be patiently waiting for rescue had apparently decided that rescue might not be forthcoming, and now they pushed toward the open deck talking loudly among themselves.

Max watched them go, wondering how they would react when they realized every last lifeboat had gone.

Fighting against his own very real fear of what was coming, Max turned and followed the

311

crowd out onto the deck. He went to join those gathered at the rail. Some men were shouting at the lifeboats to return to the ship, others were demanding to speak to the captain, sounding as if they believed he could solve their problem.

Max could no longer make out Elizabeth in any of the lifeboats and wasn't sure which one was hers. Turning away from the rail, he strode across the deck. As he passed the entrance to the first-class staircase, a small group of well-dressed men and women emerged. An attractive woman wearing a silver evening gown and a fur stole said nervously as she passed him, "The water is rising quickly inside the ship. We saw it on our way up the stairs. So hard to believe . . ."

There was panic in her voice, and Max suspected that she was one of the passengers who had remained in blissful denial for far too long. Now that she saw with her own eyes the water rising within the ship itself, the truth had sunk in, and she was terrified.

That feeling would worsen when she arrived on deck and discovered that all of the boats but for two collapsibles had already left the ship.

She had realized the truth too late.

Max went down the stairs to A deck, to see the climbing water for himself. And there it was, lapping at the stairs below him. Not very far below him, either. Staring down at the churning whirlpool, Max swallowed hard. It was coming after him, and he had no place to go to escape it.

Swallowing his own panic, he spent a few moments studying the large map where the ship's run had been posted each day. Martin Farr had remarked the day before that they were making excellent time, setting records for the journey.

And what good did that do us? Max thought bitterly as he turned to go back up the stairs, painfully conscious all the while of the sound of water below him.

On the boat deck, he went straight to the starboard rail again. Some, but not all, of the lifeboats had lights. What must the ship, sinking hard at the bow, look like from out there on the water? Did they believe it now, those people in the boats who had protested leaving the ship? Did they finally understand that the great *Titanic*, the unsinkable ship, was actually going under? Or were they still telling themselves that it would somehow be saved?

You're still hoping, a voice inside him said. You can't imagine yourself dying before your twentieth birthday, and you haven't accepted the truth, even with the deck like a slantboard beneath your feet and icy black water slurping its way up the stairwell like a thirsty dragon.

The sight of the flat, black water below him, staring up at him as if to say, I'm waiting patiently, filled Max with terror as icy as he knew the ocean itself had to be. Because no one else on deck was panicking visibly, he fought to control it.

It's just, he told himself silently, calmly, that I would have liked to see my parents once more. He pulled his coat collar up against the cold. We parted on less than pleasant terms. I would have liked the chance to make things right between us. And I wanted to see Elizabeth again.

But of course that wasn't all it was, and Max knew it. The plain truth was, it maddened him that men were still standing silently around him, though their faces were strained and pale, when to him, it seemed they should all have been screaming, "It isn't fair, it just isn't fair! We don't want to go down with this ship! We want to be saved! Someone save us, please!"

Angry tears stung his eyes and he turned away from the rail. He watched for a few moments as crewmen began wrestling to untie the only boat left that Max could see, a collapsible boat with canvas sides lashed to the top of the officer's quarters. It came crashing down, and landed upright. While the men were working at attaching it to the falls of the nearest davit, Captain Smith approached with a megaphone, calling out, "Well, boys, do your best for the women and children, and look out for yourselves."

Suddenly, the bow of the *Titanic* began to plunge swiftly, sending a tremendous wave of water washing aft from the forward end of the boat deck.

Here it is, Max thought, his heart stopping as the terror took over. Oh, god, here it comes! Though he thought he had been prepared, he was stunned by the sheer bulk of the solid wall of water as it swept over the ship. Screams and shouts for help filled the air around Max. All semblance of calm, dignified acceptance of their fate vanished as those still on deck, completely panicking under this horrendous threat, scrambled to find safety.

There was none.

Fighting despair, Max sprang like a cat for the roof of the officers' quarters . . . and made it, clutching at its edges with desperate fingers. Once there, he hung on grimly, his head turned slightly to one side to watch below him.

There was that split second or two when a valiant steward, his eyes on the wall of water coming at him, shouted for someone to cut the forward falls as people scrambled into a collapsible boat. Once seated, several people hastened to obey the steward's order. But they had barely loosened the falls when the solid wall of water slammed into them, scooping them up and yanking them back out of the boat. The collapsible was picked up and carried, slamming against a davit, then drifting into the forward funnel as the bridge disappeared under water. The last Max saw of the boat, it was floating away with only a few occupants remaining inside.

He could do nothing for himself but hold on.

Although Elizabeth's boat, number six, had pulled well away from the ship, Katie and Paddy's boat, number four, was still close enough to hear a steadily increasing roar, like the bellow of a wounded animal, coming from the ship.

She tugged on Paddy's sleeve. "What is that fearful noise?"

"Don't know," he answered, but a man sitting next to him said in halting English, "Things falling now. Ship tilting, big things fall, bump into each other. Piano. Chair. Table. Big things. Dishes, too. Lotsa broken things. Lotsa broken glass. One big mess. Lotsa noise."

Paddy drew in his breath, and Katie knew he was thinking about Brian, still on the ship. He was probably afraid that one of those big, loose objects the man was talking about might have swooped down upon his brother, crushing him, taking away any chance he had of swimming free of the ship.

Though swept by terror herself, she squeezed Paddy's hand in an attempt to comfort him.

The bow of the *Titanic* continued to dive. Still clinging to the roof of the officer's quarters, Max found himself suddenly caught up in an icy cauldron of water. His fingers were torn away by the force of it, and suddenly he realized he was off the ship and into the very sea itself. The water temperature, three degrees below freezing, penetrated instantly, in spite of his heavy coat. He could feel the biting cold in his ears, his nostrils, down his neck and chest. And then he was being pulled down, down, in a swirling whirlpool of water so dark, he might as well have been stricken blind. Sensing that it was hopeless but refusing to allow that to be so . . . not yet . . . not yet . . . Max fought valiantly to swim.

But the tug and pull of the ocean determined to claim him was far stronger than he.

Still, he managed to fight his way to the surface. He had barely gulped in several huge swallows of air when he realized with fresh, numbing despair that his arms and legs were now too frozen to move, to swim, to be of any use to him at all. "Oh, god, no," he groaned as the icy water closed over his head a second time. It dragged him beneath the surface again, his body so limp it might have been a log.

Max Whittaker did not want to die. He did not want to die in a black, graveyard-cold ocean. He meant to fight. He *wanted* to fight. Hadn't that been the reason he had never given up hope on board the ship, because all along he was convinced that he could somehow save himself?

The frigid water of the Atlantic Ocean was a far greater foe than he had expected.

As it dragged his limp, frozen body ever downward, he said a silent good-bye to Elizabeth, wondering as he did so how close her boat might be, and if she could somehow sense that he was near.

He wished she could know that his last thought was of her.

Nola Farr, watching with wide, horrified eyes as the stern of the ailing ship continued to climb higher into the air as if it meant to point out the starry sky to observers, suddenly began sobbing. The sound was heartbreaking, and was quickly joined by other similar sounds, some softer, some more agonized and louder. As for Elizabeth, she was at least relieved to see some show of emotion from her mother. But how horrible, that it had taken this fresh new shock — the sight of the great ship tilting ever higher at one end — to pull Nola out of her near-catatonic state.

Then there came from the *Titanic* a horrendous, crashing sound, as if everything inside the ship had broken free of its moorings and was careening wildly into the sinking bow.

It is happening now, Elizabeth thought numbly. The thing that everyone said could never happen, the thing that no one believed was possible even when we were forced to leave in lifeboats, it is happening now. The *Titanic* is going under before our very eyes.

And her father, and Max, were still on board.

Katie and Paddy watched in horror as the forward funnel of the ship, with the painful sound of ripping metal, suddenly toppled toward the bow. It crashed down into the water, sending out a cloud of sparks and soot. At the same time, it created a huge wave that washed free all of the passengers on a canvas boat in the water, and sent the boat itself sailing off another twenty feet, away from the ship.

Katie, watching aghast, could see people on the *Titanic* clinging desperately to anything solid to prevent being washed overboard. In vain. The deck lay at such a steep angle now, they were beginning to slide off into the water.

Terrified screams mixed with the continuing sounds of crashing objects inside the ship. People fell alone; they fell in groups; they fell in pairs, holding hands.

The ship's lights, shining all this time, went out suddenly. Passengers in the lifeboats, startled by the sudden absence of light, cried out.

The utter darkness changed everything. As long as the ship's lights had been on, a small spark of hope had remained that it might somehow survive. That spark died with the lights.

Still, no one was prepared for the sudden splitting of the ship between two of the giant funnels. The separation was accompanied by a terrible cracking sound that sent Katie's hands up to cover her ears.

As the *Titanic* broke into two sections, the bow slid below the surface, while the stern section seemed to settle back for a moment, almost on an even keel.

The settling back seemed to last a long time. Katie wondered if there were anyone left on board, who might have held on and could now float along on the level section until help arrived. Perhaps Brian?

But then that section, too, began to slide beneath the surface, the split end sinking down, the aft section rising higher and higher until it was almost perpendicular in the water.

Those in the closer lifeboats anticipated the

complete disappearance of the ship. But instead of sinking, the stern remained upright for a minute or two, and someone in Katie's boat said, "There, it's stopped! Didn't I tell you it couldn't sink?"

The words were barely out of the man's mouth before the ship began to plunge again, faster now. As the stern disappeared beneath the water, Katie heard four sharp cracks that sounded as if someone had decided to mark the dark occasion with fireworks.

Then the *Titanic* was gone, leaving in its aftermath only a slight bubbling sound, like that of a warm kettle on the stove.

One of the crewman cried, "Pull for your lives or you'll be sucked under!" Several of the women, and Paddy, grabbed oars and began to row.

As they rowed, the sea around them filled with the desperate shouts and screams of more than one thousand men, women, and children.

There were bloodcurdling sounds no one in the lifeboats would ever forget. To Katie, every other horror of the night paled in comparison to being surrounded by a sea of screams.

Then those horrifying sounds were joined by the agonized cries of women in the lifeboats whose husbands, fathers, and sons had been left behind and were at that moment fighting to survive the sea.

Just when Katie thought she would lose her mind from helplessness, Quartermaster Perkis ordered that they row back to the scene to look for survivors. Theirs was the only boat to do so immediately.

When the cries finally ended, after what seemed like hours, there was nothing. The lifeboats were surrounded now by darkness and silence. Both seemed to intensify the bitter cold.

Elizabeth wept for her father and for Max.

Nola Farr hid her face in her hands and moaned, "Martin, oh, Martin!" Other women wept for their own.

Now, when they rowed, there was nothing to break the flat stillness of the water but twenty scattered lifeboats. The giant *Titanic*, brilliantly lit, shiny and new, sitting atop the sea like a floating castle, was gone.

They were alone.

Chapter 29

Monday, April 15, 1912

Boat number four, in Quartermaster Perkis's charge, rowed back. They pulled five crewmen from the water. The men were shivering and terrified. One gasped that his friend had died in the water. Another, nearly frozen to death, had a bottle of brandy in his pocket. Perkis grabbed it and threw it into the sea.

"That mighta been useful," Paddy protested. "Brandy's a help when people are freezin'."

But the brandy was gone, floating in the sea amid other debris.

The men pulled from the water looked so near death, Katie feared they would not survive. Only one of them was conscious, and without the brandy, there was nothing in the boat with which to warm their frozen bodies.

It was the most horrifying scene Katie had

ever been witness to. The water around them was filled with thrashing swimmers, fighting to reach two of the canvas boats closest to where the ship had disappeared from sight. She could almost feel the frigid water paralyzing their bodies. One of the collapsibles had overturned, but people were climbing aboard. Katie heard warnings of swamping being shouted from one of the boats. Still, the overturned collapsible continued to fill with men standing, sitting, or kneeling. She prayed that Brian might be among them.

When the cries for help ended, Quartermaster Perkis ordered the rowing to resume. But they had made little progress when Fifth Officer Lowe, in lifeboat number fourteen, came upon them with a tiny cluster made up of boats ten, twelve, and collapsible D. He had gathered them all together, believing that a rescue ship would be more likely to see a larger object. Now his goal, he explained, was to empty his boat, distributing the passengers he was carrying among the other boats, and then take his empty boat back to pick up any survivors.

Katie couldn't believe that anyone could still be alive in that water. It had been at least half an hour since the *Titanic* went down, and there were no more cries for help. The passengers they had picked up within minutes were near death. Could someone really survive this long in a sea as cold as the iceberg that had dealt a death blow to the great ship?

But Brian had stayed behind on the *Titanic*, and if there was any chance at all that he might still be alive, she was willing to do whatever it took to find him.

"Are there any seamen here?" Lowe called out as he reached boat number four.

"Yes, sir," a crewman replied. Paddy, too, nodded. Katie could see that he was anxious to help.

"All right, then. You will have to distribute these passengers among these boats. Tie the boats together and then come with me. We're going into the wreckage to pick up anyone who is still alive."

Some people objected, fearing a swamping of one boat or another. The thought terrified Katie, since she couldn't swim. But Lowe persisted. When the exchange, with great difficulty, had been made, he ordered his crewmen to row to the scene of the disaster.

The action forced people in the boat to rouse themselves from their stupefied shock.

"They'll never find a soul alive out there," someone in boat four muttered. "Waste of time, if you ask me."

But Katie reminded herself that Brian was a strong swimmer, and young and healthy. Perhaps he had already climbed aboard one of those collapsible canvas boats. Impossible to see in this pitch-black darkness. But he might have.

It was only then that she realized, to her horror, that Paddy was no longer with her. In the confusion of the transfer, with people awkwardly, carefully climbing from one boat into another, she hadn't even noticed that Paddy was one of the passengers who had left. She knew why he had switched to boat fourteen. Because it was returning to the scene to look for survivors. He wanted to do everything he could to find his brother.

The shock of finding Paddy gone was almost too much for Katie to bear. Although she understood, she felt abandoned. Without him, the numbing cold and the utter darkness seemed far more terrifying. And without Paddy's body heat close beside her, she was quickly frozen to the bone. She couldn't imagine ever being warm again. The life vest protected her chest, but her face felt as if it were coated with a fine sheen of ice. She tried to take comfort in the fact that at least she was safe in a boat and not in the water like so many others, and the thought helped some. If it was this cold in a boat, what must it be like to be in the ocean, your body soaked to the skin and freezing? How could anyone survive that?

One of the lifeboats sent up a green flare

from time to time. When the first one went up, Katie thought it was a ship approaching. Through frozen lips, she said so aloud. A crewman said it was no such thing, dashing her hopes.

The act of rearranging the passengers had stirred some people into speech. The atmosphere in the boat ranged from optimistic about the chance of rescue to pessimistic. Some said the sea would be full of ships by morning, others said it could be days before help arrived. One woman said she could never take the bitter cold for that long and would rather be dead, and was promptly scolded for expressing such a dark thought.

But it was a thought that was on most of the despairing, frightened minds.

In boat six, Elizabeth's mother had stopped crying. But she had sunk once again into her silent depression, her head on her chest, her eyes closed to everything around her. Elizabeth felt totally alone. Everyone was in shock. Some women had lost both a husband and a son. Lives had been shattered as well as ended. And those who had lost no one were frightened half out of their minds by the vast, black sea around them, the bitter cold, and the sense of isolation they were all feeling.

Then there was Quartermaster Hichens,

who did nothing to inspire hope. Instead, he seemed determined to undermine the confidence of everyone at the oars. "Here, you on the starboard side," he yelled at Lookout Frederick Fleet, "your oar is not being put in the water at the right angle." And when the women tried to persuade him to help row, he refused, saying he was in command and would be giving the orders.

His negative attitude incensed Elizabeth. He was in charge. Shouldn't he be trying to lift their spirits, keep them going? Instead, he railed that they were likely to be at sea for days. He complained that they were hundreds of miles from land, they had no food, no water, no protection from the elements. He said everything that they didn't need to hear, and nothing that they did.

When he noticed that one of the ladies held a flask, he asked for a drink and for one of her wraps. While she passed him an extra blanket, she refused him the liquor, and a woman sitting beside her murmured, "Maybe you should give it to him. It might improve his disposition."

At some point during the night, another boat, number sixteen, drew near, and the two were lashed together. But they knocked against one another, creating a racket that got on everyone's nerves, until Major Peuchen suggested they pillow the sound with a couple of life preservers. That done, silence reigned again and everyone settled in to wait until morning. Some anticipated rescue. Others, like Elizabeth's mother, anticipated nothing.

When she had made certain that neither her father nor Max was in boat sixteen, and had dealt as best she could with her bitter disappointment, Elizabeth tried to sleep. Morning, when it came, could bring great difficulty, and she would need rest to get through the day. But sleep wouldn't come. Images of utter horror played over and over again in her mind. Her father, struggling in the icy sea, freezing to death . . . Max, doing the same . . . all those people, being torn off the deck and plunged into the deep, icy, dark water. . . . She could scarcely bear to think about it. Just a few hours earlier, they had all felt safe and protected and warm and secure. No one had dreamed this terrible thing could ever happen. Now that it had, nothing in their lives would ever be the same again.

Needing to face the truth, she told herself, My father can't swim. He is dead. I will never see him or talk to him again. When that brought no reaction beyond a dull pain, she tested further. Max, too, is dead. I was just beginning to fall in love with him, and now he's gone. Still she felt nothing. It was as if the frigid air had frozen not only her limbs and face, but her emotions as well.

She sat up and glanced around her. No one was weeping, no one was screaming, no one was tearing at her hair or clothes. The faces of those who were still awake all wore the same blank expression. We must look like a boat filled with china dolls, Elizabeth thought, a wave of sadness overwhelming her. Identical blank expressions painted on each face, as if there were nothing inside.

Still, she knew why no one was willing to feel anything. Because if we did, she told herself as she settled back into her seat, if we really let ourselves feel, we would start screaming and we would never be able to stop.

"Oh, no," Margaret Martin cried out suddenly. "I just saw a flash of lightning!"

Elizabeth realized why that alarmed the woman. Just as Hichens had said, they had no protection from the elements. If a storm should come up, they would all become soaked within seconds, and with the temperature so low, they would freeze instantly in wet clothes. And they had no way of bailing out any rainwater that collected in their boat. Too much of it would sink them.

She realized just as quickly that it was much too cold and the sky too clear for an electrical storm. The light that Margaret had seen couldn't be lightning. It had to be something else. Perhaps a shooting star.

As if she had spoken aloud, Quartermaster Hichens said, "That's a falling star, not lightning."

Then a slight boom sounded in the distance, and Margaret said, "There, did you hear that? Thunder, I warrant."

Hichens disagreed again, but could come up with no theory as to what the sound might have been.

Elizabeth, suddenly exhausted, leaned back against the gunwale, closing her eyes. She didn't care what happened, she decided. What difference did it make now? Everything was ruined, anyway. Her mother was right to give up.

Max's voice sounded in her head: "Cut it out, Elizabeth. If you want to be that dramatic, go on the stage, like Lily. Otherwise, sit up and pay attention and do anything you can to save yourself. Don't disappoint me."

Angry that he had the nerve to tell her what to do, Elizabeth sat bolt upright, her eyes flying open.

The first thing she saw was a light on the horizon. Then she saw another, and moments after that a green running light.

"It's a steamer!" Major Peuchen shouted. "Look, there, all of you, it's a steamer, and it's heading this way!"

A rocket shot up into the air over the oncoming ship. As a second rocket went up, the steamer seemed to slow in the water. Elizabeth held her breath. Perhaps it didn't see them. How visible could the boats sitting low in the water be from such a distance? If the steamer didn't see them, it would sail away, taking every last ounce of hope with it.

At the same moment, she realized with a shock that the stars overhead were slowly fading, and a faint buttery glow was appearing off to the east. Dawn. She glanced down at the watch still hanging around her neck. It wasn't five A.M. yet. Morning dawned early in the frozen north.

Now she could see the outline of the approaching ship, one dark funnel spitting smoke into the air. Smaller by far than the great *Titanic*, but far more beautiful, as well, because it promised rescue.

The sea was dotted with huge icebergs, shining pink and white under the rising sun, like giant chunks of peppermint candy. Elizabeth suddenly feared for the oncoming ship. Suppose it hit one and met the same fate as the larger, sturdier *Titanic*?

Careful, she silently warned the captain of the unidentified ship, *careful . . .*

Everyone in boats number six and sixteen, still lashed together, sat upright, eyes and ears alert.

"Has it come to rescue us, then?" someone asked Hichens.

"No," he answered. "She is not going to pick us up. She's only here to pick up bodies."

Elizabeth found that answer not only ridiculous, but macabre as well. As if any ship's captain would pick up only the dead and abandon the living! Surely no one in the boats believed that.

If she had had in her possession a large piece of tape, she would have fastened it over the quartermaster's mouth.

She needn't have worried. None of the women in the boat had any intention of allowing their pessimistic leader to keep them from rescue. A man in boat sixteen was wearing nothing but pajamas. He was so cold, his teeth were chattering, and although Hichens had ordered them to drift, Mrs. Brown now told the man to start rowing in order to keep warm. She ignored the quartermaster's protest as she gave the order.

Other women in the boat took up her cry, demanding that they, too, be allowed to row to keep warm.

A stoker, still covered with the coal dust from working on board the *Titanic*, manned an oar on the starboard side. He was shaking with cold. Mrs. Brown scooped up a fat, brown sable stole lying in the bottom of the boat and wrapped it around his legs, fastening it around his ankles. Then she directed the man wearing pajamas to cut the two boats apart.

Hichens, furious, shouted a protest, and made a move to stop her.

"I will throw you overboard if you interfere," she told him with great authority. Other women nodded in agreement.

Hichens had no choice. He gave in to the mutiny. He sank back under his blanket as the boats were pulled apart, but he began shouting insults at the Denver millionairess who had thwarted him.

"I say," the stoker called out, "is that any way to talk to a lady?"

Undaunted, Hichens retorted, "I know who I'm speaking to, and I am commanding this boat!"

No one believed that for a second now, and the women continued to row.

As the sun rose higher in the sky, lifeboat number six, manned almost solely by women, made its way slowly toward the steamer on the horizon.

Chapter 30

When Katie saw the steamer making its way toward them, she thought at first that she was seeing things. Hadn't they thought when they left the *Titanic* that a steamer was off to the east, waiting to rescue them? And there had been no ship there at all.

But others had spotted the oncoming ship, as well. Some accepted the idea of rescue eagerly. Others were more cautious, fearing disappointment. But as the steamer drew closer, everyone accepted that rescue was at hand.

We're goin' to get out of this, Katie told herself in astonishment. We are. Paddy was safe in the other lifeboat and they would meet on board the rescue ship. She could only hope and pray that Brian would be in another lifeboat as well.

Please, please, she prayed as they rowed for the ship, please let Brian be alive!

Soon they were close enough to read the name of the vessel that was about to pluck them from the cold, dark sea. *Carpathia*. Not as large or as grand as the *Titanic*, but to those in the lifeboats, it was a golden chariot.

As they approached the ship, Katie could see people standing at the rail, peering down in curiosity. Had they heard that it was the great ship *Titanic* that had sunk? They wouldn't have believed it, of course. But here was the proof, coming straight at them in a raggedy group of lifeboats.

Getting on board was not an easy thing. There were ladders and netting hanging from the *Carpathia's* side. The able-bodied boarded in that fashion. But others were unable to negotiate the ladder. To aid them, ropes were lowered and slung under arms or tied around waists, so that those who had no energy to climb could be hoisted upward. Canvas slings were used for some of the children. Boarding was quiet and orderly, though some people, either still in shock or terrified they would fall into the ocean, had to be urged on by those climbing before and after them.

When Katie reached the top of the ladder, she turned to glance behind her one last time. The more heavily loaded lifeboats were still struggling at a snail's pace toward the ship. She told herself Brian could be in any one of those boats. He had to be, for Paddy's sake as well as her own.

Instead of being rushed inside to warmth by passengers and stewardesses on the *Carpathia*, Katie remained at the rail, waiting for Paddy. She was white-faced and shivering with cold, but she was so terrified that she would miss his arrival, she refused to budge.

When she saw him, far below in lifeboat fourteen, her face was so frozen she was unable to form a smile. But she waved and called his name, and was waiting for him at the top of the ladder with outstretched arms.

When they were both safely on board, they embraced warmly, not caring who saw them. They had survived the long, terrible night. They were safe at last. And they were together.

Now all they had to do was find Brian among the survivors.

Though they were frozen through, they decided to wait where they were until every lifeboat had disembarked its passengers. If Brian wasn't among them, they would explore every inch of the *Carpathia*, hoping he had been picked up earlier.

A stewardess arrived with blankets and a tray of hot cups of cocoa. Katie accepted the blanket and a cup of cocoa, as did Paddy. Thus warmed, they stood at the rail, watching with others as the occupants of one lifeboat after another boarded. Eileen arrived, refusing to speak to Katie, although Bridey and Kevin gave her hugs and said they would see her later as they were rushed inside by two older women passengers on the *Carpathia*.

Katie watched as boat number six arrived and the pretty girl climbed aboard, her mother right behind her. The good-looking young man she'd said good-bye to on the *Titanic*, the man who had saved Bridey and Kevin, wasn't with her, and Katie hadn't noticed him climbing aboard at any other time. But then, she'd been watching for Brian. She hoped he had survived.

When the last lifeboat, a severely overloaded number twelve, arrived at the *Carpathia's* side, there had still been no sign of Brian Kelleher.

Katie's hopes rose when she saw how full boat twelve was. Brian might be in this one. The boat was so crowded, the gunwales were precariously close to the sea, and the water was becoming choppy, tossing waves of icy water over legs and feet.

"There's more than seventy people on board that one," Paddy commented, "and that's not counting the wee ones."

Katie nodded, but she was busy searching

fiercely for a tall, dark-haired young man in a worn gray jacket. There were so many faces in the boat, she couldn't sort them all out. But she couldn't say yet that Brian's wasn't among them.

A surging wave broke across the lifeboat, then a second.

"It's goin' to founder," Paddy said darkly. "They'd best get them people on board now!"

But moments later, the lifeboat rode out a third wave and then was in the shelter of the ship, bobbing like a cork on the sea as it unloaded its cargo.

When the last passenger had climbed on board, many of the survivors gathered at the rail, their eyes searching the choppy sea for some sign of husbands and sons who might still be alive in the water. Katie heard a woman say plaintively, "But he was a strong swimmer, my boy, he won medals, he was a strong swimmer!" Another woman cried, "George wouldn't have given up, he wouldn't! My George was a fighter!"

But as the ship circled the waters and no more swimmers were discovered, those watching from the rail fell silent. And when the *Carpathia* began slowly to pull away from the scene, the truth sank in. A morose silence fell. Then it was broken by heart-wrenching sobs as the women who were now widows accepted the terrible truth. They were led inside to be comforted and cared for.

The look on Paddy's face was one of utter desolation.

Katie refused to give up. "Bri could have come on board with the first survivors," she said. "We must search the ship. He could be here somewhere."

And though Paddy's expression didn't change, he nodded and followed as Katie marched along the deck in search of Brian.

Nola Farr almost didn't make it up the ladder. Exhausted and despondent, her hands numb, she hadn't the energy to climb. Elizabeth, directly behind her, shouted encouragement, urging her mother onward. But Nola had to be virtually hoisted upward by the crew on board the *Carpathia*. Once on deck, she sank quietly to her knees, weeping softly. It fell to Elizabeth to get her mother up and inside where it was warm, which she did quickly, though she herself was exhausted and frozen. Two women from the rescue ship hurried over to help her, murmuring, "Poor thing, poor thing," as they assisted the distraught woman to her feet.

"She'll be all right," Elizabeth insisted, though she was grateful for the help. "She'll be fine. She's very strong." And hoped that it was true.

With her mother ensconced in a deck chair inside where it was warm, a woolen blanket wrapped around her, Elizabeth wanted nothing more than to lie down somewhere and close her eyes. She ached almost as much for sleep as she did for warmth. But how could she give herself over to sleep? What kind of nightmarish visions would rush into her mind then?

Would she ever be able to sleep again without hearing those terrible screams?

She had never even asked Max if he knew how to swim.

Instead of sleeping, she spent the next hour wandering the decks and the public rooms, checking each pallet, mattress, and cot that held a survivor. She knew in her heart it was hopeless. But she also knew she would never be able to rest until she was absolutely certain that her father and Max hadn't survived.

She found Lily, white of face and sound asleep on a cot, a gray wool blanket covering her to her chin. But Elizabeth did not find Arthur.

Nor did she find her father or Max.

Fighting tears, Elizabeth returned to the public room. Unable to sleep, she sat huddled in a chair beside her mother's, trying to warm herself beneath a gray wool blanket. Every time she closed her eyes, she pictured Max or her father struggling in the frigid, dark water, and her throat closed and she couldn't breathe, and her eyes filled with fresh tears. She finally gave up trying to sleep and sat staring straight ahead, watching the *Carpathia*'s passengers attempting to comfort the survivors lying on cots or mattresses or reclining in deck chairs.

It struck her as odd that there was so little crying. What there was, was quiet. It was as if none of the grief-stricken wanted to disturb anyone. Or perhaps they were still in shock.

After a while, a woman approached to tell Elizabeth and her mother that two religious services were going to be held. "One," she said quietly, "will be a short prayer of thanksgiving for the seven hundred people rescued, while the other," her tone deepening, "will of course be a funeral service for the fifteen hundred who perished. You are both welcome to attend." Then she went on her way, spreading the word to other survivors.

Elizabeth swayed in her chair, clutching its wooden arm for support. Fifteen hundred? Fifteen *hundred* people had died in this one night? How was that possible? So many lives lost, so many families torn apart, so many hearts broken . . . all in one long, terrible, frigid night.

If that many had died, it was impossible to think that Max might have survived.

Elizabeth covered her face with her hands. Hadn't she known all along? Hadn't she given up, in truth, when the *Titanic* sank and she saw all those people being torn from the rail and tossed into the icy sea like rag dolls? Hadn't she known then that Max couldn't possibly have survived? Fifteen hundred people had been lost. She'd been a fool to think that he might have made it just because she needed him to. Hadn't the other women thought the same thing of their husbands and sons? And now they knew better. Now they had accepted the truth. She would have to do the same.

But it hurt so terribly.

Elizabeth leaned her head back and closed her eyes again, oblivious to the activity taking place around her. Women were being comforted by the *Carpathia*'s passengers, who seemed so willing to help. Stewards and stewardesses were moving about, warm blankets in their arms, cups of hot liquid in their hands, seeing to the ill, the exhausted, the frozen. Children unaware of the depth of the tragedy played quietly, darting curious glances now and again toward their grieving mothers, who were comforting each other. Survivors who refused to give up hope walked among other survivors, peering down into faces, searching for a husband or son lost to the sea.

But Elizabeth was lost in her own misery. What was going to happen to them? Without her father, would they still be a family? Would her mother ever recover from this terrible shock?

Even as Elizabeth thought this, Nola roused herself. She sat up, glanced around as if suddenly becoming aware of her surroundings, and noticed Elizabeth sitting off to her left. With great effort, Elizabeth's mother tossed aside the blanket wrapped around her and got to her feet. She was at Elizabeth's side in seconds, kneeling beside the chair, putting her arms around her daughter. She didn't say that much. She said only, "I am truly sorry about Max, Elizabeth. I am. But it will be all right, it will, I promise you." But that was almost enough. Elizabeth put her head on her mother's shoulder, and without tears, they clung to each other for several moments.

Then Nola raised her head and said in a voice only slightly shaken, "Now, I believe we might both feel better if we attend a service. But first" — in a normal voice now — "we must both do something with our hair. I'm sure we look a fright!"

They did the best they could, without benefit of comb or brush. Even Nola seemed to realize finally that how they looked mattered little in view of the circumstances. Still, she walked to the services with her head high and her shoulders back, as if her appearance were as impeccable as ever.

The service did help. Elizabeth said a silent good-bye to her father, though she knew he would always be with her in some way. She said another to Max, feeling a fierce pain of regret that they had had so little time, and that she had spent so much of that time arguing with him.

If her mother had broken down during the service, Elizabeth would have, too. But Nola kept her head high, held her daughter's hand tightly in her own, and any tears she shed were quiet ones. Elizabeth saw men with tears streaming down their faces, too, and wished fiercely that her father were among them.

When the service was over, Elizabeth's mother said in an exhausted voice, "I must go send a Marconigram to your grandparents, to prepare them. I doubt that word of the sinking has reached New York yet, but if it has, they mustn't receive word of their son's death from the newspapers. You go and rest. I'll be right back. Then I believe I shall find a cot to lie down on. I seem to be feeling quite tired."

Elizabeth was looking for an available cot or mattress for her mother in one of the public rooms when she spotted the red-haired girl who had boarded at Queenstown. She was in the company of one of the two young men who had arrived in separate tenders that day. The younger brother, Elizabeth decided. Where was the older one? Remembering how the Irish girl had insisted the two young children be put into a lifeboat and how it was Max who had done that for her brought tears to Elizabeth's eyes.

The two wore anxious expressions on their faces, and were moving from one survivor wrapped in blankets to another, bending down. Clearly, they were looking for someone.

I hope you find whoever it is, Elizabeth telegraphed silently to the pair as she sank gratefully into a vacant deck chair parked in front of a huge potted plant in the large, crowded public room. Perhaps they were looking for the boy's older brother. So many families had been shattered when the *Titanic* floundered. Including the Farr family.

She laid her head back and closed her eyes again, thinking that all she could ask for now was that her mother would be all right. She didn't even care if they fought constantly, without her father there to act as a buffer. What did it matter? They were alive. If there was one thing she had learned during the terrible night just passed, it was that life was too precarious to take for granted. She never would again. And it was too precarious for her to waste a moment doing what others expected of her, if what they expected was intolerable to her. Like marriage to a man she didn't love.

Had this night changed her mother as well? Possibly not. Once Nola had recovered from the shock, she might very well be as she had always been. In which case, there would be battles. It didn't matter. They would work something out, she and her mother. They were alive. That was all that counted.

At any rate, she couldn't think about the future now. It was all she could do to deal with the terrible present.

Her mother returned, her face strained, her eyes sad. She settled gratefully on the cot that Elizabeth had found for her and when Elizabeth had covered her with a blanket, she closed her eyes. Before she fell into a deep sleep, she said in a voice husky with grief and fatigue, "You'll be happy to know I thanked that Mrs. Brown. Heaven knows what would have become of us without her. Perhaps I judged her too harshly. And Madeleine Astor survived. That is good news, for her and for the baby she's carrying. They have taken her to the hospital." Nola fell silent then, and in only moments she seemed to be in a deep sleep.

She didn't notice, then, that Elizabeth had

sat bolt upright at the word "hospital." Hospital? It hadn't occurred to her that some of the survivors might be there. Of course they would. Frostbite alone would have sent some there, and there could be all kinds of injuries suffered by someone thrown from the deck of the *Titanic* into the open sea.

Don't do this, Elizabeth, a cautious voice inside her warned. *I know what you're thinking, and you're being foolish. You're just setting yourself up for more heartbreak.*

She didn't even know if Max could swim.

She stopped a passing stewardess. "Excuse me, miss, but could you tell me where the hospital on board is located?"

"Of course, miss." The directions were precise.

All the way there, Elizabeth argued with herself. Her head told her she was wasting time when she could have been sleeping off her exhaustion, while her heart told her that she wouldn't be able to sleep, anyway, until she knew the awful truth for certain. Her head cautioned, *Elizabeth, don't you think that every other woman who survived the* Titanic *is feeling as you are? You don't see them running all over the ship chasing false hope, do you?* Her heart replied, You may be right. But I'm doing what I want from now on, and this is what I want.

She was almost there when she saw him. He appeared first as no more than a figure, unrecognizable at such a distance. He was walking unsteadily toward her in an empty corridor, the last she had to pass through to arrive at the hospital.

Even as the distance between them closed, she still didn't recognize him. He wasn't wearing his long black overcoat, but a heavy gray sweater and a pair of black steward's pants. His hair was wet and slicked back, away from his finely chiseled face. And there was none of the usual jauntiness to his steps as he slowly, painfully, made his way up the corridor, his right palm trailing along the white-painted wall as if to help him maintain his balance.

Elizabeth, walking almost as shakily as he, paused in midstep. Seeing her approaching, he stopped, too. And what she recognized then, in spite of the way he looked, what made her catch her breath and raise a hand to her lips, was the way he regarded her steadily, his eyes on her face, just as he had that very first day when he boarded the *Titanic* at Cherbourg.

"*Max?*" she whispered.

He held out a hand to her.

She ran, her exhaustion gone, her feet flying along the carpeted hallway.

When she was within a foot of where he stood, she stopped short again. He stopped, too. He looked ghastly. His handsome face was gray and drawn, his eyes scarlet-rimmed, his body trembling with cold. Elizabeth, her own eyes brimming with tears, was afraid that if she threw herself at him as every fiber of her being willed her to, she might somehow injure him.

His voice when he spoke was so hoarse, she would never have recognized it as his. A fleeting image of the horrors he must have endured to arrive on this ship flew through her mind, and her tears spilled over, sliding quietly down her cheeks.

Tears appeared in his eyes, as well. "I wonder," he said huskily, letting go of the wall, "if you would be kind enough to direct me to steerage?"

Elizabeth laughed and ran into his waiting arms.

Chapter 31

Monday, April 15, 1912

"I was just on my way to look for you," Max said when he finally lifted his head. "I meant to as soon as I got on board. But I must have passed out when I hit the deck, because the next thing I knew, I was lying on a table in a big white room and a fellow in a white coat was telling me to open my mouth so he could look down my throat."

She wasn't surprised that he'd been taken immediately to the hospital, given the way he looked. And he must have looked much worse when they first brought him aboard.

She didn't want to let go of him. It would hurt too much to let go, after finding him again. "I thought —" she began, but he interrupted her.

"I know what you thought. I thought it, too, when I was being pulled down into that water."

They separated then, and Max put an arm around her shoulders and a palm on the opposite wall again as they began walking. They went very slowly. "I knew I was a goner. Couldn't quite face that, so I tried to come up with some other option. But when I kicked my way back to the surface, all of the lifeboats were out of range. I had a life vest on . . . that helped . . . but my coat was drenched and felt like it weighed a ton. I figured it wasn't going to keep me warm anymore and it was dragging me down, so I thought about ditching it. But that meant getting the vest off first." He shook his head. He was leaning heavily on Elizabeth, and his breathing as they walked seemed labored. "The thought of taking off the vest scared me to death, because even though the sea was pretty calm, I was afraid I'd lose hold of the straps and the thing would float away. Without it, I had no chance at all." He smiled ruefully. "Didn't have that much of a chance *with* it."

"But you're *here*," Elizabeth said. She could scarcely believe it herself. But the weight of his arm on her shoulders was proof.

"Almost wasn't. I was dragged down twice. Fought my way back up, but it was so cold, I knew I couldn't keep doing that. I figured if I went down a third time, I'd never see blue sky again."

Elizabeth could see that it pained Max to talk, but she needed to know how he had survived. "But you're here," she said for the second time.

He nodded. "I wouldn't be, if it hadn't been for my lifesaver. Came along just in time."

"Lifesaver? What lifesaver?"

Max grinned down at her. "A man so fortified by liquor that he was swimming like a fish, and said he was as warm as toast. Told me to grab onto his life vest and he'd get us to a boat. And that's what he did. I think it was boat number three. Or it could have been five. Hardly anybody in it, so after arguing a bit about the dangers of being swamped by our weight, they pulled us in. I must have looked like a drowned rat. But the other guy, Ralph something, looked like he'd just taken a healthy dip in a pool. The guy was laughing when he landed in the bottom of the boat, like it was all a big joke. Said he knew he was going to have one heck of a hangover later, but it was worth it."

He could barely make it up the stairs to the upper decks. Elizabeth had to help him, and he clung to the railing as they went as he must have clung to the man's life vest straps. Picturing what he must have gone through, Elizabeth shuddered again. But he was alive. He was alive, and he was here, with her.

"Max," she said as they reached the public

room where Elizabeth's mother still lay fast asleep, "I never did check in the hospital. My father . . . ?"

He shook his head sorrowfully. "He's not there, Elizabeth. I'm sorry. I don't know about anyone else. Have you seen Arthur or Lily?"

"I found Lily. But not Arthur."

Max sighed and sank into an empty deck chair. "They'll be putting out a list of survivors soon. I hope Arthur is on it, but I'm not very optimistic." He glanced up at Elizabeth with heavy-lidded eyes. "How many died?"

She told him, and his face went even grayer. "My god. That many!"

"Don't think about it. I'm trying not to. I'm just so happy that you're here." She knelt beside his chair. "I still can't believe it."

"Believe it." He took her hand. His was cold and clammy, but Elizabeth didn't pull away. "Let's just hope you remember the next time you feel like arguing with me, how glad you were to see me."

A stewardess passed by with a tray of cups, and Elizabeth reached out and took one. It was hot, and she handed it to Max, who accepted it gratefully. He sipped silently, his eyelids drooping with fatigue. When the cup was empty, he lay back against the chair. Elizabeth covered him with a blanket, and kept her eyes on his face until he had fallen asleep. Then she sat down on the floor beside him, content to simply rest there, watching him sleep and trying to take in the fact that he was actually there beside her.

The young Irish couple Elizabeth had seen earlier hurried along the deck, their faces still filled with anxiety. Whoever it was they were looking for, it was clear they hadn't found that person. They hadn't been as lucky as Elizabeth. Her heart went out to them.

Unwilling to take her eyes off Max, it was a long time before she slept.

Katie and Paddy finally had no choice. They had to give up their search for Brian. They had looked everywhere on the *Carpathia*. Though they had come across more than one drenched, pallid-faced young man lying on a pallet, most of them had been crewmen, and none of them had been Paddy's brother.

Paddy's own face had lost its usual ruddy hue by the time their search ended. "What'll I tell me ma and da?" he asked Katie as, tired and sad, they made their way to the *Carpathia*'s lounge. "Me da was partial to Bri, you know. This'll break his heart."

Katie knew Paddy's father. If he was "partial" to any one of his children, it was his younger son, not the older one. "No, it won't. Their hearts will be broken, you're right about that. But they still have you. There was people on board the *Titanic* who lost everyone, Paddy, their whole families. If your ma and da hear the news before you get a message to them, they'll think you've been lost, too. You must get word to them, and to mine, that *we* are alive. Spare them whatever heartache you can."

When he had left her in the hands of a kind stewardess, he went to see about sending his parents and Katie's a Marconigram. When he returned, Katie was lying on a steamer rug on the floor, her arms folded beneath her head, her eyes closed. She was sound asleep, her body limp with exhaustion, her face peaceful. The women surrounding her were either lost in sleep or in grief, and the public room was filled with a somber silence.

Paddy stood over Katie, gazing down at her. In spite of his sadness over his brother's loss, he knew that he was luckier than most of the people around him, all in various stages of shock and grief. Brian was gone, gone forever, and that was something he could hardly bear. But he still had Katie, a girl whose heart and soul were as fair as her face. She would help him through the worst of it. He hadn't lost everything. That was more than some who'd been on board the *Titanic* could say.

With one last glance at Katie, Paddy went to seek out a place to rest his own weary head.

Chapter 32

Tuesday–Thursday, April 16–18, 1912

Gradually over the next two days, Paddy and Katie located everyone on the *Carpathia* who had been in third class on the *Titanic*. The numbers were pathetically low. Whole families had been lost in the tragedy. Katie wept at the thought of the terrified children who had been swept into the black and icy Atlantic Ocean. Marta had survived. She, too, wept, when Paddy confirmed that Brian had not been as lucky.

It was Marta who convinced Paddy that he should accept Katie's invitation to join her at her uncle Malachy's in Brooklyn, at least for a while, until he felt at home in the great city. "Your brother would want that, ja?" she said, leaning forward to peer into Paddy's face with huge blue eyes. "He talked much about you,

357

you know. He was so proud, saying to me that you would one day be a fine writer. But he said that you would need help and he was worried that your Irish pride, that was what he called it, would keep you from accepting any help. If Katie's uncle is willing to give you a hand, you should take it, Paddy. For Brian's sake."

He finally agreed, but he told Katie later that it was only because he would be able to "keep an eye on her" that much more easily. "You'll be needin' someone to look after you in America," he said, "and if I'm livin' in the city and you're all the way out there in Brooklyn, how will I know that you're bein' taken care of?"

Katie nodded and smiled. She was thinking how amazing it would be, having Paddy right there in her uncle's house while she struggled to make a home for herself on the New York stage and he worked at becoming a famous writer. They could help each other. He could cheer her up when the hard knocks came along, as they surely would, and she could do the same for him, when every word Paddy had ever known flew right out of his skull, leaving his mind as blank as a new slate.

Together, they could do anything.

After all, hadn't they both survived the greatest of all sea tragedies? Wasn't that what everyone on board was beginning to call the sinking of the *Titanic*?

If they could survive that, they could survive anything life tossed their way.

Together.

Arthur's name was not on the list of survivors from the *Titanic*. Elizabeth noticed sadly that much of the light had gone from Lily's eyes when they first met up with her. But then, there were so many sad eyes on the *Carpathia*.

Elizabeth slept restlessly throughout the rest of the trip, half lying, half sitting in a deck chair next to her mother. Max had developed a serious cough, and she had persuaded him to spend his nights in the infirmary, away from the chill that filled the *Carpathia*, the result of a deep, damp fog surrounding the ship.

With the dawn of Tuesday came the full, painful awareness of all that had happened. As she made her way to the infirmary, Elizabeth saw dozens of women clustered together in the dining rooms, still wearing the bizarre assortment of clothing in which they'd left the *Titanic*. Most were weeping. Some were asking other women whose children were at their side, "How is it that you all managed to get to safety?" The question had a bitter edge to it.

As Elizabeth passed one room, she heard a woman wail, "Had I known there would be no lifeboat for my Andrew, I never would have left. We were married forty-seven years. I would rather have gone down with him than survived alone."

Later, on deck with Max, who couldn't seem to get enough fresh air, she heard some of the widows approaching men who had survived and asking them angrily, "How did you get into a boat when my husband did not?"

Those who had suffered most severely in the lifeboats, mainly on the collapsibles, had little patience with those who had arrived in lifeboats and were complaining of inconveniences as minor as the crewmen who'd been smoking, or blistered hands from rowing. One of the men who had undergone great hardships on a canvas boat whose sides had collapsed, leaving its passengers standing or kneeling in frigid seawater, finally cried out in exasperation, "Oh, stop your whining! You don't realize how good you had it! And you're alive, aren't you?"

When Elizabeth and Max went into the dining room for breakfast, they came upon Quartermaster Hichens, from Elizabeth's lifeboat. He was regaling an audience with complaints about how difficult it had been to maintain order on his boat, because the women had been so "uncooperative." When he recognized Elizabeth, he interrupted his story and hurried from the room.

Throughout the next two days, which were

made more difficult by a storm that arose on Tuesday night and continued through Wednesday, keeping everyone indoors, Elizabeth heard many rumors about what had taken place on the *Titanic* after she left. One that proved to be untrue was that the captain and the first officer had shot themselves rather than go down with the ship. Max was certain this was a lie, as he had himself seen Captain Smith in the water after the sinking. They also heard that some passengers had been shot rushing the lifeboats at the last moment. That, too, was later proved untrue. The most unsettling rumor spreading throughout the *Carpathia* was word that the *Titanic* had received countless messages warning about the onset of ice fields and icebergs long before the disaster, and had not only ignored the warnings, but had refused to slow its speed. This rumor persisted, and was never denied by anyone in authority.

It made Elizabeth physically ill to think that the terrible tragedy could have been averted. She could only hope the rumor wasn't true.

"If it is," Max said darkly, "there'll be hell to pay. It's bad enough we were short on lifeboats. Someone's going to have to answer a lot of questions."

A stewardess on board the *Carpathia* had borrowed clothing from two of its passengers for Elizabeth and her mother. While the apparel was not the height of fashion that Nola was used to, she was grateful. Lost in grief for her husband, she remained quiet and noncommittal, not even complaining that the ship was overcrowded, or that the lines waiting at the bathrooms to use the tubs stretched the length of a corridor. She had seemed to rejoice when she first saw Max, and though she later said she was happy for Enid and Jules, Elizabeth sensed that she was just as happy for Elizabeth. Nola never once mentioned Alan's name, nor did she send him a Marconigram saying they were safe. It seemed to Elizabeth that the sudden loss of her mother's one true love had given Nola a new understanding of just how important love really was.

Anticipating a scandal over the lack of lifeboats on board the *Titanic*, a congressman's daughter who had been in Elizabeth's lifeboat said, "I imagine there will be hearings. Investigations. I understand few people from third class survived, that whole families were lost. That will be a big scandal, too." She sighed heavily. "Nothing will ever be the same, it seems to me."

Elizabeth couldn't say whether she thought that was true or not. She only knew that life would never be the same again for the Farrs.

Nola roused herself from her grief enough to return Elizabeth's good-night hugs with warmth and affection, making it clear that she was aware of her daughter's presence and glad to have it.

"She won't stay like this forever," Elizabeth confided to Max as they were returning from lunch on Thursday. Nola, in need of a nap, had retreated to the cabin of the woman whose clothing she had borrowed. "She'll be herself again, and maybe when that happens, she'll push me at Alan again."

There was mild alarm in Max's face as he glanced over at her. Color had returned to his face, the redness had left his eyes, and except for the fact that he was still so chilled he had to wear two borrowed, heavy sweaters at a time, he was beginning to look like his old self.

Smiling, Elizabeth waved a hand in dismissal. "Don't worry. I've made up my mind. She won't change it for me." The smile gone, she added seriously, "I know that young Irish couple I watched board the ship at Queenstown lost someone they cared about. I've seen their faces. I think it was the boy's brother, who boarded with the girl. That boy couldn't have been more than nineteen or twenty. He probably thought he had his whole life ahead of him." She took Max's hand in hers, held it tightly. "So

I'm not wasting any time doing things other people want me to do, not even my own mother. I don't know exactly how I'm going to manage it, but I *am* going to college, and I *am* going to choose my own friends."

One of Max's eyebrows lifted toward the sky. "Friends? That's all I am, a friend? Do you *know* how cold that water was, Elizabeth? And I swam through it to get to *you*. Surely I deserve more than friendship for my efforts."

Elizabeth laughed. "You know you're more than that. And you know what I mean. I won't forget my promise to my father, but it doesn't worry me. I know my mother isn't going to want a daughter hovering at her side every single minute. He never saw that independent side of her, but I have. It may take her a while, but sooner or later she's going to realize we both have to live our own lives. I can wait. I can be patient. Now that I know I'm going to do what I want, there's no rush."

Max nodded. "You're right. But while you're waiting, are you going to be allowed to see me? We'll both be in New York, and —"

Elizabeth tilted her head to look up at him. "Max, weren't you listening? I just said I'm not wasting my time doing things dictated by other people. If I want to see you in New York, I shall."

"I'm going to be living in a garret," he

warned, smiling down at her. "You don't have a lot of experience with garrets."

"I don't have *any* experience with garrets. It might be fun to see one. I'll consider it part of my education. But if you ask me, your parents are going to be so thrilled that you survived the *Titanic*, they'll let you do whatever you want with your life."

"I *want* to live in a garret, and make it on my own."

"Then do it. I'm just saying if you wanted to, you could probably live in the nicest garret in all of New York City."

They were on deck by then, the chilly fog having emptied it of all but the hardiest of strollers. When Elizabeth began talking again about how glad Max's parents would be to see him, he kissed her to shut her up. They were driven inside a few moments later by lightning, thunder, and a vicious wind. They stayed inside until a steward walking by called out, "Fire Island just ahead. Only a few more hours and you'll be safely in New York."

When the storm ended, leaving a chill mist in its wake, they returned to the rail, and were soon joined by other survivors anxious for a glimpse of New York. Elizabeth, in her anticipation of finally arriving safely home, failed to notice the young Irish couple standing off to her left, also seeking refuge from the storm.

But Katie Hanrahan noticed Elizabeth, and clutching Paddy's hand tightly, she smiled with satisfaction. The pretty girl had found her handsome young man. He, too, had survived the terrible disaster at sea. Perhaps that was his reward for saving Bridey and Kevin.

They looked happy to be together again.

And although she had never met the girl or the young man, the sight of the two of them standing at the rail holding hands and looking toward the shore together filled Katie with a deep sense of peace.

She had set out for America with only high hopes and a vision for the future. She was landing on its shores with a greater appreciation of life itself and with Paddy Kelleher's hand in hers. They had lost Brian, someone they both loved deeply, but they had survived. They would mourn Brian. But they would never stop being thankful for their own lives.

Though she knew they would never forget the long, terrifying voyage, it was over now. Malachy and Lottie would be waiting for them when they stepped off the *Carpathia*. They would whisk her and Paddy off to Brooklyn, feed them hot soup and fresh bread, and listen with wide, disbelieving eyes to the tale of the sinking of the *Titanic*.

It would be a tale they would tell many

times. But for all the telling, it never would lose its horror.

She was about to step on the shores of America for the first time. And for her, as for all the others who had not been swallowed up by the dark sea, life would begin anew.

Epilogue

A light, chilly mist was falling on the city of
New York as the seven hundred survivors of
the sinking of the *Titanic*, at nine-thirty P.M. on
Wednesday, April 17, 1912, disembarked from
the steamer *Carpathia* via fore and aft gang-
ways. Wealthier passengers evaded a host of
reporters and photographers lying in wait for
them and were whisked away in private cars by
relatives and friends.

Max Whittaker's parents greeted him with
unabashed joy.

Elizabeth Farr and her mother were met by
Martin's grieving parents and taken immediately to the elder Farrs' Manhattan town
house.

Malachy and Charlotte Hanrahan of Brooklyn, New York, were forced to endure a long,
chilly wait near Pier 54 for their niece from Ireland, as third-class passengers were the last

to depart the *Carpathia*. It was close to eleven o'clock on the dreary, dismal April night when this last group of survivors began emerging from the aft gangway.

Other third-class passengers had lost everything but their lives. Without funds for hotel rooms or further travel, they were remanded to the care of the Women's Relief Committee or the American Red Cross.

There were no reporters waiting when this last group of one hundred seventy-four *Titanic* survivors straggled out into the open air. This oversight proved beneficial to Patrick Kelleher who, three years later, published a moving account of what that last night on the *Titanic* was like for passengers in third class, a story no one else had ever told as movingly as Paddy did. *The Long, Dark Night* received rave reviews, and though Paddy wrote novels throughout his life, it was that first book that made his fortune.

It was dedicated to the memory of his brother, Brian.

Katie Hanrahan found, to her great distress, that New York City was not to her liking. On the funds from the sale of his first book, Paddy took her back to Ireland, where they married and lived out their lives in Dublin, raising three children: Brian, Eugenie, and Fiona. Katie taught piano and voice to children in the area and when she wasn't starring in local theater productions, studied English grammar at length in order to do Paddy's "grammarizin'" for him.

Elizabeth Langston Farr graduated from Vassar College in Poughkeepsie, New York, with a degree in Literature. She taught at a private girls' school in Manhattan, becoming headmistress four years after her marriage to Maxwell Whittaker. She continued at the school throughout her life, with Max's support. They had no children, but Elizabeth considered herself surrogate mother to the girls in her school and was not discontented.

Max achieved modest success as a painter.

Nola Farr remarried three years after the *Titanic* disaster, to a French ambassador, and moved to Paris.

Though she missed her mother, Elizabeth put off visiting her as long as possible, reluctant to board a ship again.

But when she and Max eventually traveled to France, they sailed without incident, enjoying a safe and pleasant trip.

Resources

Ballard, Robert D. *Exploring the Titanic*. New York: Scholastic. Canada: Madison Press, 1988.

Eaton, John P. and Charles A. Haas. *Titanic Triumph and Tragedy*. 2nd ed. New York: W. W. Norton and Company. London: W.W. Norton & Company, 1988, 1994.

Lord, Walter. *A Night to Remember*. New York: Henry Holt and Company, 1955.

Lynch, Don and Ken Marschall. *Titanic, An Illustrated History*. New York: Hyperion. Canada: Madison Press Books. 1992.